P9-DNL-790

A PLACE
ON THE TEAM

·

A PLACE
ON THE TEAM

·

The Triumph and Tragedy
of Title IX

· · · · ·

WELCH SUGGS

PRINCETON UNIVERSITY PRESS

PRINCETON AND OXFORD

Copyright © 2005 by Princeton University Press
Published by Princeton University Press, 41 William Street, Princeton,
New Jersey 08540
In the United Kingdom: Princeton University Press, 3 Market Place, Woodstock,
Oxfordshire OX20 1SY
All Rights Reserved

Library of Congress Cataloging-in-Publication Data
Suggs, Welch.
A place on the team : the triumph and tragedy of Title IX / Welch Suggs.
p. cm.
Includes bibliographical references and index.
ISBN 0-691-11769-1 (cloth : alk. paper)
1. Sports for women—United States—History. 2. Sex discrimination in sports—United
States—History. 3. Sports for women—Law and legislation—United States—History.
4. Sex discrimination in sports—Law and legislation—United States—History.
5. United States. Education Amendments of 1972. Title IX—History. I. Title
GV709.18.U6S86 2005
796′.082—dc22 2004048902

British Library Cataloging-in-Publication Data is available

This book has been composed in Sabon with Kabel Family for Display

Printed on acid-free paper. ∞

pup.princeton.edu

Printed in the United States of America

1 3 5 7 9 10 8 6 4 2

CONTENTS

•

A PLACE
ON THE TEAM

INTRODUCTION

•

E arly mornings are a teenager's definition of hell. At 8:30 on a chilly November Saturday in 2003, the seventeen- and eighteen-year-old soccer players on the Potomac Mischief were having a hard time getting excited about their first game, against the McLean Mystics in the Bethesda Thanksgiving Showcase. Sleepy and cold, they made simple mistakes and let the ball spin crazily off their feet. (Luckily, the Mystics were just as sleepy.)

The summer and fall had been a long haul for the Mischief, a club consisting of young women who for the most part lived in the affluent Maryland suburbs of Washington, D.C. Most of the team had gone to summer soccer camps at colleges up and down the East Coast. Many of them got together in July and August to play in seven-on-seven leagues. A few worked with Terri Beach, their coach and a former University of Maryland star, in one-on-one sessions. When school started, so did their high schools' soccer teams, which meant practice every day and games twice a week.

The Mischief's own schedule in the Washington Area Girls Soccer league did not allow them to let up. Instead, the team fit league games, practices, and tournaments in as best it could, on early weekend mornings and whenever it could find time.

For good soccer players—and the Mischief were very good—the sport is a full-time job after school. When they kicked off for this game against the Mystics, Susan Kamenar and her teammates had played roughly twenty-three games apiece since August. And the year was far from over, with tournaments remaining in Delaware, North Carolina, and Florida before New Year's.

Why? Why devote this much time to soccer? Their parents were not forcing them; only a handful showed up to shiver on the sidelines at this game. Peer pressure was not forcing them; they played high school soccer with their friends, but the Mischief was just a group of acquaintances who happened to spend a lot of time together.

Susan hints at an answer in one of her college essays:

> Playing soccer is the one thing in my life that has remained constant
> and stable throughout my life since I was four years old. Soccer has kept

1

•

me from losing my sense of self and has prevented me from falling into the troubled world that many teenagers do. Soccer has kept my body, mind, heart, and soul alive and healthy. I am the only "original" player on my club team, the Potomac Mischief, because I have been on the team since it was formed in fourth grade. I have grown up with this team and it has shaped me into who I am today. Through my dedication to soccer and my team, I have acquired skills that help me excel in other parts of my life: time management, teamwork, decision-making, leadership, commitment, communication, social skills, determination, and other skills.

Soccer has also helped me with my faith. I use soccer to free my mind. When I play soccer I forget about everything and get into a mental spiritual zone. Before every game when we are lined up on the field waiting for the kickoff, I make the sign of the cross in the dirt and offer the game up to God. It helps to remind me why I am here, and by doing my best with the skills that God has given me, I will step off the field satisfied, win or lose.

This is why people play sports. To have fun, to excel, to push themselves and their bodies to their limits. This is why Americans have sports in schools, because of the lessons that Susan and her peers have learned from the countless hours they willingly devote to their sport.

Susan is in the first generation of women who are expected to learn those lessons on the playing field, just as men have done for centuries. Three decades after its passage, the promise of Title IX of the Education Amendments of 1972 is finally being realized.

Title IX forbids sex discrimination at colleges and schools that receive federal funds (i.e., virtually all of them). It applies to athletic programs just as it does to the rest of a school's programs.

Because of the mania that scholastic and collegiate sports inspire, Title IX's application to sports has been the most visible gender controversy of the past thirty years. Millions flock to high school stadiums on Fridays and to college venues on Saturdays throughout the fall for football games, spending hundreds of dollars per family on tickets, T-shirts, and other paraphernalia, showing team pride as a proxy for school spirit.

While fans of lower-profile men's sports like gymnastics, track, and wrestling fulminate that Title IX is killing their sports, thousands of images and trophies pay tribute to the law's triumphs. At American colleges, more than two hundred thousand women are on varsity sports teams, up from a handful in 1971.[1] More than 2.8 million girls were on high school teams in 2002.[2] There were roughly 490,000 college athletes and 6.7 million high school athletes, so women comprise about

40 percent of the total on both levels. Americans have realized that women can and ought to be competitive athletes, just like men.

No image of the law's victory is more gripping and representative than Brandi Chastain's shirtless celebration following her winning goal in the 1999 Women's World Cup. But equally important is an invisible monument—a controversy—that if made solid would take the form of several reams of densely written pages—congressional debate, federal regulations, and judges' rulings that have withstood the onslaught of scores of challenges. Taken together, these pages send American schools and colleges a simple message: If boys get to play sports, then girls do, too.

Early in the twentieth century, female coaches expressed an ideal: "A girl for every sport, and a sport for every girl." The triumph of Title IX shows how close we have come.

But "close" is not all the way. Women are a clear majority of students in higher education—7.5 million of the 13.2 million undergrads at American colleges. Women are underrepresented on sports teams, and most of their teams receive lower budgets, poorer facilities, and less attention than their male counterparts. Some argue that women are not as interested in sports as men and that the differences in participation population reflect that. Regardless, women are still getting the short end of the stick when schools and colleges allocate resources.

Title IX has a yet darker side. In mandating that women athletes be treated the same as men, the law encouraged women's sports to develop in the hypercompetitive, highly commercialized model that evolved in men's sports over the past century and a half. Teams like the Mischief play scores of games every year, cutting into schoolwork and other activities. In sports like cross-country and gymnastics, girls develop eating disorders after being encouraged to lose weight. Athletes specialize as early as their preteen years, so that only girls who have been competing in a sport since elementary school have a shot at making their high school and college teams. At the youth and secondary level, parents and schools are devoting resources to elite-style sports, not to broader participation opportunities. Susan and her teammates have learned the lessons sport has to teach because they are very good, and many of her classmates at Bethesda–Chevy Chase High School may never get the chance to learn those lessons.

The Mischief has a particular reason for being on the soccer field at this hour, and the reason is sitting on a hillock trying to wake up and keep an eye on one of Susan's teammates. Bundled in a red-and-green sideline jacket and carrying a nylon briefcase with the Mid-American Conference logo, Hugh Seyfarth is one of a hundred college coaches who have stopped here in Maryland during the national circuit of tournaments, which is designed to herd top high school soccer players together to show off their skills in the hopes of winning a scholarship or just a spot on a team so that they can dedicate themselves to soccer for another four or five years.

Seyfarth, an assistant coach at Miami University in Ohio, does not particularly enjoy the process. This year, he does not even have scholarships to offer aspirants. "We were allowed to start talking to kids on July 1, and by July 3 we'd given out all our scholarships" for players entering college in fall 2004, he said. Now, he is looking for second-tier players who might be willing to "walk on," or try out for the Miami team with no guarantee of playing time or financial aid. He is also getting an early look at next year's crop of high school talent, perpetuating the process for next year.

Miami is one of 199 universities sponsoring Division I women's soccer, each of which needs roughly twenty players to compete. That makes Seyfarth a player in a game that forces high-schoolers to make one of the most important decisions of their lives, where they go to college, based on how well they can kick a soccer ball. The better ones have to make that decision even before beginning their senior year of high school. Seyfarth worries about the process, but he points out that it's the same in most sports—basketball, field hockey, swimming, tennis, and so forth. Plus, he said, "The kids who are getting scholarships, everybody's known who they were since they were twelve or thirteen." Soccer has defined their lives for at least that long, and in many cases much longer.

That fact is thanks to Title IX, which has brought the joy and trouble of high-stakes sports to the other half of the population, radically transforming the lives of millions of girls and women.

Entering middle age, Title IX is still a mystery to most parents, coaches, and even the people charged with enforcing it. Is it a law? Is it a set of rules? Who enforces it? Who has to follow it? What does it really say? As with most laws, very few laypeople know the answers to these questions. This book is an attempt to give a full historical answer to these questions, but here is a quick primer.

In 1972, Congress passed Title IX as one of several amendments to the Higher Education Act. Its basic premise is simple: "No person in the United States shall, on the basis of sex, be excluded from participation in, or denied the benefits of, or subjected to discrimination under any educational program or activity receiving federal aid."[3] That includes every facet of education, including undergraduate admissions, laboratory space, hiring, and sports. The Civil Rights Restoration Act of 1987 made clear that if any program at an educational institution or school district received federal grants, then the entire entity is covered by Title IX and other civil rights laws. Virtually all school districts and colleges receive some form of federal money (the exceptions are private secondary schools and colleges that do not participate in federal student loan programs, such as Hillsdale College in Michigan). Thus, practically all scholastic and college sports are governed by Title IX.

How schools and colleges choose to abide by the law is spelled out in a set of regulations issued by the government in 1975 and in specific policy interpretations published in 1979 and 1986. The Department of Health, Education, and Welfare regulated educational institutions before 1980, and was split into the Department of Education and the Department of Health and Human Services. Under both HEW and the Department of Education, Title IX enforcement has fallen to the department's Office for Civil Rights.

Unlike other educational activities (or any other realm of civil rights, for that matter), nearly everyone agrees that male and female athletes ought to play in separate realms. People have fought and died to eliminate "separate but equal" schools for children of different races, but with a handful of exceptions, everyone agrees that under current conditions, men and women ought to have comparable, single-sex teams and activities. Schools and colleges do not need to offer sports programs, but if they do, Title IX makes it clear that they must provide equitable opportunities for male and female students.

Here, "equitable" covers all areas of a sports program's operations—athletic scholarships (if offered); participation opportunities; scheduling of games and practice times; travel costs and per diems; coaching and tutoring (including numbers of coaches, their salaries, and their professional backgrounds); locker rooms, practice and competition facilities; medical facilities, housing and dining services; and publicity and media services.[4] At the collegiate level, the most controversial and most litigated portion governs the number of male and female athletes institutions must have on their rosters.

The 1979 interpretation and a host of subsequent court rulings provide schools with three options. Institutions must have (1) similar participation and enrollment rates for men and women; (2) a history and strategy of expanding opportunities for women; or (3) proof that women are completely satisfied with the sports programs being offered. The 1996 clarification said that option 1 is a "safe harbor": If a college has the same percentage of women in sports programs as there are women in the undergraduate student body, it is home free.

Colleges and their lawyers now have to figure out what to do with these guidelines, on penalty of facing lawsuits and complaints filed with the federal government. The fastest and cheapest route to the safe harbor is to force the gender ratio of athletes to equal that of students. Because most institutions have more men than women on varsity teams, many have cut male athletes and even entire teams to comply with the rule.

But fastest and cheapest is not the only way. Institutions can add women's teams, complying with option 2 immediately and, over time, with option 1. Or they can attempt to demonstrate compliance with option 3, using surveys and other documents.

Cutting men's teams and telling male athletes they cannot play anymore because of a law is, on its face, heartless. To many, it is a simple matter of discriminating against real people to satisfy an abstract principle. The arguments against option 1 mirror those against affirmative action: Requiring companies or colleges to accept a certain number of people from one group, even if people from a second group are arguably more qualified or (in the case of sports) demonstrate more interest, is discrimination against individuals in the second group.

Quota has become a dirty word in discussions of Title IX, just as it has in affirmative action. Conservatives get particularly heated about this argument, particularly libertarians and most free-market advocates. A fairer law, they believe, would allow schools to make their own choices about which sports teams to offer, based on the interest shown by students.

Representatives of women's groups and advocates for women's sports offer two arguments in response. The first is the *Field of Dreams* argument, after the 1989 movie: "If you build it, they will come." How can you properly gauge interest in a particular activity if the group you are asking has never been given the opportunity or encouragement to participate? How are women going to demonstrate their interest in sports if they have not gotten the same chances to play as men have?

The second argument is subtler. Title IX requires that educational activities to be provided equitably to male and female students. Sport is an educational activity, certainly as athletes like Susan Kamenar have experienced it. Therefore, sports must be provided equitably. Schools are not required to change their course offerings or even extracurricular programs based on student interest, which of course changes every year. Instead, colleges offer the programs they do because school officials believe those programs have merit. So why should sports be offered solely on the basis of student interest?

A rich and convoluted mythology has grown up around college sports in this country. Most people, even coaches and athletic administrators, believe that men's sports were started in the mid–nineteenth century and evolved steadily to their present state. Women's sports, on the other hand, trace their history only back to 1972 and the passage of Title IX. Old football coaches look at the inequities that still remain between men's and women's athletics and say that women's sports just have not had the time to develop that men's sports have had.

But as football, baseball, and basketball were becoming national obsessions at the end of the nineteenth century, Constance Applebee, Senda Berenson, and other women in the academy had already concluded that sports offered as much to female students as to males. They developed curricula and games and teams for women at high schools and colleges, but they warned in very strict terms against following the emerging pattern of men's sports at Harvard, Yale, Princeton, and the country's large land-grant universities, the sports factories of the age. Some of their concerns were wrapped up in what we would consider antiquated notions of what women were physically capable of doing, but they had broader concerns about sports as all-consuming activities for participants.

Said Mabel Lee, one of the most important governors of women's sports in the 1920s, "The field of men's athletes is full of sorry instances of this mad worship at the shrine of technique. Now that women's athletics are developing so rapidly all over our land, let us caution our leaders to hold fast to the ideals of worthy citizenship even at the expense of fine technique."[5]

Women's sports existed at colleges all over the country long before Title IX. Women's basketball, for example, developed at precisely the same time as the men's game. But women were confined to intramural contests, under the careful control of generations of physical-education teachers. Thus exiled to second-class gyms, only a few women found it acceptable to participate, although sports became more acceptable for women in the mid–twentieth century.

Until 1981, women's sports were governed almost exclusively by physical-education teachers. They taught a particularly values-laden approach to sports, taking care to restrict recruiting, the numbers of games and practices, and other elements of team play to fit into an athlete's overall college experience.

In 1981, though, women's sports were taken over by the organizations, primarily the National Collegiate Athletic Association, that ran male sports. Creating and promoting competition has always been the NCAA's basic function, and over the past two decades especially, the intensity and pressure of that competition has turned college sports into massive, year-round enterprises for all athletes, male and female.

The most visible of these enterprises are big-time football and men's basketball programs, but athletes in other sports, male and female alike, also have been sucked into the vortex of year-round, intensely competitive college sports. Even small colleges can spend in excess of a million dollars on their sports programs, and those that compete at the highest level cannot spend less than twenty times that.

The irony is that the NCAA fought Title IX every step of the way. When the Department of Health, Education, and Welfare ruled in the mid-1970s that the law would apply to high school and collegiate sports, athletics officials fulminated that they would be forced to cannibalize football and basketball teams to pay for new women's teams. The NCAA tried to sue to prevent the law from being implemented, and called on its allies in Congress to block it. But every attempt failed, and the NCAA proceeded to take over women's sports programs in the early 1980s. Since then, the organization and its members have been struggling to figure out how to deal with Title IX, which many athletics directors see as a nuisance.

A college athletics director is a businessperson foremost. In the NCAA's Division I, athletics programs are supposed to generate enough revenue to cover the cost not only of big-time football and men's basketball, but also soccer, tennis, track, and a host of other teams. (They rarely do so, but colleges must still fund those sports at the highest possible level to have a shot at earning money from television appearances and bowl games.) Even smaller colleges use football and basketball teams to attract new students and to generate goodwill among alumni and the local community.

So the athletics director's job is to manage a small to midsized corporation whose products are winning teams in the big-money sports. The corporation pays ever-increasing salaries to coaches, buys or barters for as much new equipment as it can, and invests in new venues to attract fans and separate them from their money in new and creative ways.

The athletics director also must find the money to keep the baseball, lacrosse, and swimming teams in business, even though they do not generate any revenue. Colleges have always had these teams, and today they retain the patina of amateurism. Athletes in those sports generally graduate at much higher rates than those in the revenue sports, and they usually exemplify the NCAA's notion of the student who plays sports out of a love for the game. Many athletics directors generally care about these sports—I have met more former track coaches and former wrestlers in executive positions than I have basketball and football people—but they must treat them as sunk costs on their list of priorities.

Title IX has had a terrible time fitting into this equation. It is a law that regulates an educational program. It makes perfectly good sense in an educational context, and in most such contexts it has been wildly successful.

Women are now in the majority at most colleges, as well as law schools, and are making steady gains in engineering and medicine. But it adds a new category of sunk costs to the athletics director's budget—women's sports. Because the law requires it and NCAA rules encourage it, colleges place a higher priority on women's basketball, volleyball, and other sports than men's nonrevenue sports.

Many colleges have adopted "tiered" sports structures, in which a small number of sports (usually football, men's and women's basketball, and one or two women's sports) receive a full complement of athletics scholarships, highly paid coaches, and other resources. A second tier consisting of other women's sports and a few men's sports like baseball get limited scholarships and equipment budgets. A third tier, usually composed of men's teams in track and wrestling, gets no scholarships and is at the back of the line for equipment, gym time, and other resources.

When budgets are tight, third-tier programs are first cut. Because of an array of court decisions (discussed later in this book), most colleges cannot cut women's sports. In an era when successful football teams cost $10 million a year or more, cuts in men's gymnastics, swimming, track, and wrestling are inevitable.

Football and basketball, on the other hand, have never been in danger. A handful of colleges have dropped football teams because they could not afford them, but many more have started teams as a way of attracting more male students—as participants, spectators, and friends of the team.

Nobody can say for sure which colleges actually make money on sports, but most NCAA officials put the number at a dozen or fewer. Contracts with bowl games and television networks bring in millions for about sixty universities belonging to the six richest leagues—the Atlantic Coast, Big East, Big Ten, Big 12, Pacific-10, and Southeastern Conferences, but it is all most of these institutions can to do cover their costs. The pressure to keep up with one's rivals for coaches' salaries, facility renovations, and other improvements forces athletics directors to be ever more creative in the pursuit of new sources of revenue.

Most of these universities and the rest of the roughly two thousand colleges that sponsor sports teams for students finance them in the way they do any other extracurricular activity. They allocate general funds to pay most if not all of the costs their teams incur—travel, uniforms, coaches' salaries, athletic scholarships, facilities, and so on. The return on colleges' investment is the attention that teams get. One athletics director estimates sports teams account for 80 to 85 percent of the times any college gets mentioned in newspapers and on television; in the idiom of the football-crazed South, sports are "the front porch of the university."

All these factors are in the background when colleges decide to cut teams. Many athletics directors will say they have had to limit the number of male athletes to comply with Title IX regulations, either by dropping men's teams or limiting the number of athletes on any given team. Doing so infuriates not just those athletes and their coaches but also a wide range of political allies who say that civil rights laws like Title IX infringe on the autonomy of colleges and athletics directors to make their own decisions about how to operate. This is why the George W. Bush administration waded into the Title IX controversy when it formed the Secretary's Commission on Opportunity in Athletics in 2003. The commission was a thinly veiled attempt to rewrite Title IX regulations to protect male athletes, but it collapsed amid a steady drumbeat of negative publicity from women's groups.

The common argument by supporters of Title IX is that when athletics directors drop men's teams, they do not do so because of Title IX. Consciously or not, they decide to preserve resources for men's basketball and football instead of protecting minor sports or expanding sports offerings for women. "I used to think Title IX was responsible" for colleges dropping men's teams, a longtime college sports official told me recently. "But too often, I heard people say that and then turn around and build a new facility or hire a new coach."

The truth is that the tragedy of Title IX has nothing to do with the painful and unfortunate decisions athletics directors have made regarding men's sports. Instead, it is that female athletes and their coaches have gotten wrapped up in the high-stakes, highly commercialized model of men's sports that has developed over the past century, and the ideals held by Mabel Lee and others have been distorted or lost altogether. Athletic skill is becoming an important factor in college admissions, not just at sports powerhouses but also at small colleges. Americans see sports prowess as a proxy for other talents—sportsmanship, fair play, leadership, teamwork, perseverance—but the men's model of college sports does not always nurture those talents. The singular pursuit of winning rewards strength, speed, and skill, and not necessarily the more abstract goals of athletic participation.

Understanding the triumph and tragedy requires an understanding of the history of the men's and women's models of sports, both of which originated in the late nineteenth century at the elite colleges of the Northeast. The civil rights movement of the mid–twentieth century forced college and high school sports programs to integrate themselves along racial lines, setting the state for the integration of the sexes. The money flowing into college sports, the premium placed on competitiveness, and the political and legal climates for the late twentieth century combined to bring women into athletics departments in record numbers, fundamentally altering the American institution of college sports and forcing society to forever alter its understanding of women and athletes.

Women have not been fully integrated into scholastic sports in this country. For that reason, it may be easier to save women's sports than men's from the dangers lurking just over the horizon. The vision of a girl for every sport and sport for every girl requires a reshaping of the sports enterprise as it is practiced at American high schools and colleges. Potential reformers are starting to talk about this, but to date have had little success in turning a massive enterprise around.

Back at the Bethesda tournament, the Mischief end up losing to the McLean team 2-1. By the afternoon, though, they have woken up and roar past the Philadelphia Rage 4-0. On Sunday they defeat a team from suburban Atlanta and draw with another Maryland team. They finish the tournament in third place among the five in their division.

More importantly, though, four college coaches call Beach, the Mischief coach, in the next week. Beyond the balls they put in the back of the net, the Potomac players have scored with the people they need to impress. The factory has turned out a successful product.

CHAPTER

The Segregated History of College Sports

There was a golden age of American sports. An age when coaches were respected teachers in their field, when athletes ran out into sunlight to play for the love of the game, to match strength and skill in defending their school's honor and to stride across campus in their letter sweaters, where baseball and basketball were harmless pastimes played out in Norman Rockwell paintings.

What's missing from this picture? Men. Men's sports like football. Stadiums full of cheering spectators. In the latter part of the nineteenth and the early decades of the twentieth centuries, girls and women at American schools were the ones playing for fun under the earnest auspices of their teacher-coaches. Those coaches were in the first few generations of physical-education professionals, teaching the theories of the rapidly developing disciplines of kinesiology, physiology, and biomechanics.

The stadiums and letter sweaters were there on college campuses, no doubt about it. But men's intercollegiate athletics have always, always been a business, from the very first game contested between two schools. That side of sports has never been pure: The heroes of decades past were paid under the table, they cheated on eligibility rules, and occasionally they were not even students. Schools scheduled games and fostered rivalries because they were good excuses for a crowd to socialize, drink, and gamble.

Women's sports have always been a part of American college life, though they have never been celebrated like men's sports. Their games were always intramural, often held between classes, and conducted in a way that allowed teachers to preach the educational mission and the value of sport. For women, sport meant much more than winning.

The discipline of physical education evolved alongside organized sport in the late nineteenth and early twentieth centuries, adding a growing understanding of anatomy and physiology to the age-old philosophy that physical fitness was essential to a sound mind and a healthy life. However, teachers and students of physical education were never connected to the male sports establishment. Men's teams developed out of student-run clubs and were taken over by university administrators early in their history.

As a result, those clubs evolved much like professional teams. Interscholastic teams organized themselves into leagues based on location, such as the Big Ten Conference and the Missouri Valley Conference. Private groups, such as the Amateur Athletic Union, put on national championships in a variety of sports.

Both the men's and women's models are unique to the United States. In other countries, schools and colleges may field teams, but they do not devote to them the financial resources or the attention that American schools do. In the United States, athletes compete for secondary-school teams, perhaps for outside clubs in certain sports, and aspire to collegiate competition and perhaps the big leagues beyond. A few sports, like figure skating and baseball, have their own private developmental systems, but in all others, colleges serve as the primary means of elite athlete development.

Students have always participated in various forms of sport, of course. In the English-speaking world, organized games trace their origins to British public schools in the eighteenth century. At American schools and colleges, games and contests of all sorts took a little longer to evolve. Early-nineteenth-century American scholars, rooted in the Calvinist tradition, thought playing sports was about as moral as dancing.[1]

Furthermore, upper-class Americans and Britons frowned upon undue physical activity as something reserved for tradesmen and washerwomen. Ladies and gentlemen—especially ladies—were not expected to do anything more strenuous than take carriage rides or stroll in their gardens.

By the middle of the nineteenth century, however, even the gentry were being led to question such values. Theologians and authors like Charles Kingsley and Thomas Hughes thought the Anglican Church was becoming "overly tolerant of physical weakness and effeminacy,"[2] putting society at risk of being overrun by heathens. *Neurasthenia*, a term introduced into psychiatry by George M. Beard in 1869 that covered a range of disorders best described as laziness, was the most in-vogue malady of Victorian England and America, according to Clifford Putney.[3]

Kingsley argued that athletes would help Britain maintain its place in the world and status as the chosen people "in covenant with God." The medical profession began to advocate mild physical activity, the pursuit of bodily well-being, and, of course, careful eugenics to keep the Anglo-Saxon race pure and free from Slavic, Mediterranean, and other people of whom Britons did not approve. A similar movement arose in the United States. As immigration of people from southern and eastern Europe into America increased, Anglo-Saxons sought to maintain their physical dominance by exercising at Young Men's Christian Association chapters and pursuing exercises adapted from German and Swedish practices.[4]

As a result, education became an integral part of daily life at most northeastern colleges at that time, especially following the formation of the Boston Normal School of Gymnastics, which trained the first generation of teachers of what we would now call gymnastics, acrobatics, and calisthenics, and the success of Hemenway Gymnasium at Harvard under the direction of Dudley Allen Sargent.

Sargent was the most prominent of the early practitioners and theoreticians of physical education. He preached his gospel in halls and gymnasiums all over the Northeast and Mid-Atlantic, starting successful training programs in New Haven, New York, and Cambridge. A native of Belfast, Maine, who delighted in working out, Sargent quite literally ran away to join the circus as a teenager, becoming a professional acrobat and gymnast. Performing on the trapeze, pommel horse, and other pieces of equipment, he incessantly worked to convince friends and strangers alike that they would be better off if they exercised regularly. Men, women, children, everybody.

After semiretiring from paid performances, Sargent put himself through Bowdoin College and Yale Medical School by convincing college presidents to hire him to conduct mandatory gymnastics programs for fellow students, even though many faculty members did not believe such activities were proper for gentlemen. He strongly believed that physical prowess and mental acumen were linked. He found proof in observing that among the freshmen he taught at Yale, the top-ranked scholars also ranked high in gymnastics, and the worst in scholarship were the worst in the gymnasium.[5] He won enough debates on the subject to make a career out of preaching his creed.

Gymnastics was one of the most popular forms of exercise of the day, particularly for students with access to the necessary facilities. When Sargent came to Yale, those facilities consisted of the following:

> 8 or 10 bath-rooms, all furnished with long, zinc-lined tubs . . .
> besides the baths, there were four bowling alleys in the basement, and a
> baseball cage on one side about the width of the two alleys.
>
> The building, 150 feet over all, had a large exercising room, 80 by
> 50 feet, with cross timbers 25 feet from the floor. A running track,
> canvas-covered and filled with about 4 inches of sawdust, extended
> around the room. Over the track, along one side of the room, there was

a series of traveling rings, placed 9 feet apart and 8 feet from the floor, and on the other side, a horizontal ladder hung about 7 feet from the floor.

The equipment consisted of the usual German heavy apparatus. Two long rows of parallel bars, varying in height, fenced off two sides of the room inside the track. Vaulting bars, horizontal bars, flying rings, climbing ropes, double trapezes, climbing poles, and a set of rack bars were a few of the regular appliances. Two long spool ropes, inclined at about 45 degrees and parallel to each other, about 18 inches apart, ran along the lower end of the room. In front of the ropes, two pyramid or peak ladders, 30 feet apart at the base, extended to the tops of the cross timbers. At the same end of the room, they had 6 pulley-weight rowing machines arranged across the room, 6 or 8 pairs of pulley weights imbedded in sawdust at the front end of the room, and a few heavy iron dumb-bells and Indian clubs tossed carelessly on a straw matting in one corner. There was also a lifting machine, with about 300 pounds of iron weights, also a sand bag, weighing some hundred pounds, which was used for a punching bag. These appliances together with a leaping board, a springboard, and two large corn-husk mattresses, 12 feet by 8 feet and 10 inches thick, constituted the entire equipment.[6]

In other words, this was the forerunner of modern weight rooms. But it was not a training facility for college teams, nor was it a place where people competed against each other in gymnastics or track events. Instead, it was a laboratory of sorts—a place where Sargent could learn and teach what the human body was capable of doing, and where his students could make their bodies (and, the theory went, their minds and morals) stronger. Sargent reconstructed many of the weight machines and other pieces of apparatus to make them easier for smaller students to use and equipped other gymnasiums specifically for women and adolescents. Not long after Sargent moved on to Harvard, 80 percent of students there were exercising between one and three hours a day.

Colleges developed departments of physical education, and by century's end, an ethos of sport as a means of developing manhood was firmly entrenched in higher education and beyond, perhaps exemplified by Theodore Roosevelt. "There is a tendency to underestimate or overlook the need of the virile, masterful qualities of the heart and mind," Roosevelt wrote in 1890. "There is no better way of counteracting this tendency than by encouraging bodily exercise and especially sports which develop such qualities as courage, resolution, and endurance."[7]

Roosevelt touted his own physical prowess throughout his college days at Harvard and his political career. He began lifting weights as a teenager to overcome the crippling asthma of his childhood, rowed and rode across family estates on Long Island, and took up boxing and wrestling during college. According to Edmund Morris, Roosevelt's most recent biographer, "the most celebrated episode in Theodore's Harvard career" was a bout for the college's lightweight boxing title. Roosevelt lost, badly, but refused to give up and earned the respect of his class-mates for persisting against a bigger and quicker opponent.[8]

Roosevelt's lifestyle was popular among his classmates and other well-to-do easterners, and many of them were devoted to watching the very best college athletes perform on fields and rivers. Spectator sports first be-came popular in the United States in the second half of the nineteenth century, and intercollegiate games became a mania among the social elite.

The first organized athletic contest between two colleges is gener-ally accepted to be a rowing match featuring crews from Harvard and Yale in 1852. It was no mere challenge from New Haven to Cambridge, though. The details almost perfectly foreshadow the future of college sports.

James Elkins, superintendent of the Boston, Concord, and Montreal railroad, proposed the idea of a regatta to James Whiton of the Yale Boat Club in 1851. (Whiton later became the first American awarded a Ph.D.) Elkins offered to pay all the bills for a race between Yale and Harvard at a new resort hotel on Lake Winnipesaukee in New Hamp-shire, to promote the resort and the railroad. Ladies and gentlemen from Boston and New York rode up to the Adirondacks and, along with the crews, enjoyed an eight-day party. The only training of note was that the Harvard team abstained from pastries to prepare for the race. It was enough, as the Crimson beat Yale and won a silver plate.

In 1855, the two universities raced each other again, with Harvard again prevailing. However, the Yale team protested the race because Harvard had used a graduate student as its coxswain—the same man, in fact, who had coxed the 1852 crew. With this, college sport had its first eligibility scandal.

Within the decade, rowing became the most popular sport in the Northeast. Professional scullers such as those depicted in Thomas Eames's paintings had their followings, but collegiate fours and eights were often the main attraction. Saratoga Springs, New York, already holding its horse races, adding rowing races, and regattas often attracted more than fifteen thousand spectators. Many of them gambled on the crews just as much as on the ponies.[9]

Thus, virtually all of the ills of college sports were present at the creation:

- Companies using amateur athletes to market their products
- Colleges requiring athletes to have academic credentials, while at the same time bending those rules as far as they could stretch
- Large amounts of gambling on outcomes

In rowing, and a bit later in baseball, football, and track, students organized their own teams. College administrations quickly took over those teams, as well as the responsibility for organizing rules and contests. Faculty members were never involved, not even physical-education professors like Sargent. College sports grew up in the afternoons of academe, and the connection to the educational process was always tenuous.

The ideal of amateurism in college sports was always inconsistently upheld. Professional sports—baseball, rowing, running, and so forth—were commonplace by the end of the century, and athletes were modestly paid tradesmen. College athletes, on the other hand, were supposed to be joyously unpaid participants drawn from society's elite.

Yet college sports were at least as serious as professional ones—especially football.

Princeton and what would become Rutgers organized the first game in 1869 in New Brunswick. Rutgers defeated Princeton 8-0 in front of a few hundred spectators, in a game that signified the beginning of a national obsession.

It took a few years for some colleges to catch on. In 1876, a group of Cornell students who had been playing football among themselves were challenged to a game by the University of Michigan, to be played in Cleveland. As Mark Bernstein recounts in *Football: The Ivy League Origins of an American Obsession*, the president of Cornell, Andrew D. White, forbade it, saying, "I will not permit thirty men to travel 400 miles to agitate a bag of wind." [10]

As Harvard, Yale, and other colleges began agreeing on rules for the game, the sport quickly became a spectacle—first in the Northeast and then spreading to larger universities throughout the country. The *New York Times* reported on an 1877 game in New York between Princeton and Yale:

> The hour set down for the game was 2 o'clock, and at that time two rickety shanties provided for spectators were crowded with comely young women and portly old gentlemen, who together with innumerable young men with short hair and canes, and Scotch terriers, viewed the game from the beginning to the close, and expressed their interest in every new phase of the contest. [11]

African-American men were sprinkled on a handful of rosters in northern colleges in the early days of football, including Paul Robeson at Rutgers. Historically black colleges and universities began sponsoring teams of their own in the 1890s. Howard University founded an inter-collegiate athletics council, and baseball was a dominant sport at most institutions until football took hold in the 1920s.[12]

Enthusiasm for football was less than universal, particularly among the new breed of physical educators. Sargent had deep misgivings about "varsity" sport, especially football, which was particularly violent in its earliest incarnations. Players did not wear protective equipment, and many of their plays involved one team running into the other at full speed or flinging ball carriers over the line of scrimmage. According to Sargent,

> In consequences of the popular enthusiasm and the wide public inter-est in athletics, a large number of young men upon entering college are filled with the ambition to become athletes and get on university athletic teams. In many cases the zeal of these young men is greatly in excess of their abilities, and in their efforts to get into university form and keep pace with the stars, they often do themselves injury. In football especially a great deal of raw material is used as a temporary battering ram, or made to furnish a wall of temporary resistance to develop the defensive or attacking power of the more-stalwart rushers.
>
> The coaches cannot afford to use their time and energy in developing men, for their business is to develop football players; so they are anxious to weed out the weak ones, that they may give their undivided attention to the most promising candidates.[13]

One theme running through Sargent's writings on physical educa-tion is his desire to bring participation and athletic training to as wide a public as possible. He abhorred any pursuit that was available only to men of a certain size or athletes of superior ability. He draws a con-trast between "developing men" and "developing football players," a neat way to sum up the tension between advocates of physical educa-tion and those of athletics, even though one might consider them nat-ural allies. For educators, sport is a means to an end—developing one's body in concert with the mind, the ancient Greek ideal. Whether one's motivation is to develop a strong race of white Anglo-Saxon Protestants to resist immigrants or merely to improve the quality of one's own life, sport is only important as a means of personal de-velopment.

For coaches and players, though, the game was an end in itself. The in-toxicants of winning and the cheering crowd drowned out the moralizing of physical educators. In the words of Syracuse's rowing coach, James A. Ten Eyck:

> Who is it that gets "a hand" from the layman at the finish line? No thought is given to the losers, it is all for the victors, and no small boys are anxious to tote grips and satchels for losers, but hang close to the heels of their heroes. It is human nature, and things will not change until perhaps that far-off millennium is reached. The spirit which permeates the men in charge and the men participating is to win by "all honourable means." There is no getting behind the fact that races are entered to be won. The men who make the crew do not endure the long months of training or subject themselves to the discipline of crew life just for the fun of the thing.[14]

The students most likely to be pursuing Sargent's ideal were at women's colleges like Vassar, Smith, and Wellesley. In 1865, a member of the board of governors of Vassar wrote in the college's first prospectus, "Good health is, in the first place, essential to success in study. A suitable portion of each day is set aside for physical exercise, and every young lady is required to observe it as one of her duties."[15]

She did a strictly in moderation, however. Two powerful social prejudices kept women from participating intensely in any sport or physical activity alongside their brothers. First, upper-class women were expected to be pale and dainty, and they often wore clothing like corsets that prevented them from breathing, much less running or jumping. Muscles and tans were marks of the lower classes. Second, a woman's primary functions in society were to attract a man and bear children, and participating in sport was thought to impair the ability to do either. Until the middle of the twentieth century, a common myth was that being athletic could cause a woman's uterus to fall out.

As "muscular Christianity" took hold and more women had leisure time that could be used for sport, some forms of exercise became fashionable. While excessive exercise held dangers, moderate physical activity was thought to keep women healthy for childbirth. Bicycling, tennis, and walking were particularly popular for upper-class fin de siècle women.[16] These trends applied as well to college women. The Boston Normal School for Gymnastics began training women in the 1880s, and many of the new women's colleges springing up across the country hired graduates from Boston Normal to begin physical-education programs.

At women's colleges (and for women at coeducational schools), athletics programs were strictly the domain of women, owing to Victorian notions of modesty. Colleges found plenty of women willing to become teachers and mentors in physical education. Some truly enjoyed physical activity and competition; others could not find other jobs. (Most careers were not open to women at that time; very few colleges would hire women to teach academic subjects.)

Women's physical-education departments took root at many colleges and universities, developing their own curricula, rules, and activities and adapting Sargent's work to their students' and teachers' interests.[17] These teachers had no desire to make a spectacle of their passion. At Smith College, Senda Berenson invented the women's version of basketball shortly after and just a few miles from where James Naismith developed the game. She saw it as a pleasant alternative to the tedium of Swedish gymnastics, swinging Indian clubs, and other forms of calisthenics, but failed to account for the enthusiasm of spectators at the first contests among her students at Smith:

> We thought that just a few students would come out to watch, but the whole college with class colors and banners turned out. They filled the broad balcony. . . . They stood along the walls. . . . Except for the fact that we had nine on a side, we played the men's rules. The cheering and screaming . . . was a high-pitched sound I do believe no one had ever heard before. . . . The next day the local paper [had] a lurid description that must have made the staid citizens of the Valley wonder whether Sophia Smith had been wise to found a college in which young women might receive an education equal to that accorded to young men.[18]

Basketball became the major sport for women. Berenson published the first official rulebook for women in 1892, and on the far coast, the University of California at Berkeley launched the first team to take on rivals from other institutions.[19] After playing several girls' schools in San Francisco, Berkeley played the first-ever intercollegiate game against Stanford in 1896. Notably, the Berkeley women refused to play at Stanford or in front of a mixed audience. "Playing before a lot of college men . . . [would] be lowering a certain standard of womanhood," sniffed their coach. At San Francisco's Union Hall, Stanford won, 2-1.[20]

In 1899 Berenson helped found the National Women's Basketball Committee, which later evolved into the Committee on Women's Athletics of the American Physical Education Association. Its stated purpose was to develop common rules for the sport of basketball, but it also took on the duty of controlling "unrestrained" competition among college women.[21] They limited intercollegiate games to a very small number, preferring to emphasize intramural contests.

Women's teams were not school or college teams in any sense that twenty-first-century Americans might recognize. They did not hold try-outs or regular practices. They did not wear uniforms. Their coaches were physical-education teachers. This was nothing like men's sports of the day, and that was by design.

In old photos from the turn of the century, women stare out posed as class teams instead of teams representing their colleges. They usually have 98 or 02 or the like stitched onto the front of dark dresses—their year of graduation, not their uniform number.

Despite these limitations, or perhaps because of them, women's sports proved popular at colleges across the country. The 1909 *Silhouette* yearbook for Agnes Scott College, in Decatur, Georgia, has seventeen pages of pictures of sports teams, as well as the college's "Athletic Song":

> I'm a Hottentot from Agnes Scott,
>   A player of basket ball;
> I jump so high I scrape the sky,
>   And I never, never fall.
>   When once I get the ball,
>   I toss it above them all;
> I'll get it in, my side shall win,
>   Our foes shan't score at all.
>
> One day I went on fun intent
>   A-prancing to the gym.
> If not too late I'd learn to skate
>   Then I'd be in the swim;
>   Instead I hit the floor,
>   I'll never walk any more.
> I broke my skate, and split my pate,
>   I tell you, I was sore.
>
> Another day I went to play
>   Upon the hockey field;
> I thought it fine, oh most divine,
>   A hockey stick to wield.
>   Twinkle, twinkle star
>   I wonder what you are;
> I cracked my shin, and tore my skin
>   And had to come home in a car.
>
> Then in the gym, with greatest vim,
>   Those long ropes I did climb,
> And on the bar, I was a star.
>   Oh my! It was sublime.
>   I tried to ride the horse,
>   But dear me what remorse,
> He gave a bound, I struck the ground;
>   No safety in a horse.

And so you see at A.S.C.,
  There's something every minute.
You surely have to hustle here,
  Or else you'll not be in it.
    We're crazy 'bout the gym,
    The hockey and the swim,
So now three cheers and each who hears
Will raise it with a vim.[22]

As enthusiastic as these women were about sports, their teacher-coaches insisted on keeping games low key for two reasons. First, and perhaps most predictably, they wanted to preserve young women's modesty and accommodate their perceived daintiness. "Girls are not suited for the same athletic program as boys," wrote Ethel Perrin, a board member of the Women's Division of the National Amateur Athletic Federation, in 1928. "Under prolonged and intense physical strain, a girl goes to pieces nervously. A boy may be physically so weak that he hasn't the strength to smash a creampuff but he still has the 'will' to play. A girl is the opposite."[23]

The second was a general suspicion of competition, particularly as it was being practiced in men's sports. An excessive focus on winning games caused male participants to lose sight of fair play and sportsmanship. It exalted the most athletic and the most skilled at the expense of the broader pool of less talented players. Furthermore, men's sports, were controlled by coaches and administrators who did not necessarily understand the philosophy and morals of physical education as they were espoused by men like Sargent and women like Berenson.[24]

The way men were conducting intercollegiate sports was inherently wrong, women thought. "We must guard carefully the chances for character training, not allowing a passion for superior technique to blind us to these more worthwhile efforts," wrote Mabel Lee in 1930. "The field of men's athletics is full of sorry instances of this mad worship at the shrine of technique. Now that women's athletics are developing so rapidly all over our land, let us caution all our leaders to hold fast to the ideals of worthy citizenship even if at the expense of fine technique."[25]

Rowing teams had become de rigueur for colleges as the Saratoga Springs regattas got under way. Similarly, football flourished after the Princeton-Rutgers game. But the Berkeley-Stanford women's basketball game did not spawn a flood of imitators. Some intercollegiate events took place in the early twentieth century, but only a handful.

As women's sports evolved, so did most of the major organizations that controlled amateur and recreational sports in the United States, including many that no longer exist. Among them were the American Playground Association, the Young Men's and Young Women's Christian Associations, the Amateur Athletic Union, and the National Collegiate Athletic Association (NCAA).

In 1917, the National Women's Basketball Committee was replaced by the Committee on Women's Athletics of the American Physical Education Association (APEA). Six subcommittees, governing basketball, field hockey, swimming, track and field, soccer, and publicity were empaneled under the committee's auspices by 1922. APEA was the professional association for physical-education faculty members, formed at the same time and for the same purposes as the Modern Language Association and the American Psychological Association. The NCAA, by contrast, was never aligned with any academic organization.

The women's sports groups were established partly in response to the Amateur Athletic Union's decision in 1914 to allow women to participate in swimming championships, as well as track championships shortly thereafter.[26] Women viewed this as an intrusion of men into women's sports, and coaches and collegiate athletic administrators held their athletes out of AAU competitions. In 1920, they also organized the National Association of Directors of Physical Education for College Women (NADPECW).

This was only one of several battles for control over amateur sports, both men's and women's. The AAU, the NCAA, and the American Olympic Committee had a long-running battle over which group got to pick athletes for Olympic teams, and in 1923, dissatisfied with the AAU, the War Department organized the National Amateur Athletic Federation to provide broad-based opportunities for children and young adults, promoting physical fitness both for future soldiers and for American society as a whole. NAAF was happy to include prominent women as stakeholders, even creating a Women's Division under the auspices of Lou Henry Hoover, better known as Mrs. Herbert Hoover.

These three organizations—the Committee on Women's Athletics of the APEA, the Women's Division of NAAF, and NADPECW—had overlapping memberships and responsibilities, and it is difficult to chart or describe their precise impacts. The important point is that these organizations inherited the suspicion of varsity-style athletics from Sargent, Berenson, and others in physical education. They promoted instead an intramural, recreational approach to women's sports.[27]

The participatory goals of women's sport were woven into every bylaw of every governing organization and every meeting of coaches and phys-ed teachers from the late nineteenth century until 1982, when the Association for Intercollegiate Athletics for Women disbanded. They are perhaps best summed up in the 1924 platform of the Women's Division of NAAF, which calls on colleges and schools to promote physical activity to the masses; play for the sake of play and not to advertise corporations or even colleges themselves; and keep women in charge of women's athletics:

> The Women's Division believes in the spirit of play for its own sake and works for the promotion of physical activity for the largest possible proportion of persons in any given group, in forms suitable to individual needs and capacities, under leadership and environmental conditions that foster health, leadership, and physical efficiency, and the development of good citizenship.
>
> To accomplish this ideal for women and girls, it aims:
>
> - To promote programs of physical activities for all members of given social groups rather than for a limited number chosen for their physical prowess.
> - To protect athletes from exploitation for the enjoyment of spectators or for the athletic reputation or commercial advantage of any institution or organization.
> - To stress enjoyment of the sport and the development of sportsmanship, and to minimize the emphasis placed on individual accomplishment and the winning of championships.
> - To restrict recognition for athletic accomplishment to awards which are symbolical and have the least possible intrinsic value.
> - To discourage sensational publicity, to guide publicity along educational lines and to stress through it the sport rather than the individual or group competitors.
> - To put well-trained and properly qualified women in immediate charge of athletics and other physical-education activities.
> - To work toward placing the administration as well as the immediate leadership of all physical education activities for girls and women in the hands of well-trained and properly qualified women.
> - To secure adequate medical examination and medical follow-up advice as a basis for participation in physical activities.
> - To provide a sanitary and adequate environment and facilities for all physical activities.
> - To work for such time allotment for a physical education program as shall meet the need of the various age groups for growth, development, and maintenance of physical fitness.
> - To promote reasonable and sane attitudes toward certain physiological conditions which may occasion temporary unfitness for vigorous athletics, in order that effective safeguards should be maintained.

- To avoid countenancing the sacrifice of an individual's health for the sake of her participation in athletic competition.
- To promote the adoption of appropriate costumes for the various athletic activities.
- To eliminate gate receipts.
- To discourage athletic competition which involves travel.
- To eliminate types and systems of competition which put the emphasis on individual accomplishment and winning rather than upon stressing the enjoyment of the sport and the development of sportsmanship among the many.[28]

But the academic suspicion of women's competition did not necessarily extend to the general public. Female stars became accepted public icons in individual sports, like track (particularly in the African-American community), tennis, and swimming. Helen Wills Moody, the Wimbledon champion, and Gertrude Ederle, the English Channel swimmer, were household names in the early twentieth century, along with the multi-sport star Babe Didrickson Zaharias. Even so, team sports remained tightly governed, especially in scholastic settings.

At most, college women could hope to visit another campus during "Play Days." Charlotte West, retired women's athletics director at Southern Illinois University at Carbondale, participated in several during her undergraduate days at Florida State University. A group of athletes, especially physical-education majors, would drive to the University of Florida or another college and spend the day choosing up teams and playing basketball, volleyball, field hockey, and other sports. Teams were not "intercollegiate" in the normal sense; a random group for women from two (or more) colleges would compete against another random group of their peers. The exercise would be more social than competitive, and that was by design. By 1930, half the colleges in the country, both all-women's and coed, reported participating in Play Days, according to a NAAF survey. Play Days were common well into the 1960s.[29]

Also popular were "Sports Days," for which colleges would choose their best intramural teams and send them to compete informally against other teams in the area. By 1936, 40 percent sent teams to Sports Days. Meanwhile, 11 percent of colleges in 1930 and 13 percent in 1936 had varsity-style intercollegiate teams.[30]

The governance groups centralized in the 1930s and 1940s. The Committee on Women's Athletics of APEA became the National Section on Women's Athletics, and in 1940 merged with the Women's Division of NAAF. The following year, the new organization sponsored the first women's intercollegiate national championship, a golf tournament hosted by Ohio State. Following World War II, the championship became an annual event.

Throughout the first half of the century, governance groups for women's sports kept their activities low-key, which is one reason many people think collegiate sports for women emerged fully formed in 1972. Women's groups disdained publicity and insisted that sports remain informal, for the most part.

One could not find a starker contrast than with the NCAA, which was organized in the first decade of the twentieth century as an annual meeting of college presidents, faculty members, and athletic officials trying to curb abuses and injuries in football. Its history is one of college administrators trying to retain control over rapidly expanding sports, and taking control from other sports organizations as opportunities presented themselves. The NCAA began sponsoring championships in the 1920s, but those events were seen as secondary to the AAU's amateur championships. It took the NCAA seventy years to establish itself as the undisputed authority over competitive sports for men in the United States, and another decade to do so for women.

In October 1905, President Roosevelt summoned presidents of Harvard, Yale, and Princeton to the White House to ask them to do something about the brutal style of play in college football (although he did not ask them to ban the sport, as is commonly supposed).[31] Two months later, representatives of sixty-one colleges met in New York to form the Intercollegiate Athletic Association of the United States, which the following year changed its name to the National Collegiate Athletic Association.[32]

In its bylaws, the NCAA paid lip service to educational ideals and the need for colleges to compete on a level playing field, but it had no power to investigate violations or punish offenders, short of kicking them out. Instead, it mostly functioned as a rules-making and scheduling body, as did the conferences that began to spring up around this time, such as the Big Ten and the Southern. The pressure to win and attract crowds made the stakes too high for principles to deter opportunists.

In the 1920s, colleges across the country built megalithic stadiums, often naming them Memorial Stadium to honor students killed in World War I. College football as a focal point of campus life spread far beyond the elite northeastern institutions, even to tiny colleges like Centre in Kentucky and the University of the South in Tennessee. Both institutions had dominant barnstorming football teams in the 1920s.

Civic associations in warmer climes like Pasadena, New Orleans, and Miami organized holiday games in the teens and twenties and invited powerful teams from different parts of the country to come play each other—and bring along their fans for a Christmas vacation. This was the age of the first generation of college athletes and coaches who were folk heroes, such as Hobey Baker at Princeton and Jess Neely at Vanderbilt and Sewanee.

In the Northeast, the Upper Midwest, and the West Coast, colleges sponsored the broadest possible array of sports for men—track, golf, tennis, lacrosse, wrestling, swimming, and others beyond the crowd-pleasing football and basketball.

In 1929, the Carnegie Foundation published Bulletin 23, the first systematic critique of college athletics and its relationship to educational goals. In the words of the foundation's president, Henry S. Pritchett, investigators were supposed to ask, "What relationship has this astonishing athletic display to the work of an intellectual agency like a university?" and "How do students, devoted to study, find either the time or the money to stage so costly a performance?"[33]

Pritchett finds the university's role in "the development of the intellectual life" at odds with its function as "an agency to promote business, industry, journalism, salesmanship, and organized athletics on an extensive basis." Howard J. Savage, the principal author of the bulletin, was extremely critical of the expenses universities incurred to mount big-time football programs, noting in particular "extravagance on special personnel, including budgets for coaches, publicity agents and expenses of newspapermen, and the fictitious exaggeration of the importance of athletics, especially football."[34]

Sport was a huge part of undergraduate life at the time of the Carnegie study. According to the bulletin, between 18 and 25 percent of the student body at the 112 institutions studied were varsity athletes, and as many as 63 percent participated in intramural sports.[35] Moreover, two-thirds of the colleges had special programs set up to recruit athletes, as well as "soliciting and subsidizing" athletes with scholarships. Researcher found, though, that despite the beliefs of alumni, enrollments did not fluctuate based on how sports teams fared in competition, and that athletics were characterized by a "lack of intellectual challenge to the young and alert mind."[36]

As they do today, educators at the time complained that extracurricular activities of every type, be they fraternities or sports teams, were dumbing down the undergraduate experience. At Howard University's commencement in 1930, W.E.B. DuBois complained that "our college man today is, on the average, a man untouched by real culture. He deliberately surrenders to selfish and even silly ideals, swarming into semi-professional athletics and Greek-letter societies, and affecting to despite scholarship and the hard grind of study and research."[37]

In the years after World War II, controversies over college sports mushroomed. The debate over payment to athletes, whether in the form of scholarships or outright paychecks, became a national controversy that propelled the NCAA's members to form committees to investigate allegations of rules violations and to punish offenders. Colleges discovered how to make money from radio and television broadcasts, prompting the NCAA to begin bundling the broadcast rights to individual games into packages to sell to networks. In New York, gambling scandals threatened the survival of college basketball.

Meanwhile, the elite northeastern schools opted out of big-time football and formed the Ivy League, and the University of Chicago and a host of other institutions dropped football altogether. Some reinstated the sport later, in the "college" division of the NCAA, which later became the low-key and nonscholarship Division III.

The debate over scholarships and pay became tawdry. Southern schools such as Georgia Tech and Louisiana State had long sworn by giving out "scholarships" as if football players were getting academic fellowships, while members of the Big Ten pronounced themselves above the practice, which they said amounted to bribery. In the words of one University of Minnesota official, "The only thing we do for any athlete is to procure him a part-time job at a recognized business in Minneapolis or St. Paul."[38]

Recruiting had become a fine art. Colleges had sent many of their football coaches into the military during World War II to coach teams at training centers. Murray Sperber tells the story of Bear Bryant, en route to his first collegiate head coaching job at Maryland, forswearing recruiting in favor of marching his entire squad from the North Carolina Pre-Flight Training Center up to College Park, enrolling them, and putting them out onto the field within a week.[39]

College basketball was rocked in the early 1950s by point-shaving scandals originating with the gamblers in the corridors of Madison Square Garden in New York. Players from Long Island University, the City College of New York, New York University, Manhattan College, Bradley University in Illinois, and the University of Kentucky were all involved. The Wildcats, under legendary coach Adolph Rupp, were hit particularly hard in the new enforcement process, earning the NCAA's first "death penalty" for the 1952–53 season.[40]

During the 1960s and 1970s, the NCAA first implemented national academic standards for athletes in an effort to prevent coaches from recruiting players off the street and ones who were not prepared for college-level academics. First came the "1.6 rule," in 1966, which required colleges to admit only those athletes whose high-school grades suggested that they would be able to achieve at least a 1.6 grade-point average, or a C-minus, at the college they attended.[41]

At the end of the 1960s, men's sports were a highly developed and often controversial institution on college campuses of all sizes across the country. In the years following World War II, however, most colleges found themselves unable to compete with large land-grant institutions simply because they could not spend as much money on facilities, coaches, or scholarships. A smaller organization, the National Association of Intercollegiate Athletics, sprang up among regional universities, especially those with good basketball teams. The NCAA split into "college" and "university" divisions, with separate championship events for each.

All levels focused on championships. Most colleges were organized into conferences by the early 1960s, and conference champions earned berths in national tournaments and playoffs. These would expand dramatically later in the century, but by the 1950s and 1960s, the focus on competition had spread beyond individual rivalries and into national dramas.

This history is lavishly documented, both for individual colleges and conferences and for the NCAA as a whole. Intramural sports programs for women flourished, but in obscurity. Athletes in individual sports often achieved some level of fame, and America's first group of elite women athletes emerged in the 1950s in an unexpected location: the poorer historically black colleges of the segregated South.

The elite black institutions, such as Hampton and Howard Universities and Spelman College, disdained women's sports as unladylike and a waste of study time. Officials at Tuskegee Institute in Alabama and Tennessee State University had no such qualms and fielded top-quality basketball and, especially, track teams.

Their greatest moment was the 1964 Olympics in Tokyo, in which members of the "Tigerbelles" track team from Tennessee State swept the 100-meter dash, the 200-meter dash, and the 400-meter relay. Wilma Rudolph, Mae Faggs, and other sprinters were celebrated in a way few other female athletes ever had been, but they faded into obscurity soon after the games.

At the predominantly white colleges in the mainstream, pressure was building among female students who wanted the chance to compete, not just to play. AAU programs and industrial leagues, which had existed since the 1920s, flourished in certain pockets of the country. Especially in rural areas, girls were encouraged to participate in sports to stay out of trouble.

In 1957, several governing organizations formed the National Joint Committee on Extramural Sports for College Women to sanction events and championships for varsity-style teams. Doing so proved unwieldy, though, and in 1965 the group agreed to disband and pass its functions along to the Division for Girls' and Women's Sports (DGWS) of the American Association for Health, Physical Education, and Recreation, which in turn had been formed by the merger of the APEA Committee on Women's Athletics and the Women's Division of NAAF.

Public interest in the Olympics intensified through the 1950s and 1960s, particularly as a way of waging the Cold War against the Soviet Union and Eastern Europe. As a result, sports officials began to discuss the need for elite programs for female athletes, to give them a chance at beating the Communists. The physical educators who belonged to DGWS realized they needed to sponsor their own programs to retain control of women's sports and, hopefully, extend their philosophy of participation to accommodate the burgeoning interest in competition. In 1967, DGWS empaneled the Commission on Intercollegiate Athletics for Women to develop national championships for female athletes.

Perhaps inevitably, this brought the educational model of women's sports into conflict with the commercial model of men's sports. The women in charge of DGWS and other organizations did not want the overcommercialization and rampant cheating of men's sports, but they wanted to give women the chance to realize their fullest potential.

Before we pick up the narrative of this conflict, however, it is necessary to explain the other imperative facing schools and female athletes: a law passed in 1972 that guaranteed the latter access to all the benefits of the former.

2
CHAPTER
·

A New Paradigm of Civil Rights

The civil rights movement of the 1950s and 1960s fundamentally changed America, forcing white Americans to confront the disparities between their lives and those of black Americans, providing the cultural momentum to begin integrating schools and workplaces. As celebrated as that history is, one has to dig deep into law review articles and scholarly books to find one of the movement's most important legacies: the laws and legal theory that were designed to break down the walls separating black and white. The laws were tremendously controversial and difficult to pass, and many of the debates over them linger to this day. Affirmative action is a prime example.

The Civil Rights Act of 1964 and the government regulations that followed it provided a new framework for judging equality. The laws forced schools and employers to recognize the civil rights not only of black people, but also of women and people from all ethnic, cultural, and religious backgrounds. Agencies of the executive branch were given specific responsibilities to define discrimination and negotiate with both public and private entities to end it.

When women's rights activists and members of Congress began crafting a set of laws to bring about equality between the sexes, they imported this framework wholesale. It created many of the same controversies for women, but also brought about opportunities.

This historical conception of civil rights is where Title IX originated. It passed without fanfare and practically without debate. In 1972, when Congresswoman Edith Green and Senator Birch Bayh brought it before Congress, it represented the maturing of an educated class of women demanding opportunities to be both students and teachers, as well as the culmination of the women's movement's push for equal rights.

The civil rights background of the history of Title IX starts with the Birmingham riots of 1963, which stamped the civil rights movement on the national consciousness. Images of black children being battered by fire hoses and bitten by police dogs in northern Alabama were broadcast around the country, raising fear among members of the Kennedy administration that similar riots would break out across the country. Burke Marshall, Kennedy's assistant attorney general, recommended the drafting of a law that would end segregation in public accommodations, such as restaurants and hotels.[1]

The idea of a national civil rights bill was nothing new. In the 1950s, Rep. Adam Clayton Powell of New York regularly attached amendments to spending bills forbidding the use of funds for segregated activities and projects, such as the construction of separate schools for black and white children. The NAACP even referred to such measures as "our usual amendment."[2] Many of Powell's allies in Congress were critical of the amendments because they alienated members of Congress who were not staunch segregationists but did not want to be identified as integrationists. Many of them ended up voting against the original legislation.

Following President Kennedy's assassination in November 1963, Lyndon Johnson took up the fight for the Civil Rights Act. 'Let us continue,' he declared, promising that 'the ideas and the ideals which [Kennedy] so nobly represented must and will be translated into effective action'.[3]

The fight to craft and pass the Civil Rights Act is one of the most remarkable in congressional history, and has been amply documented elsewhere.[4] After the House of Representatives approved it 290-130 in February 1964, Senate segregationists mounted a filibuster that lasted for seventy-five days. Even after the filibuster was broken, the Senate spent another six days arguing over the bill. It was finally passed 73-27 on June 19, 1964.

At the time, the bill's Title II received the most public attention. It forbids racial discrimination in public accommodations and ended the era of segregated lunch counters. In the long run, though, Titles VI and VII proved to be even more influential in opening doors for African-Americans and people we would now describe as coming from "disadvantaged" populations.

Title VI states that "no person in the United States shall, on the ground of race, color, or national origin, be excluded from, be denied the benefits of, or be subjected to discrimination under any program or activity receiving Federal financial assistance."[5] This was known as the "universal Powell amendment," consolidating Powell's many amendments into a single, permanent law, displeasing many southerners angling for large federal allocations to bring back to their home districts for construction projects and other uses. Such projects would now have to be integrated.

Title VII forbids discrimination in hiring and employment:

> (a) It shall be an unlawful employment practice for an employer—
>
> (1) to fail or refuse to hire or to discharge any individual, or otherwise to discriminate against any individual with respect to his compensation, terms, conditions, or privileges of employment, because of such individual's race, color, religion, sex, or national origin; or
>
> (2) to limit, segregate, or classify his employees or applicants for employment in any way which would deprive or tend to deprive any individual of employment opportunities or otherwise adversely affect his status as an employee, because of such individual's race, color, religion, sex, or national origin.[6]

One key difference between Titles VI and VII is that the former says nothing about women. Congress barely broached the subject of women's rights while debating the Civil Rights Act, except by accident. Rep. Howard W. Smith, one of the leaders of the southern Democrats, offered an amendment to extend nondiscrimination in hiring practices under Title VII to women, apparently in an attempt to weaken the bill. Unions of working men, which wielded far more power then than today, opposed equal employment rights for women, fearing that women would create competition and downward pressure on wages for their members.

Historians are still debating Smith's motives. According to David B. Filvaroff, the episode demonstrates that women's rights were introduced into civil rights law as "a segregationist's attempt to work serious mischief into civil rights law."[7] Susan Becker argues that Rep. Martha Griffiths, a Michigan Democrat, deserves credit for the amendment because she campaigned for it and got it included in the bill over the objections of labor unions. Griffiths claimed to have "used" Smith to get the bill passed, according to Becker.[8]

Over the years, one of the most common arguments against civil rights legislation has been that it inevitably creates a quota system. That is, any such laws require employers or schools to absorb a certain number of people not just on their qualifications, but also to some extent on their skin color or gender or minority status in any other category. On its face, this requirement is anathema to most Americans, particularly ones in majority populations, who believe that people should be judged according to their abilities and not given blanket advantages in hiring or admissions or other situations.

The Title VI guidelines and the Title VII statute are very sensitive to quotas. They specifically forbid the hiring or firing of any individual to satisfy a quota. According to Title VII, "Nothing contained in this sub-chapter shall be interpreted to require any employer . . . to grant preferential treatment to any individual or to any group because of the race, color, religion, sex, or national origin of such individual or group on account of an imbalance which may exist with respect to the total number or percentage of persons of any race, color, religion, sex, or national origin."[9]

But to carry any weight, the laws had to be enforced in a way that truly integrated workplaces and schoolrooms, and federal agencies often took that goal to mean affirmative action, requiring companies and schools to make an effort to identify and recruit qualified minorities beyond the procedures they used to identify and recruit others. To force entities to comply, the Civil Rights Act and subsequent regulations gave the government an important tool to wield in stamping out segregation: money. The threat of losing federal funds for a school or construction project was enough to get even the most recalcitrant administrator's attention, and as became clear later, the mere act of tying up a school or corporation's resources in defending against a complaint of discrimination proved to be such a burden that administrators were prodded to open their doors a little wider to those who looked different.

President Johnson's actions went far beyond signing the Civil Rights Act into law. In 1967 he issued a series of executive orders interpreting Title VI for a variety of applications. The most important of these were Executive Orders 11246 and 11375, which required all entities receiving federal contracts to end discrimination in hiring. The first order made no mention of sex, but after strong lobbying from women's groups, Johnson included sex as a protected category in Executive Order 11375. In 1967, the National Organization for Women persuaded the government to include women in the Office of Federal Contract Compliance Programs' Revised Order No. 4, which required federal contractors to file affirmative-action plans for groups that historically had faced discrimination.[10]

Some of these plans were quite specific. The "Philadelphia Plan," for example, required potential contractors on federal construction projects in eastern Pennsylvania to state in their bids how many members of minority groups they would hire if they won a particular contract.[11] The plan was hammered out by several executive branch agencies following a series of riots over job discrimination across the country in 1966 and 1967. It did not require particular quotas, but the understanding was that contractors needed to hire a noticeable number of minorities, which was difficult for expensive technical projects that employed the lily-white trade unions of Philadelphia. The understanding, described by one critic as "creative ambiguity," ran afoul of the General Accounting Office and was abandoned in 1968.[12]

However, similar thinking shaped the federal approach to integrating minorities into previously segregated environments—and would show up later in the regulations published under Title IX. Under President Nixon, the Philadelphia Plan was revived as part of a general shift in federal civil rights enforcement away from a goal of procedural equality—making sure that a process was nondiscriminatory on its face—and toward a goal of substantive, or end-result, equality. Nixon officials used proportional representation of racial and ethnic groups as a convenient definition of substantial equality.[13]

Given the Republican Party's hostility toward affirmative action in the twenty-first century, it may seem amazing that this Republican administration was so aggressive in promoting it. Nixon's goals were not entirely motivated by his concern for civil rights, however. George P. Schultz, his secretary of labor, saw racial discrimination as a key point at which to split the Democratic Party's power base of unions and civil rights organizations. He also had an intellectual distaste for unions' interference in the labor market, according to Hugh Davis Graham.[14] He and his assistant secretary for wage and labor standards, Arthur A. Fletcher, published the Revised Philadelphia Plan in 1969, requiring officials in the Office of Federal Contract Compliance Programs to assign a target range of percentages for jobs to be filled by members of minority groups in any given construction trade. These did not require fixed numbers of black or Hispanic or female workers to be hired, because that would have violated Title VII's ban on quotas. However, the target percentages were supposed to increase over time, with the idea that they would eventually mirror the proportion of minority members in the population as a whole. For example, plumbers and pipefitters on Philadelphia-area projects were given a 1970 goal of being 5 to 8 percent minorities. By 1973, that goal was supposed to escalate to 22 to 26 percent minorities.[15]

This logic was adopted in other contexts, including, eventually, women in education. It represents one part of the paradigm shift in the government's pursuit of civil rights that occurred during the Johnson and Nixon presidencies. In congressional testimony in 1995; Graham laid out examples of the sea change.

> What were the shared attributes that linked civil rights reform and social regulation? One was a common origin in social-movement mobilizations, first on behalf of African Americans, then on behalf of women, students, consumers and workers, the environment. . . . [To] provide this protection Congress established an array of new regulatory agencies—the Equal Employment Opportunity Commission (1964), the National Transportation Safety Board (1966), the Environmental Protection Agency

(1970), the Occupational Safety and Health Administration (1970), the Consumer Product Safety Commission (1972), and others. Additional enforcement subagencies were established by the executive branch, for example the Office for Civil Rights (OCR) in [HEW] in 1965, the Office of Federal Contract Compliance in Labor in 1965, the Office of Minority Business Enterprise (OMBE) in Commerce in 1969.[16]

These agencies developed a new model for regulating society. Instead of boards of inquiry and commissions set up to respond to complaints, they published scientifically established standards in a broad array of areas in an attempt to eliminate risks and hazards as well as discrimination, emphasizing compliance over punishments for misdeeds. These agencies were designed to cajole citizens and organizations into abiding by the law, with punishment as a last resort.[17]

While Congress could pass laws to allow the executive branch to regulate such matters as water and air quality, forcing public and private entities to open up their hiring processes was another matter entirely. Hence the reliance on federal contracts. "One of the doctrinal things that came out of the executive order [11246], and made clearer in Title VI, was the idea that the government, when it spends money, the right to put reasonable conditions on spending that money," says Jeffrey Orleans, a former civil rights lawyer for the Health, Education, and Welfare Department. "It's just like a contract for asphalt or concrete—if you break a contract, there are repercussions. Similarly, the government has the right, unless it's asking you to do anything unconstitutional, to say to you, 'Don't discriminate.'"[18]

In three cases settled in 1971, the U.S. Supreme Court gave its imprimatur to the kind of statistics and numerical formulas set down in the Philadelphia Plan to solve discrimination problems. In *Swann v. Charlotte-Mecklenburg Board of Education*, the Court ruled that a North Carolina school district had to desegregate by busing students to schools out of their neighborhoods, by redrawing attendance areas, and by other means. A related case, *North Carolina State Board of Education v. Swann*, held that finding new ratios of white to black schoolchildren was a "useful starting point" in integrating school districts. Finally, *Griggs v. Duke Power Co.* established that tests or other means to determine fitness for employment were not allowed if they disproportionately excluded women or minorities, as demonstrated by statistical evidence.[19]

When the federal Department of Health, Education, and Welfare began crafting Title IX regulations for sports a few years later, it relied on these cases, the Philadelphia Plan, and other uses of proportions and statistics to integrate schools and workplaces along racial lines as a way of defining "fairness" in athletics.

Although it was focused on attaining equal rights for black Americans, the civil rights movement helped create the environment necessary for the women's rights movement to advance its own platform after fifty years of frustrations. After 1920, when the states ratified the Nineteenth Amendment to the U.S. Constitution to give women the right for vote, Congress would introduce bills for a new constitutional amendment, the Equal Rights Amendment, guaranteeing women equal rights under the law. The bills all failed quietly.

By the 1960s, the swirl of activism around civil rights and the war in Vietnam helped reinvigorate the movement. So did the publication, in 1963, of Betty Friedan's *The Feminine Mystique*, which put forth a controversial account of the anomie of young mothers and housewives, disenfranchised in their homes in a way that women before World War II were not. Activist groups like the National Organization for Women (NOW) coalesced on a national level, proudly embracing the mantle of radical feminism. Somewhat less radical groups also were organized and began attracting chapters and members, most notably the Women's Equity Action League (WEAL).

These groups found a ready audience. More women were working, after a dip in women's employment following World War II, and they could not help but see that they were getting paid less than men and had far fewer opportunities for advancement.

At the same time, an aggressive group of women's leaders in Washington were learning to work the system from the inside. Congress had its share of powerful female members, including Edith Green and Martha Griffiths, and members of the new women's groups learned how to use the regulatory process to push civil rights agendas into social regulations, just as civil rights lawyers had.

Women's groups lobbied the Johnson administration to include women in executive orders, with a fair amount of success. In 1969, Bernice R. Sandler made the contacts she needed in the executive branch to begin using the orders to force colleges to change their hiring practices governing women.[20] Sandler had been a doctoral candidate in psychology at the University of Maryland. Her activist career emerged after she was told she was "too strong for a woman" to be considered for a job on the faculty there. At that time, female employment in the academy had plummeted, and women routinely lost out on jobs to men because male applicants were supposed to be breadwinners, and women's employment was thought to be optional.

In fighting for the job at Maryland, Sandler's research led her to Executive Order 11246, which applied to colleges because they received federal funds, mostly in the form of research grants, student loans, and congressional earmarks. Emboldened, she called up the Department of Labor's Office for Federal Contract Compliance, which connected her to Vincent G. Macaluso, the director. "He said, 'Yes, [the order] definitely covers sex discrimination at universities. Come on in and let's talk about it,'" Sandler recalls. "It turns out he had been waiting for someone to make the connection."

He introduced Sandler to Katherine East of the Labor Department's women's bureau, which had been an outgrowth of a Kennedy-era commission on the status of women. East not only was the center of a developing network of women's activists in the government and throughout Washington, she also had what in those days was an activist's most powerful weapon: a Xerox machine.

Macaluso and East encouraged Sandler to file a formal complaint, citing data and patterns of discrimination against women. She used studies of women faculty from Columbia University and the University of Chicago, and collected her own data on Maryland faculty members. Her report charted inequities in faculty rank, pay, interviews, and so on. In January 1970, she and other members of WEAL started filing complaints against colleges and universities, charging them with violating Executive Order 11246 by discriminating against women in the hiring of faculty members. The complaints charged that a pattern of discrimination against women existed in the academy, citing admissions quotas for female students at undergraduate and graduate programs and inadequate financial aid in addition to discriminatory employment practices.

Sandler made two hundred copies of the report and sent it with a press release to the Washington newspapers, other media, and members of Congress. Macaluso followed up by asking congressmen to write to the secretary of Labor urging him to enforce the executive order.

"Higher education was hysterical, saying, 'Nobody's going to tell us what to do,'" Sandler says. Courts had traditionally given colleges broad latitude as a matter of academic freedom, but did not shield them from the new antidiscrimination laws. The Department of Labor began investigating the University of Maryland in April 1970, and ever so slowly, doors began to open for women.

Over the next two years, Sandler filed 250 complaints against colleges and universities. WEAL and NOW also filed similar complaints.

This activism did not go unnoticed. After numerous discussions with Reps. Martha Griffiths of Michigan and Edith Green of Tennessee, both Democrats, Sandler got a job as a consultant to Green's Subcommittee on Higher Education in 1970. The following year, Green empaneled hearings on sex discrimination in education. They came at one of the rare times when women's issues were near the top of the congressional agenda. Both houses were debating the Equal Rights Amendment, and the legislation had a chance of passing for the first time in fifty years of similar efforts.

In putting together the hearings, Sandler and the rest of Green's staff identified a number of leaders from WEAL and women throughout higher education who would, testify. The American Council on Education and other members of Washington higher-education establishment refused to send representatives to testify, claiming that sex discrimination was not a problem in American colleges.

Green's original plan was to submit legislation to amend Title VI of the Civil Rights Act to cover women. Other politicians discouraged her out of fear that bringing the act up for amendment might inspire conservative southern members of Congress to tinker with it themselves.

Green's legislation therefore adapted the language from Title VI—"no person in the United States shall, on the ground of race, color, or national origin, be excluded from participation in, be denied the benefits of, or be subjected to discrimination under any program or activity receiving federal financial assistance"—to academe: "no person in the United States shall, on the basis of sex, be denied the benefits of, or be subjected to discrimination under, any educational program or activity receiving federal financial assistance."

Sandler, Green, and others working on the legislation saw it as addressing employment primarily. Other issues were secondary, they thought "With students, we're really thinking, when hearings began, that okay, there's discrimination and quotas, and there was some testimony about discrimination in [the awarding of] scholarships," Sandler says. "We knew vocational counseling was bad, that there were pink forms for girls and blue forms for boys, but we really didn't know enough about discrimination."

As a result, only a few moments of the two weeks of hearings in June and July 1970 focused on student, and scholarship sports were mentioned only twice in passing. The hearings themselves, packed with testimony about classified-advertisement sections of newspapers, which had special spaces for women's jobs and postings of jobs "for men only," became enormous history. A two-volume set of the hearing transcripts made its way through congressional offices and the headquarters of women's organizations, generating widespread support for Green's legislation.

The stir on Capitol Hill finally got the attention of college presidents and the American Council on Education, their lobbying organization. Harvard, Princeton, and Yale had recently begun allowing women into their student bodies, and Dartmouth was on the verge of doing so. After some lobbying, Green agreed to support an amendment to her bill to exempt private undergraduate admissions. The exemption was narrowly written, stating that colleges had the right to remain single-sex, but that if they were in the process of changing from single-sex to coeducational, they had to comply with the law within seven years.

During floor debate over what would become Title IX, the question of whether it would apply to sports finally came up. Senator Peter H. Dominick, a Republican from Colorado, was quizzing the bill's Senate sponsor, Democrat Birch Bayh of Indiana. Dominick asked, "In what way is the senator thinking here?" referring to the bill's call for all programs and activities to be free from discrimination by sex. "Is he thinking in terms of dormitory facilities, is he thinking in terms of athletic facilities or equipment, or in what terms are we dealing here? Or are we dealing with just educational requirements?"

Bayh, who was drafted to sponsor the bill because of his endorsement of the Equal Rights Amendment, responded: "I do not read this as requiring integration of dormitories between the sexes, nor do I feel it mandates the desegregation of the football fields. What we are trying to do here is provide equal access for women and men students to the educational process and the extracurricular activities in a school, where there is not a unique facet such as football involved. We are not requiring that intercollegiate football be desegregated, nor that the men's locker room be desegregated."

That seemed to satisfy Dominick, although he had one further comment: "If I may say so, I would have had much more fun playing college football if it had been integrated." Bayh said he would restrain himself from responding.[21]

This was the only discussion of college sports during the entire debate over the sex-discrimination bill. Although even Bayh, a liberal and a champion of women's rights to this day, thought football was an exception, he made it clear that the new law would apply to extracurricular activities at a college. In subsequent years he has said in public appearances and private interviews that he intended all along for the law to cover sports. He is fond of quoting his father, who went to Congress in the 1930s to ask for funds for physical education for girls in the District of Columbia public schools. "He was going to tell them that little girls needed strong bodies to carry their minds around, just like little boys," Bayh told a federal commission in 2002. "And you know, that theory is true today for girls and young women of all ages, and really is sort of a bedrock of Title IX."[22]

Both the House and the Senate approved versions of the law in 1971, but the Senate did not approve House amendments introduced later. The law finally passed as a conference report on June 8, 1972, and was signed into law by President Nixon fifteen days later. The Equal Rights Amendment finally passed the same year, but failed to win enough support among state legislatures.

A full copy of Title IX may be found in appendix A, but in summary, it reads, "No person in the United States shall, on the basis of sex, be excluded from participation in, be denied the benefits of, or be subjected to discrimination under any education program or activity receiving Federal financial assistance."[23] Admissions to private institutions are exempted, as are the operations of institutions controlled by religious organizations if compliance would violate the tenets of their faith. Military academies are also exempt.

In addition, the law specifies that the prohibition on sex discrimination

> shall [not] be interpreted to require any educational institution to grant preferential or disparate treatment to the members of one sex on account of an imbalance which may exist with respect to the total number or percentage of persons of that sex participating in or receiving the benefits of any federally supported program or activity, in comparison with the total percentage of person of that sex in any community, state, section, or other area: Provided, That this subsection shall not be construed to prevent the consideration in any hearing or proceeding under this title of statistical evidence tending to show that such an imbalance exists with respect to the participation in, or receipt of the benefits of, any such program or activity by the members of one sex.

This language forbids the explicit use of proportionality as a singular means of defining compliance, as required under the Philadelphia Plan, but just as explicitly, it permits the consideration of the ratio of female students to males in judging whether a school is denying members of either sex the chance to participate or receive the benefits of an educational program.

The law applies to educational institutions receiving federal funds from any agency, and requires each such agency to set up a compliance program to monitor its funding recipients.

One difficult point remained. The law did not specifically define an "educational program or activity receiving federal financial assistance." Student loan programs backed by the federal government certainly were covered. Activities in buildings financed by congressional earmarks might be. What about extracurricular activities like sports? That was unclear, and the ambiguity laid the foundation for many of the coming debates.

As with the Civil Rights Act of 1964, the executive branch had to publish a series of regulations and guidelines to explain how educational institutions should comply with Title IX. The Civil Rights Act had required pages and pages of specific discussions of rules and punishments, which were clarified by President Johnson's executive orders. By comparison, Title IX is short in length and broad in scope, and the specifics were left to the Department of Health, Education, and Welfare, known as HEW. The department hired Jeffrey Orleans straight out of law school at the University of North Carolina in 1971 as one of six civil rights lawyers, plunging him into one of the most contentious periods in American higher education. Within two years, President Nixon signed an executive order forcing HEW to oversee contract compliance and employment regulations for the nation's schools and colleges; Congress passed Title IX; and the father of Kenneth Adams, a schoolboy in Charlotte, sued the department to force it to move faster to enforce its own desegregation rules. The case, *Adams v. Richardson*, became a landmark requiring federal agencies to enforce their rules in a timely manner. The Women's Equity Action League also sued the department on similar grounds, but a judge ruled their case moot when the Supreme Court ruled in favor of Adams.

Orleans and his colleagues worked on racial-desegregation cases as well as the first set of regulations for Title IX, and their experiences in the former influenced the latter. They began requiring schools and colleges to submit data on admissions and employment to the department. They also ran into some trickier issues with Title IX, according to Orleans. "We saw that there was value to letting federal funds continue going to private institutions that were single-sex," he says. "There's a different set of issues for private undergraduate education that's single-sex than for either public institutions that are single-sex or for private institutions that racially discriminate."

For a variety of social, cultural, and psychological reasons, a plausible case can be made, or could have been made in 1972, for permitting private institutions to teach members of only one sex, Orleans says, even though the concept of "separate but equal" educational opportunities for black and white students had been ruled illegal.

HEW had no intention of establishing gender quotas for undergraduate or graduate admissions, Orleans says, but its lawyers did apply the same kinds of standards they had applied in school-desegregation cases. They began by looking at the demographics of a given population, for example, children in a particular school district. If substantial discrepancies marked a single school in the district, then investigators might take a close look at the school. If the reasons for the disparity included discrimination, such as the school principal refusing to let black students transfer in, the department attempted to negotiate an "agreement to resolve" that would eliminate the discriminatory practice. After HEW and the school signed the agreement, the department monitored the school for some years to make sure it performed the actions specified. Upon the conclusion of the monitoring, if the discrimination had been eliminated, the department would give the school what amounted to a clean bill of health.

The thinking behind the Philadelphia Plan and the Supreme Court's 1971 decisions thus found its way into the rapidly expanding landscape of civil rights law and practice. Using numbers and population statistics was acceptable in an analysis of a potential violation of civil rights laws, but employing them in a formula to determine whether a violation had taken place was a much trickier matter. Quotas, of course, were to be avoided at all costs.

Lawyers and policymakers have always sparred over quotas and whether they are ever permissible. Titles VI, VII, and IX, along with other civil rights laws, are meant to improve the lot of minority groups as a whole, but never as a benefit to, or as a cost to, one individual. This group-versus-individual struggle has shaped the debate over Title IX since Congress passed the law.

3
CHAPTER
·

Heroines as Well as Heroes

Title IX threw open the schoolhouse doors. It also threw open the doors to the gym—for female students and for coaches both. Competing became acceptable, training became acceptable, and schools sent teams out to play almost immediately. Teams require not just players, but coaches, coaches like Sylvia Rhyne Hatchell, Judy Wilkins Rose, and Pat Head Summitt, who met each other in Knoxville as graduate students in physical education in the fall of 1974. That fall they started three of the most remarkable careers of any women in college sports.

They did not start with much. Summitt, training for the 1976 Olympics and rehabilitating a knee injury, was put in charge of the fledgling varsity women's basketball team at Tennessee. She asked Rose to be her assistant, and Hatchell was put in charge of the junior varsity club. "I had a graduate assistantship when I arrived here in the fall of 1974," Summitt says. "I expected to be the assistant coach, but the head coach took a sabbatical. I remember Judy and I walking from the HPER [Health, Physical Education, and Recreation] building to Alumni Gymnasium when I really started talking to her about coaching, and one thing just led to another."[1]

All three women had grown up in the last era when girls who played sports with their brothers and friends were called tomboys. None of them recall being criticized for being unladylike; Rose thinks that their parents figured that playing sports kept them from doing less savory things. "Maybe because it was a small town, and there wasn't much else to do," she says of her sporty childhood in South Carolina in the 1950s and 1960s. "We had a movie theater, but then it went under. But this was prior to all the drug issues, alcohol, smoking, all of that. It was more of, 'Hey, it keeps the kids occupied,' that kind of mentality in a small town. The town took a great deal of pride in us, and I really was not hassled for being a tomboy."

Hatchell had a similar experience growing up in Gastonia, North Carolina, where she played both junior high and high school basketball. Gastonia had basketball and a handful of other sports for girls, but that was more than the nearest big city, Charlotte, which had no high school sports for girls well into the 1970s.

The basketball the three women played had three things in common with boys' basketball (and the kind played by women today): two hoops and a ball. They played six-on-six ball, which dictated that players had to stay in the front court or in the back court, playing two nearly separate three-on-three games. Sometimes they had "rovers"—one player per team who got to run the entire court. Gradually, toward the end of high school, they began playing the same five-on-five game boys had been playing since the nineteenth century.

All three women went to small colleges and became basketball stars— Hatchell at Carson-Newman College in Tennessee, Rose at Winthrop College in South Carolina, and Summitt at the University of Tennessee at Martin. They graduated with bachelor's degrees in physical education in 1974, just as college officials were starting to realize that a new law passed in Washington required they rethink how they offered sports for women. Tennessee-Knoxville was the best-known physical education program in the region, so that is where they went.

When they got there, they found themselves in charge. "That showed the level of importance they placed on [women's sports]," Rose notes wryly. "Granted, Pat was very good and had been to the World University Games, but she had no coaching experience, and she was a graduate student. Yet her first head-coaching job was to coach the University of Tennessee."

Across the country, women like Hatchell, Rose, and Summitt found themselves in the right place at the right time. Men did not coach women; colleges were adding or upgrading hundreds of women's teams, and they needed coaches.

"When we started applying for jobs, some guy [in our class] would say, 'Hey! I just got offered the job at Knox Junior High to be the football coach!'" Rose recalls. "Then a girl would come in . . . and say, 'Y'all, I just got offered the job to coach girls' tennis at the University of North Alabama. I have to coach basketball, too, but I think I'm going to do it.' Every day, somebody was getting word back. The guys were getting junior high and high school jobs, and the girls were getting college jobs. People got serious [about expanding women's sports]. It was real definite that federal funds would be taken away if they didn't do something. So they started implementing Title IX, and it became very strong."

Summitt stayed at Tennessee; Rose considered jobs at Francis Marion and Lenoir-Rhyne before accepting an offer to coach at the University of

North Carolina at Charlotte, and Hatchell took the Francis Marion job. They did not start with much.

"We had a limited budget," Summitt says. "I think there was a ten-thousand-dollar budget for five women's sports. There were no scholarships, we didn't charge admission, and it was really just a cut above the intramural level of play. We played local schools—Maryville College, Tennessee Tech, Carson-Newman. The longest road trip we took was to Rock Hill, South Carolina, for a tournament, or to Western Carolina. We traveled in vans and sold doughnuts to buy uniforms."

When Rose, Hatchell, and Summitt took their teams onto the court, they did not do so under the auspices of the NCAA or the smaller National Association of Intercollegiate Athletics (NAIA). Those were men's organizations. Instead, they played in the brand-new Association for Intercollegiate Athletics for Women, an organization conceived by the physical-education associations to give female athletes expert coaching and better competition on varsity-style teams.

AIAW officials, all of whom were physical-education teachers, still saw competition as desirable, but only within limits, so they built into rules safeguards to maintain the amateur, educational approach to sport. But their efforts to promote a distinctive brand of women's sports were ultimately in vain. Even before Title IX passed, the NCAA was eager to start its own set of championships. NCAA officials say that they were trying just to do the right thing for female students; their critics say the NCAA was trying to consolidate its power as a monopoly over amateur sports. As college presidents began to accept the wide-ranging implications of Title IX, they grew uncomfortable with having women's sports under the supervision of the physical-education department while men's sports operated as a separate entity. They decided that equality meant men and women should be under the same umbrella.

Ironically, the AIAW's own rules came into conflict with Title IX regulations, which used the male model of college sports to define equality between the sexes. This provided even further incentive to move women's sports programs out of physical-education departments, out from under the supervision of faculty, and into men's athletics departments, which were run to promote men's basketball and football.

The public mind-set about women in sports had begun to change in the mid-1960s in part as a result of the Cold War. The public watched women were compete on television, mostly in individual sports like tennis and gymnastics. Any competition in which Americans could beat Soviets was met with general approval. Although colleges had cut back on most sports offerings for women in the years following World War II, by the middle to late 1960s more colleges were experimenting with intercollegiate athletics for women.

As mentioned earlier, the first college championship for female athletes was the 1941 golf tournament at Ohio State sanctioned by the National Section on Women's Athletics of the American Association for Health, Physical Education, and Recreation, or AAHPER. The tournament became a yearly event in 1946, and a decade later the various organizations governing women's sports formed the Tripartite Golf Committee. By 1958, that group had expanded to form the Joint Committee on Extra-mural Sports, which was designed to unite and streamline the efforts of the dizzying array of organizations that had some jurisdiction over sports for women at the time: the AAHPER women's section, which soon became the Division of Girls' and Women's Sports; the National Association of Directors of Physical Education, and the Athletic and Recreation Federation of College Women.

The task of the joint committee was to satisfy the fast-growing interest among college women in competitive sports in the late 1950s and early 1960s. As women broke down barriers in all facets in society, their interest in sports also grew, after watching Wilma Rudolph, tennis players like Margaret Court and Billie Jean King, and other athletes.

At the same time, the women in charge of the physical-education associations were worried about losing control over women's athletics. Dissatisfied with what they were getting in college settings—especially in comparison to what male athletes got in uniforms, training table meals, and facilities—some women were playing tennis and competing in semipro sports at private clubs, corporate teams, and AAU programs.[2] Some women were also competing on men's teams when they could.

"I was playing almost-semipro softball in the 1960s with the Raybestos Brakettes, playing against outside amateur teams," says Donna A. Lopiano, a four-sport athlete who became athletics director at the University of Texas at Austin and later director of the Women's Sports Foundation. "I played in four national championships, and we drew crowds in the thousands in small towns in Connecticut."

Administrators with the Division for Girls' and Women's Sports realized that women were going to find opportunities to compete in elite, Olympic-style sports and decided that it would be better for those women to compete within the American educational system, under the supervision of qualified women, rather than allowing the AAU or NCAA to take command. In 1963, Sara Staff Jernigan of the DGWS addressed the NCAA's annual convention, asking the association to stop allowing women to compete on men's teams. She said she and other educators feared that women would be in danger of getting roughed up in games against men, and that women's sports would not develop if the best athletes were skimmed off by men's programs. Women leaders were also deeply suspicious of the regular scandals in men's sports—stories of players being allowed to skate through classes, boosters handing out bribes to recruit talented players, and point-shaving to help gamblers.

"The women in the sixties were historians, students of what had happened in intercollegiate athletics, and one thing they all recognized was that men's sport had gotten to where it was because physical educators, male physical educators, had taken a hands-off approach, saying, 'I don't want to have anything to do with that,'" Lopiano says. Women educators "were faced with repeated history. They took responsibility. They knew highly competitive sport for women was going to come in an educational construct, and that they needed to control it and keep it educational."

At the time, the NCAA did not object. In 1964, the association satisfied Jernigan by passing a rule to limit championship participation to men. It also created a "special liaison committee on women's athletics" the same year.[3]

At the same time, DGWS officials began to explore the idea of creating an organization to sponsor women's championships, which would involve creating a new structure to govern women's sports across the country. Again, NCAA officials approved. In a 1966 memorandum, Charles S. Neinas, the top assistant to NCAA director Walter F. Byers, wrote that the "NCAA limits its jurisdiction and authority to male student-athletes. . . . Consequently, a national organization assuming responsibility for women's athletics would not be in conflict with this Association."[4]

In 1967, AAHPER announced the formation of the Commission on Intercollegiate Athletics for Women (CIAW) "to give college women more opportunities for high level competition in athletics." A news release announced that a national college championship in gymnastics would be held in March or April 1969, with a track meet scheduled for April or May. The schedule called for swimming, badminton, and volleyball championships in 1970, and the golf tournament was subsumed under the new slate.[5]

Katherine Ley of the AAHPER was to be in charge of the new organization, which would replace all of the competing committees and associations. Her platform for the new organization was as follows:

> Children growing up need heroines as well as heroes. We suspect that the naming of national champions each year in the different sports will make sports activity seem more desirable and will motivate less talented girls all over the country to learn sports skills and to enjoy sports on their own.[6]

Within three years, AAHPER officials decided they needed a separate and more formal structure for the championships slate, and they spun off the CIAW into the AIAW in January 1972.

Developing their own association free from the influence of men, the women of the AIAW had a great feeling of ownership and protectiveness over their organization. They were able to reinvent the "girl for every sport, and a sport for every girl" philosophy from the history of their organizations, and the teams and championships they sponsored were structured to promote broad participation more than competition. They banned athletic scholarships and placed significant restrictions on recruiting.

This sentiment was reflected in the AIAW Policy Statement, adopted in May 1974:

> We believe sport is an important aspect of our culture and a fertile field for learning. The sense of enjoyment, self-confidence, and physical well-being derived from demanding one's best performance in a sport situation is a meaningful experience for the athlete. These inner satisfactions are the fundamental motivation for participation in sports. Therefore, programs in an educational setting should have these benefits as primary goals.
>
> In keeping with this belief, the following program elements are vitally important:
>
> **1.** The enrichment of the life of the participant is the focus and reason for the existence of any athletic program. All decisions should be made with this fact in mind.
>
> **2.** The participants in athletic programs, including players, coaches, and support personnel, should have access to and representation on the policy-making group on campus and in sport governing organizations.
>
> **3.** Adequate funding is necessary to provide a comprehensive program. Sufficient funds should be provided for
> - A broad spectrum of sports experiences;
> - A variety of levels of competitive experiences;
> - Travel using licensed carriers;
> - Appropriate housing and food;
> - Rated officials;
> - Well-trained coaches;
> - Equipment, supplies, and facilities which aid performance and appeal to the aesthetic aspects of sport;
> - Competent staff for administering and publicizing the program;
> - Qualified medical and training personnel;
> - and regular opportunities for social interaction with opponents.

4. Careful consideration is needed for scheduling practice sessions and games. The athletic schedule should ensure sufficient time to gain personal satisfaction from skill achievement, but should not deny the student the time to participate in other activities. Factors to be considered include:

- Equitable competition at all levels;
- Adequate pre-season conditioning;
- Appropriate spacing and length of practice sessions;
- Sufficient number of events in each sport; and
- Comparable length of seasons between sports.

5. Separate but comparable teams should be provided for women and men. In addition to separate teams, intercollegiate coeducational teams comprised of an equal number of women and men competing on opposing teams is desirable in those sports in which such teams are appropriate.

Athletic ability is one of the talents which can be considered in the awarding of financial aid to students. However, students should be free to choose the institution on the basis of curriculum and program. Staff time and effort should be devoted to the comprehensive program rather than to recruiting efforts.[7]

This is more a manifesto than a set of playing rules. The women in charge of the AIAW were fighting for equal funding and equal recognition on their own campuses, accustomed as they were to having to pile into players' and coaches' cars to get to a road game. While they wanted their fair share of funding, they really wanted to maintain the independence to conduct their own sports programs with their own values.

Among those values was a certain egalitarianism. In the first AIAW championship, in volleyball in 1972, participants ranged from huge urban campuses like UCLA to tiny rural ones like Sul Ross State in Alpine, Texas. In fact, Sul Ross beat UCLA in the championship match. The NCAA had separated into college and university divisions fifteen years earlier, and was on the verge of creating even more divisions.

Early rules were carefully drawn to be restrictive. The AIAW forbade flying recruits onto campuses for visits, a common practice among men's basketball and football teams. Christine H. B. Grant, one of the AIAW's presidents, described the organization's approach to recruiting as "a system that attempted to achieve three goals: (a) to avoid the harassment of high school athletes; (b) to create a system that was financially reasonable to all member institutions; and (c) to prevent the burnout of coaches who spend excessive time in the recruitment of athletes."[8]

The AIAW was accepted widely and quickly. A total of 275 colleges and universities signed on as charter members, including junior colleges, women's colleges, liberal-arts colleges, regional universities, and state flagship institutions (a complete list can be found in appendix B). However, women were still in a world of postgame meals of fast-foot hamburgers and self-transportation while their male counterparts ate steak and took chartered planes and buses. In 1973, Margaret Dunkle of the Women's Project on Education catalogued the following complaints:

At a prestigious private institution the women's and men's physical education departments were separate and the instructional courses available to female and male students varied considerably. For example, women could not take wrestling and men could not take self-defense or volleyball.

At a southern state university female students could not take coaching courses for credit, with the result that they were not "qualified" to coach teams. At an Ohio liberal arts college women majoring in physical education must take a service course each term. There is no similar requirement for men.

At a Pennsylvania college women must show proficiency in two sports in order to graduate. Men need only to show proficiency in one sport.

Men, but not women may be able to exempt required physical education courses by taking a skills test.

Male, but not female, varsity athletes may be exempted from physical-education classes.

Men, but not women, may receive academic credit for participating in intercollegiate athletics.

Women, but not men, may be able to fulfill their physical-education requirements by taking such courses as square dancing, bowling, or archery.

At a major state university, women were prohibited from participating in any of the five team sports in the "All Campus Division Program." They could only compete in the individual or dual sports.

At one Ohio institution a woman could not use the handball courts unless a male signed up for her.

At a large Midwestern university, the intramural pool was specifically reserved for "faculty, administrative staff and male students" for approximately two hours each day. That is, this was a time for men only.

At an Ivy League college the women's crew team was given inferior equipment because the coach of the men's team did not believe that women could handle the newer, better shells. At another Eastern college, the crew coach authorized the use of funds designated for both the female and male teams to purchase a shell designed for men only, rather than for a shell both sexes could use.

At a private Eastern university, members of the male football team at a "training table" which featured high-protein food. No similar provisions were made for any female athletes.

At a west coast state university, certain insurance programs are available to men athletes only.

The women's varsity basketball team at an ex–women's college had difficulty practicing because they were allowed to use the gym only when the men's teams did not want it.

The women's swimming team at one elite eastern school had to practice on weeknights after dinner because no other time at the pool was made available for the women to practice.

In some stadiums, women are not allowed in the press box, with the result that they cannot adequately cover games.

Women at a prestigious western university protested so-called "honey shots" of women spectators at sports events. The women said they neither wanted nor needed "the defense of their physical attractiveness by [the] sports information director nor the media."

A large Midwestern university spent over $2,600,000 on its men's intercollegiate athletics program. There was no comparable program for women's intercollegiate athletics. In fact, no university money whatsoever was officially spent on women's intercollegiate athletics.

At a formerly all-female college, men compete in five sports (with an annual budget of $4,750), while women have three sports (with a $2,060 budget).

At a larger Midwestern football power the men's sports programs are controlled by the athletic department while the women's programs are under the auspices of the physical-education department.

At a western state university, the women's athletics department is an administrative subsection of the men's department.

A woman who had worked for several years in the women's physical education department applied for an opening on the men's athletic staff. Though qualified for the job, she was not even considered. Instead, a recent male graduate was hired.

At a major Midwestern university the men's athletics director is paid $10,000 more than the women's athletic director, even though they perform essentially the same work.

Coaches at a state university in the South are paid to coach the men's teams. The coaches for the women's teams are not paid to coach. They are paid as physical education instructors only, and coach (without compensation) in addition to their full-time teaching responsibilities.[9]

The issue of whether female athletes should be competing on male teams remained controversial. The *Athletic Director*, a newsletter published by the National Council of Secondary School Athletics Officials, said in 1974 that "while positive experiences for the exceptional girl competitor may occur through participation in boys or men's competitive groups, these instances are rare and should be judged acceptable only as an interim procedure for use until girls' programs can be initiated."[10]

This was a crucial issue. The NCAA had reconsidered its decision to ban women from its championships in 1974, fearing it could be sued for violating women's rights under the Fourteenth Amendment to the U.S. Constitution, even before Title IX had been introduced in Congress. Some male athletics directors believed they could accommodate women in sports simply by opening tryouts to everyone, male and female: Women could go out for a team and get cut because they were too small, too slow, or lacked other skills, but the school would have protected their legal obligations.

But that end run around the law never became popular. Women's officials pressed the point that women needed sex-segregated sports programs, and men's officials and employees of HEW never pressed the point. Thus, women created perhaps the only context in civil rights law where "separate but equal" was tolerated and even endorsed. According to an undated memorandum from Dorothy McKnight and Joan Hult of the University of Maryland addressed to AIAW members,

> It is time for adoption of an affirmative action which demands full support for separate teams for women on an equitable basis with that afforded men. In addition, mixed (co-ed) teams should be encouraged as important to the total athletic programs for college men and women.
>
> . . . Our counterpart, the NCAA, has made a clear verbal statement, if not a written policy, supporting the right of women to "try out" for membership on men's teams. This practiced policy has helped prevent discriminatory claims being filed against NCAA or a member school. This policy is the vehicle being used to provide "equality of opportunity"; when, in fact, it is actually a type of tokenism for the exceptional woman athlete.
>
> There may be immediate relief from this new situation as a result of the guidelines of the Education Amendment Act of 1972, Title IX. There seems to be clear evidence that there can be NO TOKENISM in "Competitive Athletics." However, legal counsel advised that cooperative sponsorship of a policy supporting separate teams by the governing bodies of intercollegiate athletics for both men and women would hasten the reality of equality of opportunity.[11]

Some male officials were extremely supportive. The National Association of Intercollegiate Athletics' leadership sent the AIAW a letter saying, "The NAIA Executive Committee is fully aware of the problems which face our member institutions in financing separate men's and women's programs of intercollegiate competition. . . . We are free to admit we have no magic or painless solution. However, NAIA is most sympathetic to the AIAW program and is committed to give every assistance to make it possible for opportunities for athletic competition for women to develop."[12]

Even as women won these initial battles for separate programs, however, they found themselves embroiled in a bigger war: the struggle to decide who would ultimately govern women's sports. In the mid-1960s, the NCAA decided that it needed to begin sponsoring women's programs. Its espoused reasons were legal—as the women's movement was so ably demonstrating, institutions available to men ought also to be available to women. AIAW leaders believe to this day that the NCAA was angling to cement its control over all of collegiate sports.

The first steps were cautious. In 1966 the NCAA's Neinas wrote again to CIAW officials asking if they planned to conduct championships. "Please do not misinterpret this letter," he wrote. "The NCAA has enough problems of its own without irritating DGWS or the gals. It should be recognized, however, that some of the athletic directors in the NCAA believe that national competition for women will stimulate activity at the grass-roots level."[13]

In 1967, the NCAA Council, a group of athletic administrators and college presidents that served as the organization's board of directors, appointed a study committee to consider "the feasibility of establishing appropriate machinery for the control and supervision of women's athletics."[14] In explaining the council's actions, Arthur W. Nebel of the University of Missouri wrote,

> All of us are aware of women's important role [in society]. They now are becoming more interested in intercollegiate athletics. NCAA championships are limited to male students. Also, the Association's rules and regulations governing recruiting, financial aid and eligibility apply only to the male student.
>
> It was recently brought to the Council's attention than an increasing number of NCAA institutions are sponsoring intercollegiate athletic activities for women. Some of these institutions have sought the advice of the Association as to the proper administrative procedures for an intercollegiate program for female students.
>
> As a result, the Council has appointed a committee to study the feasibility of establishing appropriate machinery to provide for supervision and administration of women's intercollegiate athletics. . . . This should not be misconstrued as an effort on the part of the NCAA to establish women's championships or extend present Association regulations to women's intercollegiate athletics. It is possible that this may be the eventual result.[15]

That fall, the NCAA became more direct. Walter F. Byers, the association's cantankerous executive director, fired what many women considered a shot across the bow in October 1967. In a letter to women's leaders, he wrote, "The question of whether the NCAA is the organization to take this job [of governing women's college sports] is a question yet to be determined. Likewise, I presume that the question of whether the AAH-PER (through DGWS) is the appropriate organization to supervise and control women's intercollegiate sports has not been determined."[16]

Byers continued to press the question as the decade turned. In 1971, he wrote to Elizabeth Hoyt of the AIAW to say that he had asked the NCAA's lawyer, George H. Gangwere, to evaluate whether the men's association could be held liable for not permitting women to participate in its championships. This letter predated Title IX by a year and a half, and was written four months before Edith Green held hearings in the House of Representatives about inequities in education. "It appears that the NCAA is in a difficult legal position on the basis of its present posture and I suspect that it is quite likely that we will proceed to remove such barriers and, in fact, provide competitive opportunities for women as well as men," he wrote.[17]

A month later, Byers reported to his members on Gangwere's opinion.

> Because there are numerous opportunities for female athletes to participate (e.g., the Olympic Games), they would have justification to complain that the NCAA does discriminate by preventing females from competing in events against other female athletes. (If the United States constitutional amendment for women's rights is adopted, there probably no longer would be any legally tenable grounds for disqualifying an athletically-talented female from competing in an NCAA event against males.)
>
> For the present, action, if any, will more than likely come on the grounds of the equal protection clause of the Fourteenth Amendment. . . . It could be argued that any illegal discrimination is that of member institutions, not the NCAA.[18]

Neinas told AIAW officials that he hoped their organization would be the appropriate venue for collegiate female athletes, but that the NCAA had to make plans if AIAW leaders felt "that you cannot make the adjustments necessary to accomplish that end."[19] The implication was that the AIAW's emphasis on participation would not provide female athletes opportunities "comparable" to those of male NCAA athletes.

The NCAA by this time was well established as the largest athletic organization in the country, sponsoring championships for hundreds of schools of all sizes and missions. The NAIA was very viable, especially in basketball, but NCAA officials controlled the airwaves for football and basketball broadcasts, and their championship events were becoming fixtures on the American sporting scene.

Contempt might be too strong a word, but the men of the NCAA were not very impressed with the AIAW's attitude toward sports. To NCAA officials, the AIAW's model was one of playing sports and having postgame teas, while the men were the "real" athletes. They were dubious that a professional association of educators could manage a sports program, and they certainly did not think the women's organizations were up to the task of administering women's athletics.

Neinas recalls approaching DGWS officials in the 1960s in one of the conversations about improving the United States' medal count in the Olympics. The U.S. Olympic Committee "was willing to put some development money into women's sports, and I said, 'Can you [in the DGWS] help us channel it?' The response was, they weren't interest in competition. That was the group that believed in Play Days, and they didn't want to have too high a level of competition."[20]

Byers's 1971 memo brought a furious response from Rachel Bryant of the AIAW:

> No action the NCAA could take would be a bigger mistake [than to try to co-opt female athletes or the AIAW]. A group of professional women educators have designed an organization and a program in accordance with their accepted philosophy and standards to meet the needs and interests of college women students. To have it now threatened by an organization designed for men and controlled by men would cause such a furor that the NCAA would have a real battle on its hands. The possibility of one girl instituting a court suit to participate on a male varsity team would be a very pale issue in comparison.[21]

The passage of Title IX in 1972 and the kickoff of the AIAW's championships pushed the issue of the NCAA and women's sports to the forefront. The women's movement, according to Byers, made Title IX a national battle instead of a local one: "It's tough for a woman to do battle with the football coach on a Division I-A campus, but a collection of determined women at the national level—with political support and media attention—could take on the NCAA and look very good indeed," he theorized.[22]

While mounting its own challenges to the law, which will be discussed in chapter 4, the NCAA pushed ahead on the question of whether to start championships for women. In 1975 the association sent another of Byers's assistants, Thomas A. Jernstedt, to address the AIAW's convention in Houston. Jernstedt remembers a very chilly reception. "I flew to Houston and made a very brief presentation to say that the NCAA sent me here to share with this organization that the NCAA had been involved in discussions to establish women's championships, perhaps in the next academic year; that hadn't been totally resolved."

According to the AIAW's minutes, Jernstedt said that.

> The association has attempted to cooperate with women's amateur sports organizations for more than eleven years.
>
> This is not a new area of concern for the Association; it is simply that the emphasis and problems involved here have increased markedly over the past two years.
>
> In response to the membership's request for direction in this matter, the Council directed the NCAA staff to prepare a report and recommendations regarding NCAA's role in women's intercollegiate athletics. That report was received by the Council. It recommends that the Association move now to provide the same meaningful services in high quality national championship competition, backed by the same administrative support, for women student athletes and teams of its member institutions as it does for men student athletes. It recommends that the only satisfactory approach, considering the demands of court decisions, to the necessary institutional control of all of its intercollegiate athletic programs is to place men's and women's programs under the same administration, the same legislative body, and the same eligibility rules. It further recommends that the NCAA begin immediately to offer national intercollegiate competition for women in selected sports. Your Council approved the concept of that report and referred the recommendations to the Special Committee on Women's Intercollegiate Athletics for implementation at the earliest possible time.[23]

Before he had finished speaking, Jernstedt says, delegates were streaming off the convention floor, heading outside to call their campuses to see if their presidents would support an effort to quell the NCAA's plan.

Carol Gordon, chairwoman of the AIAW's executive council, fired off a telegram to the NCAA's convention, which was taking place at the same time in Washington:

> AIAW views with grave concern the announced intention of NCAA to commence a pilot program of intercollegiate athletics for women. For the sake of future harmony in administration of intercollegiate sports programs for all students and to restore an atmosphere of cooperation in which a mutually beneficial exchange of views and exploration of future alternatives might continue, the Executive Board of AIAW urges the Executive Council to reconsider immediately its decision to initiate any pilot program in women's intercollegiate championships. AIAW has no choice but to view failure to reconsider as an effort by NCAA to undermine the existing women's intercollegiate championship program.[24]

"So it was not met with any noticeable enthusiasm," says Jernstedt of his efforts.

> "I think there were individuals like Linda Estes [the women's athletic director at the University of New Mexico], and I'm sure others in the crowd, who understood it and thought, "This was very interesting," and that it may be better for women student-athletes, and they were silent. This was a very genuine desire and effort by the NCAA to see if we could provide better and more extensive competitive opportunities; [media and public] exposure, I think, was one of the primary components. . . . The NCAA, because of the broad scope of the program on the men's side, was in a stronger position to move women's athletics to a higher level.

The time was not quite right, however. The mass exodus from the convention that Jernstedt's address caused came back to swamp the NCAA. Enough of the AIAW women had prevailed with their presidents and male athletics directors to force the NCAA convention to table the matter.

The campus debates over the governance of women's sports mirrored the national one. As college presidents realized that they would have to provide "equitable" programs for female athletes, many of them decided they ought to make women's programs look like men's programs. They moved women's sports out of physical-education departments, often making the women's athletics director an associate athletics director (in addition to her teaching responsibilities) and placing her under the supervision of the men's athletics director.

Said one women's sports administrator: "I think what started us actually doing anything about moving into 'athletics' as such was a group of students in the early 1970s who said, 'We are world class and national class athletes. And when we are swimming in the summer, we are just as good as the guys, and we get [the same competitive opportunities and benefits].' And it was those students who stirred up such a ruckus in the early 1970s. Then came the emphasis of Title IX when it started to come along in 1972. The combination of the two got the attention of the administration in this school."[25]

State legislatures and universities often kicked in money from general funds to help start women's programs, and the number of women participating in varsity programs spiked immediately after the law's passage. The NCAA puts the number of female athletes on varsity teams at 15,182 in 1966–67. In 1971–72, even before the passage of Title IX, that figured had doubled, to 29,977. By 1976–77, the number of women playing sports had doubled again to 62,886. (The number of male athletes also increased, from 151,918 in 1966–67 to 168,136 in 1976–77.)[26]

But the increases were not always comfortable. Many women had to learn that varsity sports were not "church league," according to Judy Rose. Another female administrator described the transition in the administration of women's sports.

> The first cuts were made in team selection, but you still didn't have extensive schedules and you didn't practice all the time. In 1972 things changed a little bit more and we renamed our women's sports organization the Women's Intercollegiate Sports Association. And several sports were dropped as concentration was put into about five sports, because we had only $5,000 at that point. And that was the beginning of the change to an intensified coaching situation which was mild by comparison with today.
>
> And then in 1973 the chancellor appointed a task force to take a look women's athletics and decide what to do with it. The upshot of the task force was that women's athletics should become part of the Athletics Department and not be part of physical education any longer, because they determined that it wasn't appropriate, from a financial standpoint nor a philosophical standpoint. And so in June of 1974, two weeks after the task force made their report, I was hired as the Assistant Athletics Director, and we moved into the Athletics Department. At that point our women's budget jumped from $10,000 to $83,000. The men's budget at that time was about $2.5-million.[27]

The first major conflict between the AIAW's idealism and the pragmatism of implementing Title IX came a year after the law passed. Female tennis players at Marymount College and Broward Community College in Florida sued the AIAW in 1973 over the ban on scholarships. No matter what good reasons the AIAW might have for banning scholarships, the plaintiffs argued; if colleges were going to provide men with a certain benefit, they needed to provide women with an equitable benefit.

Many college administrators believed that they needed to provide scholarships for members of both sexes. Even before the Florida lawsuits were filed, some colleges experimented with scholarship programs, leading to even more chaos among women's programs. A memorandum indicates the precariousness of the situation:

> Pennsylvania State University did not use the DGWS sanctioning approval for the National Intercollegiate Women's Fencing Association Championship held on April 6–8, 1972. Della Durant, Coordinator of Women's Varsity Sports, Penn. St. U., reported that the directors of the event felt that they could not rightfully use the sanctioning since three to four schools would not sign a statement asking for specific information regarding the status of scholarships at their institutions.[28]

The AIAW settled the case and changed its rules to permit scholarships to avoid losing members that wanted to avoid scholarships, but tried to convince administrators to stick to educational criteria for awarding scholarships rather than athletic ones:

> The DGWS reaffirms its concern that the provision of scholarships or other financial assistance specifically designated for athletes may create a potential for abuses which could prove detrimental to the development of quality programs of athletics. Specifically, the DGWS deplores the evils of pressure recruiting and performer exploitation which frequently accompany the administration of financial aid for athletes.
>
> The DGWS is concerned that many collegiate athletic programs as currently administered do not make available to female students benefits equivalent in nature or extent to those made available to male students. While a curtailment of programs of financial aid to female students involved in athletics does eliminate the potential for abuses inherent in any such programs, this remedy is overly broad because it operates inequitably to deny to female students benefits available to their male counterparts. Specifically, these benefits might include the recognition of athletic excellence and the opportunity for economic assistance to secure an education.
>
> Therefore, DGWS believes that the appropriate solution in our contemporary society is one directed to avoiding abuses while providing to female students, on an equitable basis, benefits comparable to those available to male students similarly situated.[29]

Many female administrators viewed the awarding of scholarships as a critical change for women's college sports. They had built their paradigm around the idea of providing the best experiences to women who were already enrolled. They did not allow coaches to recruit off-campus, nor to send prospective students anything more than a simple brochure describing their programs. Colleges were not supposed to compete for prized women athletes as they did for males, and coaches were restrained from recruiting so that they could devote their time to teaching.

Scholarships shifted the emphasis from women already enrolled to those who could be recruited. Armed with scholarships, coaches needed to go out and find the best possible recipients. They had to choose athletes on the basis of athletic ability, not as a way of providing students with a healthy extracurricular activity.

This may seem like an obscure point to someone familiar with the NCAA's scholarship system, but it meant that women's programs in the 1970s "would take a 180-degree turn," in the words of one administrator. "I'd been here all these years trying to develop a program for the young women who came to this university to get an education, and [also] liked to compete in sport. As they came we tried to allow our program to grow as rapidly as they could take that growth. Now suddenly, with this act, we were going out to find the student-athlete who we thought the university should have. And then we were going to have to provide the program for those student-athletes. And as soon as we began to do that the emphasis for women's sport changed."[30]

Lopiano says that the AIAW held firm to its philosophy, keeping coaches from going off-campus and instead permitting them to hold on-campus "auditions," just like college drama or music programs would. "It was a very healthy experience in that parents came to college with the kid [prior to enrolling], and after it was all over, both parents and kids knew whether they belonged," she says. "The organization didn't look to the NCAA model and say, 'We're going to do this,' but said, 'We don't believe in off-campus recruiting; we believe the kid should recruit the school, and play with the program to see if there's a fit.'"

Grudgingly, the AIAW set caps of eight scholarships a year each for basketball, field hockey, gymnastics, lacrosse, softball, swimming, track and field, and volleyball; and four per year for archery, badminton, bowling, crew, golf, fencing, riflery, skiing, squash, and tennis. Scholarships required athletes to pass minimum academic standards to renew them, and were limited to tuition, room, board, and fees, excluding books. In men's sports, the NCAA had no limits on scholarships.

NCAA studies show that women's sports grew rapidly in the 1970s. By 1977 women were getting 14 percent of athletics department budgets nationally, but 55 percent of their budgets were coming from nonathletic sources, such as campus general funds, donors, and state appropriations.[31] Given the meager size of those budgets, colleges were clearly not choosing to cut men's programs to finance women's.

Some colleges even got into a bidding war over coaches. In 1976, the University of Kentucky tried to lure Pat Summitt away from Tennessee by offering her nine thousand dollars a year to coach the Wildcats. The sum was only one hundred dollars more than Summitt was making at Tennessee, though, and so she stayed in Knoxville. (Male coaches at that time were making sixty to seventy thousand dollars in base salaries.)[32]

"Being at Texas, you win a national championship and they love you," Lopiano says. Her budget went up exponentially in those years, often doubling. She and her basketball coach, Jody Conradt, made women's sports a cause célèbre in Austin, taking lessons from the men's department in marketing their programs to the public. "There's nothing wrong in marketing," Lopiano says. "We had great graduation rates, articulate kids, and great coaches. . . . It can be done."

Texas financed its women's program with mandatory student fees, proceeds from campus soft-drink machines and from leasing their facilities back to the university, and "making every effort to find money from nonacademic sources," Lopiano said. Not until the late 1980s, when money began pouring into college football from new television and bowl-game contracts, did the women's department at Texas get funds from the men's athletics department.

At the national level, Byers had not given up. He pressed the NCAA's annual convention every year to inaugurate championships for women, but throughout the 1970s the delegates from the association's colleges turned him down. But a few voices joined his. In 1975, John A. Fuzak of Michigan State University told delegates that the NCAA Council "recognized that the moral obligation to provide meaningful services for the female student-athlete of its member institutions is greater today than ever before, and that to temporize further is to deny the NCAA's own statements of purpose and fundamental policy."[33]

The council further concluded that

It is not feasible or desirable for the NCAA to confine future services and programs only to male student-athletes;

It is not possible under the provisions of the law to restrict application of NCAA rules only to male student-athletes competing on intercollegiate varsity teams; and

It is not permissible or plausible for the NCAA to enter into agreements with other organizations that, for example, would accord the NCAA exclusive authority over male intercollegiate athletics and accord a like monopoly position to an organization for control of women's athletics.

Existing rules of law and policy contemplate that qualified females will participate on teams which formerly were exclusively male. The NCAA cannot legally or practically limit its services and programs so as to exclude such qualified females.

While the argument may be made that it is legally possible to provide . . . programs through separate but equal facilities and staff, economy probably will dictate that there be a minimum of duplication of personnel and facilities. Furthermore, administrative necessity and the need for equitable eligibility requirements will require coordination and similarity not only at the institutional level, but also on a national level. Integrated

or coordinated programs at the national level cannot be achieved if separate male and female national organizations are left to accomplish it
through . . . bilateral agreements.[34]

This was a declaration of war, or at least was taken as such by the
AIAW. The NCAA had asserted not only its desire to start a national-
championship program as an alternative to the AIAW, but also its belief
that only one organization ought to govern all of collegiate sport. And
that organization was not the AIAW.

In his autobiography, Byers said that some individual women in college sports were less hostile than the AIAW's leaders. He recounts a 1980
meeting with Mary Alyce Hill of San Diego State University and Linda
Estes of New Mexico. "They wanted women in key positions in the
NCAA, and they wanted the NCAA to be the national governing body
for women's athletics," he writes. "Both of them were key players in the
burgeoning world of women's athletics, and their decision in favor of the
NCAA gave my dwindling confidence a shot of adrenaline."[35]

In 1980, Byers got his wish. Divisions II and III voted to hold women's
championships in basketball, field hockey, swimming, tennis, and volleyball beginning with the 1981–82 academic year. The following year in
Miami at the association's annual convention, the entire NCAA membership voted to expand its committees and allocate positions to women,
and to create a three-year transition period to allow colleges to adapt
from AIAW to NCAA rules. The vote was 383 for and 168 against. The
convention then voted to establish Division I championships in basketball, cross-country, field hockey, gymnastics, softball, swimming, tennis,
and outdoor track and field. That measure passed 128-127, and for all
practical purposes, the AIAW was rendered irrelevant.[36] Byers was not
very sympathetic to those who regretted the undermining of the AIAW.
"The men and the NCAA itself didn't discriminate against women,"
he writes. "Women's athletics leaders discriminated against themselves
through the years by refusing to accept competitive athletics as a proper
pursuit for teenage women."[37]

The AIAW sued the NCAA to prevent it from starting women's championships, arguing that the association was exercising an illegal monopoly power over college sports. No federal judge agreed with them, and
the lawsuit was dismissed.

Byers and other NCAA historians largely neglect a crucial fact about
his drive to start women's championships: It was plan B. The NCAA
spent much of the 1970s trying to kill off Title IX in Congress and in the
courts, a fight that will be detailed in chapter 4. Once those efforts
failed, the next best option was to acquire women's sports.

Not everybody in women's sports was sorry about the NCAA's taking charge. The NCAA was and is the "big time" in college sports, and for women's coaches like Summitt the move to the NCAA represented a step up in competitiveness, legitimacy, and prominence. "I think it changed the face of women's basketball," she says.

> It's different when it's the NCAA. I've been around the game a long time, and I'm appreciative of all the pioneers, the women who fought for women's championships under the AIAW, but I also recognize that what really gave our sport the boost in the eyes of the country was the NCAA. That gave us some clout, and eventually brought about the television package that otherwise we never would have gotten.
>
> I definitely saw [the AIAW model of governance and recruiting] as restrictive. Players had to come to you. . . . [Recruiting in the NCAA] has really brought about an opportunity for student-athletes to have choices, because they can, regardless of financial background, select colleges of the greatest interest, visit, and have their way paid. It just opened up the door of opportunity.

Summitt, Hatchell, and Rose adapted quickly. The first two have become two of the most famous coaches in the country, and Summitt has won more basketball games than any college coach in history, male or female. Hatchell has a national championship to her credit. Rose moved out of coaching in 1990 and has been athletics director at UNC-Charlotte ever since.

They have not forgotten their roots, though. At her annual camp for teenaged players in July 2003, Hatchell got word of a minor catastrophe, an air conditioner that had leaked condensate all over the floor. So she swung into action. "I just walked out of my office with rubber gloves and a mop, and everybody just stared at me," she says. Hatchell may be making a six-figure income from coaching and sponsorship deals and may be one of the biggest names in the business, but she still thinks like the graduate student who had to do it all when she got her big break at Francis Marion in 1975.

4
CHAPTER
·

College Sports and Civil Rights

itle IX's basic text is the least controversial aspect of the law. Even in the early 1970s, nobody in an official position would have argued that women did not deserve equal rights to educational opportunities. Over the past three decades, the legal and cultural battles have been fought instead over the assortment of rules and regulations the government published to implement Title IX, particularly in sports. Congress and the Department of Health, Education, and Welfare took the better part of a decade to debate and finalize these rules, even as the AIAW came into being and then folded in the shadow of the NCAA.

The federal officials who developed the rules and regulations had little experience with college sports, and they moved much more slowly to write and implement their plans than they had in other civil rights programs. Despite an active lobby from the NCAA and proponents of college football, though, the final rules ended up being fairly strict, at least on their face.

In her subcommittee's deliberations, Edith Green had been very careful not to make athletes part of the debate over Title IX, according to Bernice Sandler, because both women knew the subject might kick up a protest that would overshadow the broader intent of the legislation. As a result, it took about a year before colleges and athletic associations like the NCAA realized what Title IX meant for them.

By that time, big-time colleges were spending millions of dollars on football and men's basketball programs. The idea that he might have to double these expenses was enough to curdle the blood of any athletics director, particularly as the recession of the 1970s hit.

This challenge was unique to athletics. No other segment of academe was required to maintain single-sex programs, so in most cases, the task of regulators and educators alike was to ensure that women did not face discrimination as programs were integrated and opened. Female students might not choose to go to engineering schools or business schools for assorted reasons—reasons that might need to be addressed—but it was relatively straightforward to devise regulations to cover most aspects of a school's operations.

Athletics were a different case. A handful of women chose to participate on men's teams: Cindy Meserve earned a spot on the varsity basketball team at Pratt Institute in 1974, and Francie Larrieu, a star distance runner, trained with the men at UCLA the same year.[1] For the most part, though, the leaders of women's sports demanded separate teams for their athletes, owing to the differences in size, strength, and (at least in those days) skill between most male and female athletes.

By and large, nobody argued with that position, but the NCAA and its allies in Congress were worried about protecting men's athletics. Colleges and associations have often opposed various governmental regulations when they saw potential dangers to academic freedom, threats to institutional autonomy, or the imposition of an unfunded mandate, and Title IX could be seen as either of the latter two.

In May 1974, as the Department of Health, Education, and Welfare was finishing up a first draft of its regulations on college sports, Sen. John Tower of Texas offered an amendment to the pending Elementary and Secondary Education Act. The amendment, strongly supported by the NCAA, would have exempted "revenue-producing sports" from Title IX: "This section shall not apply to an intercollegiate activity to the extent that such activity does or may provide gross receipts or donations to the institution necessary to support that activity."[2]

In a speech on the floor of the Senator Tower, a Republican, declared that "at most colleges and universities, intercollegiate athletics are funded in whole or in part by monies raised, for example, through the sales of tickets to men's football or basketball games and through fundraising campaigns for general, scholarship, or other specific purposes." Other sports at other colleges, such as ice hockey at Ohio State and wrestling at Lehigh, were also major moneymakers, he said. "Impairment of the financial base of the revenue-producing activity threatens not only the viability of that activity, but the viability of the entire athletic program."

Colleges were not providing enough sports opportunities for male or female students, Tower continued, and further demands were likely to place a strain on athletics budgets in the future. Congress, he said, did not intend Title IX to extend to sports, and thus it ought to hold hearings to determine whether a separate piece of legislation ought to be passed to guarantee equal opportunities for women in sports. In the meantime, Tower commented "Grave concern has been expressed that the HEW rules will undercut revenue-raising sports programs and damage the overall sports program of the institution. Were HEW, in its laudable zeal to guarantee equal athletic opportunities to women, to promulgate rules which damaged the financial base of intercollegiate sports, it will have thrown the baby out with the bath water."[3]

Tower did not say specifically how he thought guaranteeing equal athletic opportunities for women would damage the financial base of intercollegiate sports, but the common argument goes something like this. Colleges would not get more money to pay for the sports they were being forced to add for women. Thus, they would have to divert money from football and men's basketball operations to finance the new women's sports, which nobody would actually pay to come watch. With less money, the quality of the football and basketball teams would drop. Fans would lose interest, stop coming to the games, cease buying tickets and making donations. With less money coming in, there would be less to go around for all sports, dooming every team to mediocrity.

The draft regulations were issued by the HEW the following month. They did not exclude revenue sports, as Tower had requested, but instead required colleges to take proactive steps to create and publicize opportunities for women (see appendix C for the full text). They required colleges to "operate or sponsor separate teams for members of each sex where selection for such teams is based upon competitive skill." Colleges would be required to "determine annually, using a method to be selected by the [federal funds] recipient which is acceptable to the director, in what sports members of each sex would desire to compete." Furthermore, they would have to publicize athletic opportunities for women, offer coaching, practice, and competitions "designed to improve and expand their capabilities and interests to participate in such opportunities."

Affirmative action would be mandatory, requiring schools to provide sports and teams in a manner "as will most effectively equalize opportunities for members of both sexes." However, "nothing in this section shall be interpreted to require equal aggregate expenditures for athletics for members of each sex."

The last paragraph seems to save colleges from having to duplicate the budget for the men's football team with the women's lacrosse team, and could have alleviated Tower's fears. By the 1970s, football had grown into an enormously expensive sport, requiring rosters of scores if not hundreds of players, each requiring a full set of pads, helmets, and other equipment to keep athletes from breaking their necks. Stadiums were growing as well, with some edifices topping eighty thousand seats. The prospect of spending the same amount of money on football and any women's sport was infuriating to NCAA officials, who argued that they could give women the same quality of opportunity for far less money.

A curious portion of the regulations is the requirement for an annual survey of interest in sports for both male and female students. This is unlike any other requirement placed on schools and colleges, who are not required to change their academic offerings yearly based on students' interest. It would have been a violation of academic autonomy that college officials would never countenance, although popularity certainly plays a role in determining course offerings.

While HEW was receiving comments on the draft regulations, Congress moved forward on the Elementary and Secondary Education Act. A conference committee of senators and congressmen met in July and deleted the Tower amendment, supporting an alternative offered by Sen. Jacob R. Javits, a Democrat from New York:

> The Secretary of [HEW] shall prepare and publish proposed regulations implementing the provisions of Title IX of the Education Amendments of 1972 relating to the prohibition of sex discrimination in federally assisted education programs which shall include with respect to intercollegiate athletic activities reasonable provisions considering the nature of particular sports.[4]

This seemed to authorize HEW to issue public regulations much like those in the draft proposals. They would not require precise equality or equal distribution of funds: Spending more money on football than on women's lacrosse did not mean a college was discriminating against the lacrosse players. The amendment did assert, however, that Title IX gave HEW authority over varsity sports.

That was too much for the NCAA. In September 1974, Byers sent out a blistering memo about the Javits amendment and the draft regulations. Both were illegal, he asserted, because sports programs did not receive federal funds. The regulations were "vague, ambiguous, and lacking in specific standards," meaning that "enforcement necessarily will be subjective and erratic." "To the extent that the regulations compel educational institutions to eliminate differences in athletic programs which result from differences in the level of income generated by particular sports activities, they are arbitrary, exceed DHEW's statutory authority, and will seriously damage athletic programs for student-athletes of both sexes."[5]

Byers's standard was a strictly capitalistic one. Teams should be entitled to keep the money they generate, he argued, even though some make much more money than others. He rejected the idea in the 1974 regulations that colleges themselves were responsible for allocating money, staff, and other benefits to male and female teams without reference to their business practices.

For their part, women's activists were already upset that it had taken the Department of Health, Education, and Welfare nearly two years to issue draft regulations, particularly in the aftermath of the *Adams v. Richardson* lawsuit, as a result of which the U.S. District Court for the District of Columbia ordered the department in 1973 to enforce its own regulations and investigate complaints in a timely manner. Women's groups did endorse the Javits amendment, which they saw as a victory over the NCAA and its allies.

After HEW published the draft regulations, it received over 9,700 comments. That prompted Casper W. Weinberger, then the department's secretary, to quip that he had not been aware that the most pressing issue facing higher education was the preservation of football.

Weinberger's writings and interviews indicate that he was not particularly interested in the subject of sports under Title IX. In a tart letter to President Ford accompanying the final draft of the regulations, he said that sport was less important that other areas covered by Title IX, but that it "[raises] the most controversy and involves some of the most difficult policy and legal points."

> The department received substantial comment on this issue. These comments generally fell into three categories: those filed by women's groups, such as the National Organization for Women, those filed by the Association for Inter-Collegiate Athletics for Women, and those filed by many colleges and by the men's athletic organizations, such as the National Collegiate Athletic Association.
>
> NOW suggests that the "separate but equal" concept is inappropriate for any civil rights regulation and that open access should be required for all athletic teams with one exception. Where women are effectively excluded from open teams (where skill in the given sport is the criteria, it is still conceded by all that open competition for a tackle football team would result in an all-male team), separate teams should be provided for them on the basis that the training and sports traditionally available to women have been limited and that provision of separate teams until such time as the training gap is closed would best fulfill the purpose of the act.
>
> The AIAW suggests that separate men's and women's programs be allowed under all circumstances and that institutions be required to provide proportionate funding for each program. AIAW is opposed to what they call the "commercialism" of men's athletics and want to be allowed to use the money allocated for women to provide opportunities for more women instead of expending large sums for recruiting and scholarships.

The NCAA argues that athletics is not covered by Title IX because athletics receives no federal assistance. They also argue that, if athletics are covered, revenue-producing sports should be exempted because they support all other sports and institutions cannot afford to offer sports to women on the same scale as men.

The HEW General Counsel, as well as the Department of Justice's Office of Legal Counsel, advised me that athletics are a part of the educational program and activity of an institution whether or not the athletics department itself received federal funds, and athletics are, therefore, covered by Title IX.[6]

The Javits amendment, Weinberger added, resolved any legal doubts about whether Title IX applied to sports, including revenue sports: "If Congress wants to exempt athletics, they will have to do so by changing the law."

In May 1975, HEW published the final regulations, which to this day are the only section of federal law that deals explicitly with sports and gender equity (for the full text, see appendix D). They included a number of more specific provisions:

Single-sex sports. If a college offers a team for men and not for women,[7] and if the team plays a noncontact sport (contact sports are defined as boxing, wrestling, rugby, ice hockey, football, basketball, "and other sports the purpose or major activity of which includes bodily contact"), then women must be allowed to try out for the men's team.

Definition of equal opportunity. To ascertain whether equal opportunity is provided, HEW will consider a list of ten factors: "whether the selection of sports and levels of competition effectively accommodate the interests and abilities of members of both sexes"; the provision of equipment; scheduling of games and practice times; travel and per diem allowances; the availability and compensation of coaches and tutors; practice facilities; competition venues; locker rooms; medical and training facilities; housing and dining; and publicity.

Spending. Larger budgets for men's sports than for women's is not sufficient to prove a violation of Title IX, but the department may consider unequal spending in assessing whether women's and men's opportunities are equal.

Period of implementation. Schools and colleges have three years to come into compliance, an unheard-of grace period in civil rights law.

The regulation got rid of the yearly survey requirement and in its place created the idea that schools must "effectively accommodate the interests and abilities of members of both sexes." While vaguer than the 1974 draft regulations, this version of the regulations packs four important concepts into answering the question of how many female athletes a college needs to have: which sports to offer; the level of competition at which each team should be expected to compete (such as intramurals, low-key extramural clubs, or elite varsity squads); what sports students are actually interested in; and whether the college has enough athletes with the requisite abilities to field a competitive team in a given sport at a particular level of competition. This view may seem obvious and innocuous, but it is the first step toward putting a number or at least a guideline on how many women ought to be on a school's sports teams.

In the 1975 regulations, though, the participation requirements were only one of the ten items on the list of areas to consider. The list reflects a certain understanding, or lack thereof, of how sports operated at high schools and colleges. For one thing, two of the ten topics concern the provision of academic tutors. Principal among the AIAW's precepts was the idea that athletes ought to be matriculating and progressing through college on the same terms as other students. Thus, they should not need tutors apart from those offered to all students. Similarly, the topic of housing and dining reflects the common practice at big-time athletics programs of providing special dormitories and training tables for male athletes, primarily football and basketball players. (Jock dorms have since been abolished and training tables curtailed under NCAA rules.) The regulations seem to have been written with the idea of male athletes at a college like Penn State in mind, not female athletes at, say, Yale, or any athletes at the high school level.

The regulations also put to rest the idea that athletics programs could satisfy gender-equity obligations simply by allowing women to try out for traditionally male teams. Peter V. Holmes, then the director of HEW's Office for Civil Rights, highlighted this point in a letter to college officials that accompanied the 1975 regulations:

> If by opening a team to both sexes in a contact sport an educational institution does not effectively accommodate the abilities of members of both sexes (see 86.41(c) (i)), separate teams in that sport will be required if both men and women express interest in the sport and the interests of both sexes are not otherwise accommodated. For example an institution would not be effectively accommodating the interests and abilities of women if it abolished all its women's teams and opened up its men's teams to women, but only a few women were able to qualify for the men's teams.[8]

Holmes also warned schools and colleges not to consider the "adjustment period" a waiting period. "Institutions must begin now to take whatever steps are necessary to ensure full compliance as quickly as possible.

Schools may design an approach for achieving full compliance tailored toward their own circumstances; however, self-evaluation, as required by section 86.3(c), is a very important step for every institution to assure compliance with the entire Title IX regulation, as well as with the athletics provisions."

Holmes also stated flatly that Title IX applies to all areas and programs for any educational institution receiving federal funds, including sports, "whether or not that segment is the subject of direct financial support" through HEW. Echoing Weinberger in asserting Title IX's coverage of areas like athletics, Holmes was taking a controversial stand in a debate that would dominate much of the first twelve years of Title IX's existence.

Holmes also addressed the revenue debate directly. "The fact that a particular segment of an athletic program is supported by funds received from various other sources (such as student fees, general revenues, gate receipts, alumni donations, booster clubs, and non-profit foundations) does not remove it from the reach of the statute and hence of the regulatory requirements," he wrote.

He also became the first federal official to declare that cheerleading is not a sport. "Drill team, cheerleaders, and the like . . . are covered [by the law] more generally as extracurricular activities."

Holmes also addressed the concerns of AIAW leaders, noting that nothing in the statute precluded colleges from directing men's and women's sports through separate departments. He did warn institutions that "changes in current administrative structure(s) or coaching assignments which have a disproportionately adverse effect on the employment opportunities of one sex are prohibited by the regulation."

Under the terms of the adjustment period, colleges and school districts were supposed to file self-evaluations of their entire programs by July 1976, a year after the regulations were published, assessing their own efforts at gender equity. Athletics programs had to address inequities in athletic scholarships provided to male and female athletes. They also had to assess the levels of interest of male and female students in sports and decide not only which sports to offer, but also whether to have single-sex or coed teams, depending on the relative abilities of male and female athletes and the number of interested members of each sex.

The 1975 regulations required institutions to "develop a plan to accommodate effectively the interests and abilities of both sexes, which plan must be fully implemented as expeditiously as possible and in no event later than July 21, 1978. Although the plan need not be submitted to the Office for Civil Rights, institutions should consider publicizing such plans so as to gain the assistance of students, faculty, etc. in complying with them."

Holmes cautioned that the overall objective of Title IX and the 1975 regulation was not duplication, even between similar teams such as men's and women's basketball squads. Instead, compliance was to be determined by comparing the number and quality of athletic opportunities available to women to those available to men. "The thrust of the effort should be on the contribution of each of the categories to the overall goal of equal opportunity in athletics rather than on the details related to each of the categories," he wrote. Educational institutions should carefully consider the "impact of expenditures for sex-identifiable sports," and "the pattern of expenditures should not result in a disparate effect on opportunity. . . . The fact that differences in expenditures may occur because of varying costs attributable to differences in equipment requirements and levels of spectator interest" is understandable, but it "does not obviate in any way the responsibility of educational institutions to provide equal opportunity."

For all their talk of *not* requiring institutions to field identical programs for male and female athletes, some in Congress thought that they actually did. During a hearing, with football coaches Jerry Claiborne of the University of Maryland and Bo Schembechler of the University of Michigan providing testimony, Rep. James G. O'Hara of Michigan complained that "this is the classic way of doing it. They say you don't have to do this but they say one way that you can avoid having your university declared ineligible for federal contracts and whatever is to do these things. . . . So in effect, what it does is put a tremendous amount of pressure on you to comply with these things because you recognize that if you do this, you are safe. . . . So the easy way out or the simple way out is to say, well, let us do it even if they say we don't have to. I think that is the problem you face."[9]

O'Hara, a Republican, argued that the threat of losing federal funds would be so great that colleges would take the simplest path to compliance, even if it was not the fairest to either male or female athletes. This would be a common complaint about the law in future years.

Finally, the 1975 regulations had a separate and specific policy requiring colleges to allocate the same proportion of their athletic-scholarship budget to women as there were women on varsity teams, absent nondiscriminatory circumstances.

"The thrust of the athletic scholarship section is the concept of reasonableness, not strict proportionality in the allocation of scholarships," Holmes wrote. Allocating athletic scholarships should depend on "the degree of interest and participation of male and female students in athletics," and "neither quotas nor fixed percentages of any type are required under the regulation." Later in the letter, Holmes said that "where the sports offered or the levels of competition differ for male and female students, the institution should assess its athletic scholarship program to determine whether overall opportunities to receive athletic scholarships are roughly proportionate to the number of students of each sex participating in intercollegiate athletics."

The 1975 regulations and the Holmes letter offer a clear insight into the thinking of HEW's staff on Title IX and sports. Separate-but-equal sports were fine, as long as institutions made sure women had equal opportunities to participate. Here is the problem: The regulations offered no singular statement or formula to define equal opportunity. Instead the rules left it up to HEW to decide whether an institution was in compliance.

The vagueness is intentional. It was designed to preserve an institution's autonomy to decide for itself the best means to comply with the law. It gives a school some flexibility, but the regulations also allow it to drag its feet until and unless federal investigators show up on the doorstep. A school cannot determine for itself if it is in compliance, so the only way to know if the steps it has taken to ensure equal opportunity are adequate is to invite the government in.

That was the NCAA's first complaint. Its council said the 1974 regulations were "unreasonably vague, ambiguous and lacking in specific standards," so "confusion, conflict, and controversy will characterize efforts to comply. . . . Virtually no coeducational institution of higher learning in this country can possibly be assured that it is in compliance with the regulations . . . and no such institution can tell what it should do to attempt to comply or even whether the greatest good-faith on its part would suffice."[10]

This system of compliance is common throughout the regulations that evolved out of Titles VI and VII of the Civil Rights Act of 1964. The Department of Health, Education, and Welfare and the Department of Labor investigated and adjudicated claims of discrimination against almost any entity receiving public funds. In the case of athletics, the generality of the regulations has pushed colleges to look for safest harbors and simplest routes to Title IX compliance, trying to find numbers and formulas to immunize themselves against lawsuits.

At the time, Congress was allowed to review regulations within forty-five days of their publication. Conservative congressmen, particularly those sympathetic to big-time sports, took full advantage of the opportunity. North Carolina's Jesse Helms offered a resolution to disapprove the regulations in their entirety, as did Rep. David T. Martin, a Republican from Nebraska.

In June 1975, the House Subcommittee on Post-Secondary Education held hearings on the regulations, hearing testimony from panels of football coaches, AIAW officials, and representatives of the Department of Education. "As we read the guidelines of the HEW, we first read that we will not be requested to match necessarily dollar for dollar the money that is being spent on men's intercollegiate athletics with a like sum for women's programs. However, as we read on, we see the guidelines that are laid out for us in the form of equal salaries and coaches, equal housing, equal training table facilities, equal equipment, equal everything," protested Darrell Royal, legendary football coach at the University of Texas. "Any way we look at it, we can't see that it is going to do anything other than eliminate, kill, or seriously weaken the programs we have in existence."[11] He found some sympathy among members of the panel. "The bureaucrats in HEW are all wet on this proposal," said Rep. Ronald M. Motti, who had been a baseball player himself as an undergraduate at Notre Dame. "I think a moratorium should be invoked until there can be further study. We want to be fair naturally in our collegiate institutions but I think this is not the way to go about it."[12]

In July O'Hara introduced yet another bill to strike down portions of the regulations. The subcommittee recommended to the full Committee on Education and Labor that it support O'Hara's bill, but the latter committee chose not to. O'Hara then introduced a bill to allow educational institutions "to use money earned from revenue-producing sports only on that sport or first on that sport, regardless of inequities." It suffered the same fate.

In July, the Senate went through the same exercise, with a flurry of bills to strike down the regulations all dying in committee. Senators Helms, Tower, and Laxalt (the Utah Republican) introduced bills, and the Senate Subcommittee on Education held its own hearings, but none of the bills was able to muster enough support to make it out of committee.

All this meant the regulations moved forward, albeit slowly. Thanks to the three-year transition period, schools and colleges were dragging their feet on compliance, according to activists. "The problem for athletics in higher education was that with this transition period, it was possible to find some discrimination, but because of the flexibility in this idea of transition, the practicality of enforcement really meant that schools were sort of looking at it as a grace period before they had to get serious," said Marcia D. Greenberger, cofounder of the National Women's Law Center. "There never was any effort to say, 'Okay, we haven't seen any progress for you to get there.' There was always this fiction that by year 3, everything was just going to happen."[13]

Colleges were assuredly unhappy with the regulations, believing that despite the generalities, they represented a significant breach of institutional autonomy. The NCAA itself sued HEW, claiming that it had outstripped its authority. Dallin H. Oaks, president of Brigham Young University, called the regulations "one of the most significant inroads on [academic] freedom in many years" and said, "I am only sorry that no individual colleges or universities have joined the NCAA in that suit. I find it sad that a position of vital interest to the independence of higher education has to be litigated by the athletic establishment, as if athletics were the only program in a college or university that was concerned about maintaining its freedom from illegal control by HEW."[14]

However, no colleges joined the NCAA in its suit, and the lawsuit eventually died in 1980 with the U.S. Court of Appeals for the Tenth Circuit, which ruled that as an independent association, the NCAA did not have legal standing to sue HEW.[15]

By July 1978, when the regulations were supposed to take full effect, ninety-two complaints had been filed against high school and college athletics departments. In an effort to address complaints about the vagueness of the regulations, HEW published a draft "policy interpretation" (appendix E). It stated that a college would be ruled in compliance with the law if it had "eliminated discrimination in financial support and other benefits and opportunities in its existing athletic program" and followed "an institutional policy that includes procedures and standards for developing an athletic program that provides equal opportunities for men and women to accommodate their interests and abilities."[16]

It judged equality of opportunity by reckoning whether the money a college spent on male and female athletes, on a per capita basis, was roughly equivalent in the awarding of athletic scholarships, the provision of recruiting budgets, and the allocation of operating budgets. It also emphasizes colleges' obligation under the 1975 regulations to publicize women's sports and make extra efforts to recruit female athletes.

Using "average per capita" measures of expense caused widespread protests for two reasons. First, it flew in the face of the Javits amendment and the 1975 regulations, which permitted reasonable differences in funding for men's and women's teams. Second, it looked like a quota system of sorts. Not so, the HEW protested. "The average per capita standard was not a standard by which noncompliance could be found," wrote one drafter in response to a later comment. "It was offered as a standard of presumptive compliance. In order to prove noncompliance, HEW would have been required to show that the unexplained disparities in expenditures were discriminatory in effect. The standard, in part, was offered as a means of simplifying proof of compliance for universities."[17]

That approach, however, has its own problems. By creating a standard of "presumptive compliance," the drafters of the 1978 policy interpretation created three levels of compliance: "presumptive compliance" or supercompliance as a standard that would be obvious to everyone; ordinary compliance that could be determined only by the Department of Health, Education, and Welfare; and noncompliance. O'Hara's earlier objections are apt here: While protesting that a guideline was not an absolute standard, the department was pushing institutions toward that guideline.

HEW received more than seven hundred comments and complaints about the 1978 draft policy interpretation. "Many of those same commentators noted an absence of concern in the proposed Policy Interpretation for those institutions that have in good faith attempted to meet what they felt to be a vague compliance standard in the regulation," the department noted.[18] Following the formal comment period, HEW officials brought college presidents and athletic officials to Washington for formal meetings on the policy interpretation, and also visited eight campuses, including Stanford, to see for themselves how sports programs worked. A year later, it issued a final policy interpretation, which differed substantially both from the 1975 regulations and the 1978 draft interpretation. The per capita standard of "presumptive compliance" was dropped, and the interpretation addressed some of the nitty-gritty, day-to-day challenges an athletics program has to cope with.

The 1979 policy interpretation (appendix F) is, from a legal standpoint, the most influential document issued to explain how gender equity should work in college sports. It divides a school's obligations under Title IX into three areas: the provision of athletic scholarships, "general athletic program components," and the accommodation of students' athletic interests and abilities through the number and type of opportunities available.

The section on scholarships is fairly simple. Absent nondiscriminatory circumstances, colleges must award athletics-related financial aid in a manner that reflects the gender makeup of athletes on varsity teams. That is, if an athletics department has one hundred male athletes and one hundred females, it must award 50 percent of its budget for scholarships to athletes of each sex. However, under many circumstances—athletes leaving school unexpectedly, different numbers of athletes receiving in-state and out-of-state scholarships—schools can be justified in awarding differing amounts of aid to males and females. Here is another example of the three levels of presumptive compliance, ordinary compliance, and noncompliance.

The general athletic program components are a reprise of the areas in which colleges must provide equitable benefits to male and female athletes:

Equipment and supplies
Scheduling of games and practice times
Travel and per diem allowances
The opportunity to receive coaching and tutoring
The assignment and compensation of coaches and tutors
Locker rooms and practice and competition venues
Medical and training facilities
Housing and dining facilities
Publicity
Recruiting resources and opportunities
Support services

The regulations on the accommodation of interests and abilities would prove to be the most troublesome and controversial. The interpretation said that colleges must determine the "athletic interests and abilities of their students," offer an appropriate selection of sports, and offer appropriate levels of competition, including team competition. Colleges have three choices of strategy, which have become known as the "three-part test." They can comply with any one of these three options:

    1. Have substantially the same proportion of female athletes on varsity teams as the proportion of female students in the undergraduate population
    2. Be able to demonstrate a "history and continuing practice" of expanding programs for women
    3. Be able to show that the institution is fully and effectively accommodating the interests and abilities of women on campus[19]

In structure, the test appears to govern what kinds of teams colleges ought to offer for men and women. In reality, however, it came to determine how many women ought to be participating on varsity teams. It appears far more flexible than the Philadelphia Plan: Instead of requiring that colleges provide an increasing number of opportunities to the underrepresented group, it gives colleges a series of options, one of which could at least in theory be accomplished by adding one woman to one team per year.

But the test soon acquired the same compliance problem as the scholarship test described previously and the per capita test of the 1978 draft. The first test became a threshold for "presumptive compliance" and the other two means of ordinary compliance.

In a three-part series published in 1980, the *NCAA News* was quick to point out that the policy interpretation did not have the same force of law as the Title IX statute itself or the 1975 implementing regulations.

Instead, the policy was supposed to serve as a series of guidelines to help colleges comply with the law. At least in theory, a college's lawyers could walk into court and claim that even though their institution was violating one or more sections of the policy interpretation, it was complying fully with the letter and spirit of the law. This claim would be tested—often—but not until nearly twenty years later.

As one might have imagined from the Weinberger letter, enforcing Title IX in sports was never a major priority for HEW. Nor was it for his successors in the Carter administration, given the challenges they had trying to enforce the integration of public schools and then managing the transition of HEW into the separate departments of Education and Health and Human Services, which took place in 1980.

Coming into office in 1981, officials in the Reagan administration were actively hostile to the civil rights revolution that took place in the 1970s. Title IX faced its first major legal challenge from a small religious college in Pennsylvania, and when the case reached the Supreme Court, nobody from the government bothered to show up to defend the law.

5
CHAPTER
•

Legal and Logistical Challenges

As Title IX evolved into a contentious set of bureaucratic guidelines and the NCAA and AIAW fought for control over women's sports, the idea that high school and college women ought to be out playing on the fields and courts of academe evolved from a theory to a practice around the country. In many cases athletics directors simply upgraded existing informal teams, or they created new teams to attract athletes who had been active in intramurals.

This happened fairly quickly. Between 1966–67 and 1976–77, the number of women participating in college athletics jumped from 16,000 to 64,375, according to a report by the U.S. Commission on Civil Rights. From 1970–71 to 1978–79, participation by high school girls jumped from 294,000 to over 2 million.[1] (The number of male athletes in high school and college increased as well, but only incrementally.)

Budgets and equipment did not keep up with the rise in numbers, by all reports. Women's teams traveled in coaches' cars and vans, eating at fast-food restaurants, while football teams traveled by chartered airplane. Practices like these led many women to file complaints against athletics departments at their host universities or with the Department of Health, Education, and Welfare. At the same time, athletics directors and other college officials were trying to make sense of what they saw as vague and ponderous new legal requirements.

As noted before, the only way to know if an athletics program is in compliance with Title IX is for the education department's Office for Civil Rights to review it. If investigators find a violation, they are charged with negotiating an agreement with the institution to resolve the violation. If they cannot, they can initiate proceedings to strip a college of its federal funds, including research grants, capital allocations, and student financial aid. Removing funds from unrelated programs would be such a massive penalty that the civil rights office has never even moved in that direction in a Title IX case in athletics. Instead, the mere threat of an OCR review has often been enough to provoke colleges to do a better job with women's sports. Answering questions and supplying information for a review consumes an immense amount of time, money, and effort, not unlike an Internal Revenue Service audit.

Athletics directors get immensely frustrated with OCR investigators, whom they often see as inflexible, bureaucratic, and, most of all, ignorant of how athletics programs operate. People love to tell tales about the investigator who accused a small East Coast university of discriminating against women because they did not have equal numbers of racquet presses for the men's and women's tennis teams. (Presses are used to keep wooden tennis racquets in shape, and wooden racquets have been out of favor for almost as long as Title IX has been in force.)

A manual issued to OCR investigators in 1980 offered a wealth of thought and tactics but gave investigators a contradictory mission. They were supposed to conduct what amounted to an audit, collecting a broad range of information before they got to a campus to interview as many coaches, athletic administrators, and athletes as they could. Then they were supposed base their decision on whether a college was complying with the law "upon an overall evaluation of an institution's athletic benefits and opportunities."[2] Investigators were to collect "data on each individual program component and examin[e] each component separately to determine whether equivalent treatment, benefits, and opportunities are afforded members of both sexes. . . . Disparities which favor members of one sex may be offset by disparities which favor the other sex." However, they could find a college to be out of compliance in any given area if it did not have a plan to correct whatever disparity investigators had found.

This scheme offered a curious way to look at athletics programs. At least in theory, a college could give athletes far less scholarship aid, but still be in compliance if it gave them greater per diems and locker room space. How can such different characteristics be weighed? The manual does not offer persuasive answers.

Beyond athletics, the Department of Health, Education, and Welfare faced persistent criticism in the 1970s for dragging its feet on enforcing Title IX. Civil rights groups were annoyed that the department took three years to issue the 1975 regulations; the typical time period for issuing implementing regulations is closer to eighteen months. The U.S. Commission on Civil Rights echoed that complaint in a 1975 report, saying that by delaying so long, the department "had effectively nullified the will of the Congress."[3] Throughout the 1970s, the National Organization for

Women's Project on Equal Education Rights released a series of reports accusing the department of stalling on both regulation and enforcement of Title IX, calling its efforts negligible.[4]

A 1980 report from the civil rights commission pointed out that most colleges had not complied with the 1975 regulations by the 1978 deadline. Although ninety-two complaints against colleges had been filed by 1978, the commission could not determine how many had been resolved.[5]

In the early days of the law, though, the Office for Civil Rights was the only ally for women in a position to accuse universities of violating the law.

Lamar Daniel, an investigator in OCR's Atlanta field office, led the first Title IX investigation ever mounted against an athletics program, the mammoth one at the University of Georgia. "They were obviously out of compliance on everything," recalls Daniel. Two complaints of sex discrimination in sports had been filed against the university, the first in 1972 by the student government. The complaint was held in abeyance while HEW began the long process of writing regulations. The second, filed by female athletes in 1975, was also held up by the three-year grace period included in the 1975 regulations. Most of the regional offices interpreted the three-year "adjustment" as meaning "you gave them three years and left them alone."[6]

In the fall of 1978, though, time was up, and the Atlanta regional director sent Daniel to Athens. "I went over there and looked at the program and oh, it was enormously controversial," he says. "Attorneys were in on all the interviews." It was no surprise that Georgia was in violation of the law "up one side and down the other. I remember in one of the interviews they had, five women basketball players came in to talk. They might have been the starting five, and they brought their game ball. It was a used ball from the men's team." The entire women's coaching and administrative staff was crammed into cubicles in the trophy room in the university's basketball arena. There were far fewer - female athletes than men, and hardly any of them were receiving scholarships.

Like Dallin Oaks and other campus leaders, Georgia's president was also a vehement opponent of the law. Daniels says that he and Davison "just went at it" during a conference closing the investigative stage.

Daniel went back to his office to begin writing up the investigation. In the winter of 1979, he recalls, "My boss comes to me and said, 'Hold off on doing anything more with Georgia. Headquarters is preparing a policy interpretation, and we're going to want you to go back and use the interpretation.'" It took the rest of 1979 to prepare the interpretation.

In 1980, Daniels went back to Athens: "Lo and behold, Georgia had a new program," he says. "They were in compliance with everything except athletic financial assistance [scholarships] and office space, and they had a plan for the office space." The plan was to build a new office complex for the football staff and the athletic administration—Vince Dooley was Georgia's athletics director and football coach—and leave the old offices for the women.

Georgia still had a long way to go. In the early 1990s, women's basketball and gymnastics coaches sued the university, protesting their pay scale. But this was one of the few instances where OCR was able to push colleges toward compliance. It may have taken the better part of the decade, but by 1980s standards, Daniel says, Georgia was doing well by its female athletes.

While the Office for Civil Rights tried to figure out what its role should be in enforcing Title IX in sports, the broader question of how gender equity applies to higher education became a topic for the courts.

The first major case starred Geraldine G. Cannon, who sued the medical schools of the University of Chicago and Northwestern University in 1975. Cannon was thirty-nine at the time, and had been refused admission to both schools despite having adequate grades and test scores because they both had policies banning students older than thirty. She argued that this amounted to discrimination against women because many more women than men interrupted their education to start careers, get married, and have children. Federal district and appeals courts rules against Cannon, saying that Title IX did not give an individual the right to sue an institution. The Supreme Court, however, reversed that decision because Title VI of the Civil Rights Act of 1964 and other civil rights laws on which Title IX was based did allow an individual to sue, or, in legal terms, offer an individual a "private right of action." Because of the similarities in these laws, and owing to other legal factors, the government had come to expect Title IX to allow people to sue to compel its enforcement, Justice John Paul Stevens wrote in the court's majority opinion.[7] "The Federal Government and the federal courts have been the primary and powerful reliances in protecting citizens against invidious discrimination of any sort, including that on the basis of sex," he wrote. "Moreover, it is the expenditure of federal funds that provides the justification for this particular statutory prohibition."

But how far does that justification extend? The government was using federal funds to change social policy, but how far into a school's own policies could it reach?

Virtually all school districts and colleges get some form of money from the federal government—research grants, student loans, congressional earmarks, and so on. Title IX bans sex discrimination in any "educational program or activity" receiving federal funds. But does a "program" mean an individual office or department that *directly* receives government funds, or does it mean the entire educational institution, because many other offices and departments will *indirectly* benefit from the federal money?

The Department of Health, Education, and Welfare had made its position clear in Holmes's letter accompanying the 1975 regulations. "These sections apply to each segment of the athletic program of a federally assisted educational institution whether or not that segment is the subject of direct financial support through the Department," Holmes wrote. "Thus, the fact that a particular segment of an athletic program is supported by funds received from various other sources (such as student fees, general revenues, gate receipts, alumni donations, booster clubs, and non-profit foundations) does not remove it from the reach of the statute and hence of the regulatory requirements."[8]

The Carter administration did not enforce the law very actively, but it did intervene on behalf of Colleen Pavey, a basketball player at the University of Alaska at Anchorage who, along with two of her teammates, sued the university in 1979. Carter's Department of Justice filed a motion accusing Alaska of giving fewer scholarships and issuing ragged uniforms to women, as well as paying women's coaches less.[9]

College lawyers and others who believed that the federal government should not be in the business of dictating college policies disagreed, saying that Title IX's application should be limited to programs that directly received federal aid. Two lawsuits alleging illegal discrimination against women in sports brought this controversy to the fore. In 1981, the U.S. Court of Appeals for the Fourth Circuit ruled in favor of the University of Richmond, which responded to a Title IX complaint against its athletics department by claiming that sports were not subject to Title IX. The following year, a three-judge panel of the U.S. Court of Appeals for the Second Circuit reached the opposite conclusion in a case filed against Temple University.

In the Richmond case, the Education Department notified the university in February 1981 that it had received a complaint of sex discrimination in the Spiders athletics program.[10] The complaint came two months after the Office for Civil Rights had concluded an investigation into graduate programs at Richmond, finding that they were in full compliance with Title IX. Dewey E. Dodds, director of OCR's regional office in Richmond, told university officials that his staff would turn its focus to the athletics department. He also asked that they submit a full report on their sports operations, including details of budgets, policies, practice schedules, and modes of transportation, as well as lists of all teams, locker rooms, and weight and training facilities.

Richmond officials responded that the Education Department had no jurisdiction over the athletics department because Richmond received no federal funds for sports. They filed a federal lawsuit to press their position. In July, a district court agreed, finding that the department had no authority to assert Title IX jurisdiction over sports or other programs at Richmond that did not receive direct federal financial assistance.

In his opinion, Judge D. Dortch Warriner accused the Education Department of trying to use Title IX to expand its own authority, asserting that Congress had in fact declined a chance to pass a law that applied to an entire institution. " "Having failed in its straight-forward lobbying effort to obtain institutional coverage in Congress, the ED has apparently taken the law into its own hands and decided it knows better than Congress," he wrote. "Perhaps they do, but they lack the legislative authority under the Constitution to amend acts of Congress. Moreover, delegation of authority pursuant to [Title IX] did not authorize the ED to subvert the will of Congress that the programmatic rather than the institutional approach be established."[11]

In the Temple case, the National Women's Law Center and another civil rights group, Trial Lawyers for Public Justice, backed a group of women athletes claiming that their teams had inadequate supplies and facilities. Rollin Haffer, a badminton player, was the lead plaintiff in the case, which she filed in 1980.

The Temple plaintiffs claimed that Title IX dictated that colleges spend the same proportion of athletic operation budgets on female athletes as the proportion of women on varsity teams. Temple was actually ahead of most college athletics programs of the day: Women were 42 percent of varsity athletes. But they were getting only 13 percent of the Owls' athletics budget.[12]

The judges on the Second Circuit court agreed with Haffer, expressly pointing out that Title IX did extend to an entire university. A separate panel of the same court had made a similar ruling just months earlier in a case involving Grove City College, a small Presbyterian college in central Pennsylvania, where officials had argued that they were not covered by Title IX even though its student received federal financial aid in the form of Basic Educational Opportunity Grants, commonly known as Pell grants (after former Senator Claiborne Pell).

Looking at Title IX's legislative history and the statute itself, the Second Circuit ruled that the "all-inclusive terminology" of Title IX "encompass[es] all forms of federal aid to education, direct or indirect."[13] This was the argument put forth by Carter's Justice Department in defending the Education Department, but when Reagan took office, the new slate of officials he appointed to run both departments took a substantially different view of civil rights and the government's responsibility to protect them.

The second-ever secretary of education (Carter had appointed the first, Shirley Hufstedler) was Terrel H. Bell, former commissioner of education under Nixon and Ford. In his memoir, *The Thirteenth Man*, Bell paints himself as a moderate who believed that the federal government had a vested interested in preserving and strengthening the American educational system. (He does not mention that the National Organization for Women had given him a "Silver Snail" award for failing to help women and girls.)[14] This was not a popular position in Reagan's cabinet, dominated as it was by Ed Meese and other conservatives who believed that the fledgling Education Department should be abolished and education left entirely to the states. Meese and his assistants, W. Bradford Reynolds and William French Smith, also thought the government should not be in the business of imposing civil rights laws on schools and colleges.[15]

Furthermore, the Republican staffers at the White House and the Office of Management and Budget were derisive of civil rights and openly made racist and sexist jokes, Bell recalls, referring to Title IX on more than one occasion as the "lesbian's bill of rights."[16]

When it came to enforcing Title IX and other laws, Bell's department and the Justice Department were split philosophically and ideologically.

> ED's problems with the Department of Justice emerged from differences in reading and interpreting the words in the laws both departments were required to enforce. In ED, we read the law from the perspective of educators who had worked in schools and colleges and understood admission, placement, and promotion procedures. We read the law broadly to assure equal educational opportunity. Justice lawyers were reading to find ways to "get the government off the backs of the people."[17]

Apparently, then, at the behest of Justice, the government began a widespread revision of its policies and practices. In 1982, Bell announced that the Education Department would not appeal the Richmond case, even though the U.S. commissioner for civil rights, Clarence M. Pendleton, warned that failing to fight Warriner's decision "would decimate civil rights protections in education."[18] Brad Reynolds, then the head of the Justice Department's civil rights division, said that "there was little room to argue" Warriner's ruling, and that the opinion "is pretty sound as a matter of law."[19]

Bell, whatever his private feelings might have been, introduced a new era in enforcing Title IX in sports. In announcing the settlement of a complaint against the University of Akron's athletic program, the secretary criticized what he called a "shoot first, ask questions later" approach to investigating complaints of bias.[20] He declared the university to be in compliance with the law, despite the fact that it was in violation of numerous regulations, because it had a plan for remedying its problems. The department wanted schools to solve their bias problems "over a period of time, not all at once," he said.[21] "We are going to listen to what the institution is doing to resolve discrimination and take that into account," Bell told a reporter. "I am certain that the final result will be more effective and entail less conflict."[22]

Furthermore, the Education Department was going to stay out of the debate over sports and gender. In testimony before the Senate Budget Committee, Bell said, "It is not the policy of the Education Department to specify what sports you have to offer."[23]

Reagan's Task Force on Regulatory Relief, a group looking at all areas of government operations, also targeted Title IX and sports. The group

> expressed concern about the application of a policy interpretation of Title IX and its implementing regulations relating to intercollegiate athletic programs. In particular, the Task Force cited requirements for record-keeping, overall coverage of intercollegiate athletics programs, and comparable expenditures for both sexes as areas for review. The ED Office for Civil Rights (OCR) has initiated a review of the policy interpretation. As a result of this review, we anticipate making amendments to the regulations that will reduce fiscal and administrative burdens on recipients of Department assistance.[24]

After the University of Richmond decision, the Justice Department decided to reinterpret Title IX and other civil rights laws on a program-specific basis, abandoning Bell and previous administrations. Bell protested, forcing Meese to make a decision whom to support. Bell recalls that at a meeting to discuss the new policy, Meese asked him if the pattern on his tie was a hammer and sickle. Predictably, Meese sided with the Justice Department's program-specific interpretation.[25] That meant changing course in the Grove City College case, which the Supreme Court had decided to hear.

Grove City was one of a handful of colleges that refused to accept federal funds of any sort because it wanted no federal oversight or interference. Many of its students, however, applied for and received Pell grants, which are based on financial need. In 1977 the Department of Health, Education, and Welfare said that because the college benefited by receiving this money for its students, it was covered by Title IX and thus was obligated to produce a gender-equity plan. The college refused, the department initiated plans to cut off the grants, and Grove City and four of its students sued.[26]

A district court agreed with the college's interpretation of the law, but the Second Circuit appeals court reversed and ruled in favor of the government. The Supreme Court agreed to take the case to resolve the inconsistencies with the Fourth Circuit's decision in the Richmond case, and as oral arguments approached in 1983, Bell and the Department of Justice found themselves at odds. Bell actually believed that Grove City should not be held accountable under Title IX because it received only the Pell grants and not other forms of federal aid, and he was excoriated by women's groups for holding that position.[27] He did, however, believe that for institutions that received federal funds, Title IX should apply in all programs. William French Smith, however, argued the opposite position before the Supreme Court. According to Bell,

> The brief filed with the Court argued that Pell grants were, indeed, aid to Grove City College. But the pleading before the Court went on to state that the "program or activity" applied only to the student aid office and not to the entire institution. So, despite the administration's view that Grove City College received federal aid by admitting students who had received Pell grants, the entire institution was free to discriminate, if it chose, except for the student aid office. . . . This action of Justice was, in my view, mean-spirited. Bill Smith's complaint to me that he had come to Washington to make a difference and that I was obstructing his good intentions was just a harbinger of more Justice Department actions.[28]

The Court agreed with Smith, to Bell's surprise. Justice Byron White, himself once a star football player for the University of Colorado, wrote in the majority opinion that "we have found no persuasive evidence suggesting that Congress intended that the Department's regulatory authority follow federally aided students from classroom to classroom, building to building, or activity to activity." Title IX should be applied, he wrote, to Grove City's financial-aid program, thanks to the Pell grants, and nothing else at the school.[29]

This effectively gutted Title IX, along with other civil rights laws directed at recipients of federal funds: Title VI and Title VII of the Civil Rights Act, Section 504 of the Rehabilitation Act of 1973 (which forbade discrimination against people with disabilities), and the Age Discrimination Act of 1975. The decision also shut down all investigations of educational programs not specifically marked as recipients of federal funds.[30]

Within weeks, the Office for Civil Rights closed files on active investigation, including twenty-three involving large universities, and narrowed or reinterpreted twenty-four more.[31] Opening new cases now required first proving that a particular department or office accused of discrimination received federal funds directly. A Philadelphia judge ordered that Rollin Haffer's lawsuit against Temple be restricted to claims about athletic scholarships and other forms of financial aid.[32]

It is commonly thought that the expansion of women's sports screeched to a halt in the wake of the Grove City decision. In the aggregate, that was not entirely true. Colleges continued adding teams here and there, but during the middle 1980s, the NCAA declared that sports as a whole faced a funding crisis. The association makes such an announcement at least once a decade, and what follows is a wave of cost-cutting that primarily affects nonrevenue teams. This time, both men's and women's teams were on the chopping block. Louisiana State University got rid of its softball team amid murmurs that many of its players were lesbians.[33] LSU and many other colleges in the South also dropped men's wrestling squads. In all, NCAA members dropped 167 men's teams between 1981 and 1989.[34]

Later, women's leaders would claim that this pattern is proof that Title IX is not responsible for cuts in men's sports. If colleges were dropping men's sports even at a time when Title IX was not being enforced, then the law itself cannot be the reason for the cuts in wrestling, gymnastics, and other men's sports that followed in the 1990s.

Members of Congress from both parties, including Republican Bob Dole of Kansas, immediately criticized the Supreme Court's decision. Shortly after it was announced, Dole and his colleges sponsored a "Civil Rights Act of 1984" to make it clear that Title IX, Title VI, Title VII, the Rehabilitation Act, and the Age Discrimination Act applied to all programs operated by recipients of federal funds. The goal was explicitly to overturn the Grove City decision. A resolution to support a broad interpretation of Title IX and the other laws passed in the House by a vote of 375 to 32.[35]

The Reagan administration was split on Dole's bill. Reynolds declared that it "represents a monumental, drastic change in the civil rights enforcement landscape. It rewrites our status to the point that the Federal Government would be involved in every facet of state and local activity. Under this bill, if a Ma-and-Pa grocery store takes food stamps, it would probably have to put in a ramp to provide access to the handicapped."[36] Bell and other moderates were said to favor the bill, as were some of Reagan's political advisors, who thought that opposing the measure would kill off any chance Reagan had of attracting women or minorities for the 1984 election.

Unlike the original debate over the Title IX, the potential for women's sports was a major talking point for sponsors of the new bill. According to Rep. Tom Coleman, a Missouri Republican,

One of the best examples of women gaining equal access in education thanks to Title IX has been in the area of athletics. Before Title IX was passed, practically no college or university offered scholarships to talented female athletes. For every 100 athletic scholarships awarded in 1974, an average of 1 went to a woman. Today, 22 out of every 100 athletic scholarships are awarded to women. In my own state of Missouri alone, the dollar amount of female athletic scholarships awarded at the University of Missouri at Columbia has climbed from $8,000 in 1975 to $364,000 in 1984.

I am unaware of a program of Federal financial assistance that directly supports an athletic program on a college campus. Yet, since the enactment of Title IX, athletic programs across the country have felt its tremendous impact. During 1981, over 10,000 athletic scholarships were awarded to female high school students.

[The bill] must be enacted swiftly so that the tremendous gains that we have made for women and girls in education are preserved.[37]

The final version of the bill passed the House overwhelmingly, but it was stalled in the Senate by Utah's Orrin Hatch, who in 1980 had introduced legislation of his own to limit Title IX in much the same way the Grove City decision later did.[38] After a fierce debate in the Senate's final 1984 sessions, the bill was tabled for the next term.

Dole and other sponsors reintroduced it in 1985 and 1987, opposed each year by the Reagan administration. In his annual message to the Senate in 1987, Reagan criticized what had become known as the Civil Rights Restoration Act as being "vague and sweeping," subjecting "nearly every facet of American life" to government intrusion.[39]

The act (appendix G) added a section to Title IX and other civil rights laws that specified that the terms "program or activity" and "program" referred to all the operations of any entity—including colleges, universities, other postsecondary institutions, public systems of higher education, local educational agencies like a school system, or any department of state or local government—that received any kind of federal funding.[40] Both houses of Congress passed the bill after a debate in the Senate over whether to insert a provision stated that the law was neutral on the topic of abortion, meaning that a recipient of federal funds (such as a hospital controlled by Baylor or Brigham Young) was not required to provide abortions.[41]

But Reagan was not done. He vetoed the bill in March 1988, urging Congress to pass instead a bill that would have exempted religious institutions and some private businesses from coverage under civil rights laws.[42] In his veto message, Reagan said that

Congress . . . has sent me a bill that would vastly and unjustifiably expand the power of the Federal Government over the decisions and affairs of private organizations, such as churches and synagogues, farms, businesses, and State and local governments. In the process, it would place at risk such cherished values as religious liberty.

. . . The bill would seriously impinge upon religious liberty because of its unprecedented and pervasive coverage of churches and synagogues based on receipt of even a small amount of Federal aid for just one activity; its unprecedented coverage of entire religious elementary and secondary school systems when only a single school in such a system receives Federal aid; and its failure to protect, under Title IX of the Education Amendments of 1972, the religious freedom of private schools that are closely identified with the religious tenets of, but not controlled by, a religious organization.[43]

Both houses of Congress took the bill up to decide whether to override the veto, despite an onslaught of protests from evangelical Christians, including the Reverend Jerry Falwell.[44] Within a week, both the Senate and the House did vote to override the president's veto, dealing the administration a harsh defeat as Reagan prepared to leave office. It was only the eighth Reagan veto overridden by Congress.[45]

The civil rights and women's rights establishments swung back into action. In Philadelphia, lawyers for the National Women's Law Center and Trial Lawyers for Public Justice had amended the original Rollin Haffer lawsuit to claim that Temple was violating Pennsylvania's state equal rights amendment and the U.S. Constitution's equal-protection clause embodied in the Fourteenth Amendment. They also got their case certified as a class action and in 1987 began meeting with female athletes at Temple. That provoked a spat with Temple officials, chronicled in court papers, who evidently encouraged players not to meet with Arthur S. Bryant of Trial Lawyers. The judge in the case, Joseph S. Lord III, agreed with the plaintiffs that they had shown enough instances of possible discrimination in the number of participation opportunities for women, scholarship allocations for female athletes, and inadequate budgeting for women's teams to allow the suit to go forward.[46] Temple settled the case in 1988 and agreed to give more scholarship money to female athletes.[47]

While these battles raged in courts and Congress, college sport was undergoing seismic changes. In 1984, the Supreme Court ruled that the NCAA could no longer control the broadcast of regular-season football games, on which it had held a monopoly since the 1950s. A new breed of cable television channels, led by ESPN, all hungry for programming on the cheap, began to offer colleges money and publicity for putting their teams on the air at all hours of the day and night.[48] That gave athletics directors the opportunity to get more university money to invest in football and men's basketball teams and facilities, arguing that improving high-profile teams would guarantee their college more visibility across the country.

This development put nonrevenue men's sports and all women's sports in a bit of a bind. Athletics directors were on record saying they wanted to improve opportunities for women and preserve opportunities for men, but they were also caught up in an escalating salary race for big-time coaches and needed to invest in expensive facilities to impress recruits. So they began looking for ways to cut costs in other areas, that is, lower-profile sports.

In 1987, the NCAA considered a measure to cut scholarships 10 percent across the board—even in women's sports, which were already underfunded at most institutions under the terms of the 1979 policy interpretation.[49] The measure was tabled, and some colleges moved forward with plans to drop women's sports. The University of Toledo abolished its field hockey team, and the University of Oklahoma tried to drop women's basketball before a public outcry forced the Sooners to bring back the team.[50]

Meanwhile, college sports as a whole were taking a bit of a beating. The NCAA punished college after college for violating recruiting rules, bribing players, and overlooking players' drug habits and violent behavior. The culmination of the scandals of the 1980s was the decision in 1987 to ban Southern Methodist University from competing in football for a year. Colleges also were castigated for recruiting athletes who were incapable of keeping up in their classes, and Congress held hearings featuring athletes who were given degrees despite being unable to read.

Following the override of Reagan's veto of the Civil Rights Restoration Act, newspapers also started asking hard questions about whether schools had done enough to comply with Title IX. Most such stories were sympathetic toward college administrators, charting the struggles of those who wanted to expand women's programs but just did not have the money. But college presidents and NCAA officials began talking about the responsibilities they had toward female athletes.

"It's more than a Title IX and a financial issue, it's a moral issue," the NCAA's new executive director, Richard D. Schultz, told the *Minneapolis Star Tribune* in 1992. "We need the opportunity on the playing field, but we also need the opportunity in coaching and athletic administration. We know what the problems are in gender equity; we need the solutions."[51]

Schultz also may have been trying to warn his members of impending legal dangers. Following the resolution of the Temple case, women and public-interest lawyers began suing universities in an effort to get them to expand their sports programs. These cases (covered more fully in chapter 7) were either successful or settled out of court, forcing colleges to commit to offering more women's teams or better facilities, or both.

The NCAA published its first Gender Equity Report in 1992, in time for the law's twentieth anniversary. Using data from the 1990–91 academic year, it found that women were only 30 percent of the athletes on varsity teams and were receiving only about 30 percent of scholarship budgets, 23 percent of operating budgets, and 17 percent of recruiting funds.[52]

Schultz, only the second executive director of the NCAA, announced the formation of a Gender Equity Task Force in 1992 to study the status of, and problems facing, women in college sports. The committee consisted of male and female coaches, athletics administrators, and college officials, and it held three meetings over the course of the next year to listen to the NCAA's members as well as the general public.

The most contentious issue they faced was not how to treat women. Everyone agreed with the general idea of equity, and those who did not were smart enough not to challenge it in public. Instead, the key issue was what to do about football and its ravenous appetite for equipment and personnel. Previous cost-reduction measures had brought the number of scholarships down from an unlimited number in the early 1970s to 105 to 95 and finally 85 in an effort to level the playing field for poorer institutions. No other NCAA sport, however, is allotted more than 28 scholarships per institution. That means that colleges trying to devise an equitable distribution of roster spots and scholarship dollars among male and female athletes must come up with a multitude of women's teams to offset the needs of the football team.

Football representatives, including LSU athletics director Joe Dean and Baylor head coach Grant Teaff, argued that they needed to preserve the full complement of scholarships as a matter of safety to protect injured players, as well as a way of having enough talented athletes around to keep the game popular among spectators. "We're competing against professional football in many areas, and I've got to keep my game exciting," Dean told the *Chronicle of Higher Education.* "I need skilled people. People say we could live with 60 scholarships, and if we had to we would. But we'd be rolling the dice, and that scares me."[53]

Despite these concerns, the committee's recommendations included some radical propositions, particularly the pronouncement that "the ultimate goal for each institution should be that the numbers of male and female athletes are substantially proportionate to their numbers in the institution's undergraduate student population"[54]—in other words, meeting the first part of the three-part test outlined in the 1979 policy interpretation.

This would have been a heady goal for almost any college to meet, given that undergraduate student bodies nationally were now more than 50 percent women, but women were barely 30 percent of athletes. By wiping out the second and third parts of the three-part test, this standard was much tougher than any set forth by the Department of Education.

This goal threatened to foment a revolt among the larger football-playing institutions, some of which had been chafing under the NCAA's other rules for years. "It may be that the NCAA is no longer the institution we can ride with," Dean told the *Houston Chronicle* during a meeting of the College Football Association. "I know a lot of people hate to hear me say it, but we have to do something."[55]

LSU and other colleges sponsoring the largest and most expensive athletics programs have periodically discussed seceding from the NCAA, leaving behind the many restrictions it places upon members in the name of creating a "level playing field" for its diverse set of member institutions. None of these discussions has led to action, and Dean's suggestion that gender equity provisions might force top colleges to abandon the association did not move much farther than the College Football Association meeting.

To head off these grumblings, however, the NCAA endorsed only a general principle that all colleges ought to comply with the government's gender-equity regulations, and that "an athletics program can be considered gender-equitable when the participants in both the men's and women's sports programs would accept as fair and equitable the overall program of the other gender. No individual should be discriminated against on the basis of gender, institutionally or nationally, in intercollegiate athletics."[56]

The panel also recommended increasing scholarship limits for women's sports, but the association never acted on the suggestion. It did, however, adopt a system of "emerging sports," supposedly a group of women's sports that had a chance to grow: rowing, ice hockey, team handball, water polo, synchronized swimming, archery, badminton, bowling, and squash.[57] Interestingly, many of these had been recognized as varsity sports during the AIAW era, but did not "emerge" during the first decade of the NCAA's involvement in women's sports. In subsequent years, bowling became a popular sport at historically African-American colleges and universities, while rowing and ice hockey have attracted a national following of fans and participants. The rest of the sports continue to languish, with only a handful of teams sponsored.

Although many colleges cut back on sports programs in the 1980s, women's sports in the aggregate expanded dramatically over the decade. Overall, the number of NCAA women's teams increased by 20 percent from 1981 to 1989. Certain sports, like gymnastics and swimming, suffered major cutbacks, as did men's fencing and wrestling, among others. Sports like women's soccer and track exploded.[58]

As the numbers increased, so did interest in and the intensity of women's sports. The coaches who had learned their skills in the late 1970s began to develop a new ethos for making women into the best athletes they could possibly be. In certain niches across the country, those athletes began to attract a devoted following.

6

CHAPTER

•

The First Generation

Apart from, and often oblivious to, the concurrent legal battles, a generation of girls entered junior high and high school in the 1980s and early 1990s. Most of them had the opportunity for some kind of athletic experience, mostly in recreation programs and YMCAs in the suburbs but quite often in both urban and rural areas.

In certain niches of the country, girls' and women's sports became socially acceptable, not only for participants but also for spectators. Small communities like Shelbyville, Tennessee; Hart County, Georgia; the Crow reservation in South Dakota; and Oregon City, Oregon, became girls' basketball hotbeds. Just as they had done for boys' teams for generations, parents and townspeople turned out in droves to watch and cheer and discuss. Girls' sports became communal focal points.

The 1980s also were the decade when soccer established itself as one of the preeminent sports of the American suburbs. Fields sprung up alongside (and in some places in place of) baseball diamonds and football fields, and the ease of play and low equipment costs made the sport tremendously popular among both boys and girls in the towns surrounding Washington, Atlanta, St. Louis, Dallas, San Diego, and elsewhere.

The widening and deepening of the talent pool meant a greater demand for places to play at the college level. Independent of the legal issues, hundreds of colleges added teams in both sports, as well as others, for women.

Some colleges made only a token effort to support their teams. At others, however, dedicated coaches and supportive administrators created the first powerhouse programs. With all the resources of the University of Tennessee behind her, Pat Head Summitt built a dynasty that supplanted earlier basketball champions like Delta State University and Immaculata College. At the University of North Carolina, a male law student named

Anson Dorrance agreed to coach both men's and women's soccer teams. The men became pretty good; the women, the most successful program in NCAA history.

Summitt turned the Lady Vols into a machine—not just a winning machine, but a cash machine. Her relentless courtship of Knoxville and its environs won her players a community of devotees, some of whom were fans of the "men Vols" and some of whom were not. Dorrance was as successful as Summitt in tallying wins and championships (maybe even more so), and systematized a new psychology of teaching women to compete as hard as men did.

Following the 1976 Olympics, Summitt dedicated herself full-time to the Lady Vols. Also that year, Tennessee decided to operate two parallel athletics departments—one for men and one for women. The entire budget for the women's department was $126,000, including $25,000 for athletic scholarships. Of that scholarship budget, $3,000 went to the basketball team.[1]

Her teams grew dominant first on a statewide basis, then on a regional one. Attention and interest in Tennessee grew accordingly. Summitt had started the Boost-Hers club to support the team in the late 1970s, and fans in the area invited players over for cookouts and small parties. Speaking to the Big Orange Club of nearby Oak Ridge, Summitt made an impression on one newly converted fan: "She had all those leadership qualities in the generals I had worked for," Tom Haynes told the *Chattanooga Times-Free Press*. "I could recognize that right away." He bought season tickets that night and remained a fan for the next twenty-five years.[2]

When the Lady Vols moved into the 24,000-seat Thompson-Boling Arena in 1987, they were a national powerhouse. Their fans loved them: Attendance hovered around 3,000 per game in the first half of the 1980s, and the team qualified for two Final Fours in three nears. The team won its first national title in 1987, defeating Louisiana Tech's Lady Techsters in the finals, 67-44. That year, attendance jumped to 4,000 per game, and the following season, nearly 7,000 fans per game watched the Lady Vols run to a 31-3 record.

Along the way, the Lady Vols established an identity for themselves in the marketplace. They had different logos and different uniforms than the men Vols, featuring a light blue to go with the Big Orange. Not more feminine or feminist (like the University of Minnesota, where the women's department replaced the block-M logo with a "Ms."), just distinct.

After the Lady Vols' third national championship, in 1995–96, attendance surged to 10,500 a game, making Tennessee the first women's team to average more than 10,000 fans. The same year, the women's athletics department hired its first full-time marketer, Ron Goch.[3] After the team won another title, in 1997, attendance jumped to 14,659, and after a third straight in 1998, the first stood at 16,559—more than thirteen of the twenty-nine National Basketball Association teams and about 800 more than the men Vols' basketball squad. In 2002–3, the University of Connecticut's Huskies became the first team in six years to top the Lady Vols in attendance, 12,859 fans per game to 12,585.

Goch, later with the Utah Starzz of the WNBA, brought a big-league marketing style and game-management attitude to Knoxville. At a 1999 game, a full cohort of cheerleaders (both male and female) did cartwheels across the floor during pregame festivities while a marketing intern dressed as a hamburger danced across the floor, promoting a local fast-food chain.

"We'll have a laser-light show with the players' signatures on the floor," Goch said. "We have fireworks, and this year, we've got this new wiener gun. One of our interns will have it down on the floor, and they can shoot hot dogs into the stands, or T-shirts, or whatever. We've already got three sponsors for it—we just swap out the decals."

Attendance grew at all kinds of women's events across the country during the 1990s, and interest in women's basketball jumped after the American team's success at the 1992 and 1996 Olympics. Yet the Lady Vols stayed ahead of the game. The women's basketball team turned a tidy net profit of $498,000 in 1998–99 with revenues of slightly over $2.8 million and expenses of a little under $2.4 million. That made them one of only a handful of women's teams, in any sport, that actually make money.

Of that $2.8 million, almost $1.3 million came from gifts and endowment income. Season-ticket buyers whose seats are in the lower bowl of Thompson-Boling Arena must donate at least $1,000 per ticket on top of its price, a practice most colleges reserve for football and men's basketball ticketholders.

Not all income can be reckoned in dollars, though. Goch and his colleagues trade tickets for goods and services, such as the laser-light show. Signs for Philips Electronics, Adidas, and State Farm dot the inside of the arena, and tickets, posters, pamphlets, and other promotional materials for the team are plastered in corporate logos.

Even with all this, though, the Lady Vols athletics department does not turn a profit on its sports as a whole. The women's department receives more than $3 million annually from the men's department and the university, including $1-million in student fees and over $500,000 in licensing income. Will the women's athletics department ever be able to balance its budget?

"Probably not," said its director, Joan Cronan. "I would like to think so, but . . ." She shrugged philosophically. Even at a powerhouse like Tennessee, fans are not going to support a women's team with quite the degree of fanaticism reserved for men's sports. The football team attracts nearly 110,000 fans per game here in Knoxville, and high school boys' sports are a religion. Women's sports occupies a niche, and the Lady Vols basketball team happens to fill it particularly well. But it is still a niche.

Along with all their accomplishments on the court, Summitt and Tennessee officials are fond of bragging about what their players do when they are not playing. The Lady Vols have never been in trouble with the NCAA, and two-thirds of their players earn degrees within six years of entering college, compared with less than 30 percent of male basketball players at Tennessee.

Dorothy Stulberg, a civil rights lawyer in Knoxville, was one of the Boost-Her Club's earliest members. She and her husband Mel still attend games, and for a time had season tickets next to a couple from Iowa who flew in for as many games as they could—not because they had any connection with the university, but because they saw the Lady Vols in an NCAA tournament and were hooked on the players and the way they comported themselves.

To any fan of Southeastern Conference sports, the hoopla cuts both ways. The Lady Vols have clearly arrived as a subject of passionate interest among fans in Knoxville and beyond. However, men's teams in football and basketball have consistently gotten in trouble for bribing recruits, committing academic fraud, and having pathetic graduation rates. There is a danger associated with the big time.

"You're afraid they'll get like the boys," Stulberg said, gazing out over the full arena at the 1999 game. "But on the other hand, I wouldn't give this up for anything."

A few teams have had success on par with Tennessee's. Texas Tech University, the University of Texas, Connecticut, Southwest Missouri State University, and a handful of other women's clubs draw well, and others, like the University of Notre Dame, do well at the ticket counter when their teams are winning. Purdue University even had student riots when the Boilermakers lost to Notre Dame in the 2001 national finals.

Other women's sports have flourished in their own niches. The University of Nebraska's volleyball team attracts several thousand fans to its games in Lincoln, and gymnastics teams at the universities of Alabama, Georgia, and Utah have well-established followings. These, though, are the exceptions. In 2002–3, four women's basketball teams (Connecticut, Tennessee, Texas Tech, and New Mexico) averaged 10,000 fans per game, but in the aggregate, the 322 women's teams in Division I of the NCAA averaged only 1,619 fans per game. Men's teams averaged 5,732.[4]

As a result, most colleges put barely a fraction of the resources into women's sports that they put into men's. The exceptions dominate their sports—Nebraska in volleyball, Alabama in volleyball, Louisiana State University in track, to name a few.

No team, however, has ever been as dominant as North Carolina in women's soccer. Beginning in the waning days of the AIAW, Dorrance developed an approach to coaching unlike any of his competitors'. By emphasizing aggressiveness, teamwork, and fitness, he brought a new attitude to coaching women, resulting in seventeen NCAA titles in the first twenty years they were handed out. By 1990, and even more so today, the Tar Heels were the dominant force in women's soccer, not just collegiately but throughout the world. On the 2004 Olympic team, twelve of the thirty-seven players were Tar Heels alumnae, and the team's coach, April Heinrichs, was Dorrance's first big recruit.

Coaching women is different from coaching men, according to Dorrance. Women need more nurturing, and they need to learn the take-no-prisoners attitude that seems to come naturally to male athletes.

He coached both the men's and women's teams at Carolina for a decade, from 1979 to 1989, and picked up responsibility for the national women's team as well. In training players of both sexes, he said, he did not condescend to women, but expected as much out of them as he did from the men.

"Originally, people felt like if you were going to coach women, you had to be gentler with them," he says.[5] "The periods in the international game were shorter, just like there was a period where women were not allowed to run marathons because it was feared that their uteruses would descend and fall out. The evolution of women's sports is the evolution of understanding how strong they are."

He continued, "I had a younger sister, one year younger, who was the best athlete in the family. So in my experience, there was nothing I could do that my younger sister couldn't do. I never had this illusion that women were the gentler sex. The impression I had was that they were a collection of savages, because that was what my sister was. I didn't have any preconceived notions about being easier or softer on my women. So I started training my first women's teams the same way I trained my first men's team."

That included a heavy dose of physical conditioning—wind sprints, long-distance runs, and other elements to make his players fitter than any opponent they could possibly face. Tar Heel players regularly say that their practices are much tougher than games, and Dorrance says he trains his players to be strong and enthusiastic for the entire ninety minutes of a game, "not just the first twenty minutes when you've got the adrenaline flowing."

"A lot of what we do comes from the men's game," he says. "The standards we aspire to are men's standards."

At the same time, women need a different approach from their coach, says Dorrance. Women desire a "connectiveness" in a team setting in which players and coaches all have a relationship with each other. It took Dorrance a while to realize this. In trying to recruit Heinrichs, for example, he gave her the same spiel as he did for male recruits—what kind of scholarship money he could give her, how much playing time she could expect. "But she sort of skipped over that and instead asked, 'How does your team get along?'" he recalls. "I couldn't figure out at the time why it made any difference, but each time I called her, she asked the same question."[6]

So Dorrance worked hard to create an almost-democratic environment on his team. "We have a no-cut policy," he says.

> Any kid that tries out makes it, and the only kids we cut are the ones who are a royal pain in the ass. We've always had that as a philosophy. Some of the finest people we coach are people who can't play, so we foster a community of great people and great players.
>
> The question we ask kids is, "Do you really want to continue to do this?" We challenge them to quit. They have to convince us they enjoy not playing [in games]—that they enjoy being part of our team, competing with and against household names. We respect these people. A lot of them are great students and fine leaders.

Carolina typically has around twenty-eight players on its roster. In 2001–2, the average for Division I teams was twenty-two.

The other important aspect of coaching women, Dorrance says, is teaching them to be more competitive, especially in practice. In *Vision of a Champion*, he writes:

> Uninhibited competition is usually harder for females. Because of the importance of their relationships, they struggle with separating competitive anger from personal anger. In general, females don't like direct confrontation. This is true from a young age. . . . If two young girls show up at a basketball court, they don't customarily fight for turf in a game like

one v. one. Their tendency is to play a cooperative, turn-taking game like HORSE. But this doesn't really train you for the competitive arena.[7]

"Women don't really enjoy competing with their friends," he says. "It separates women, and some women pull in their claws a bit when they're competing with their friends. The challenge in coaching women is getting them to train with intensity, to compete in practice. Part of competing against opponents, for women, is to actually dislike them in some fashion, and that's a difficult environment to create in practice."

He tries to do so by recording everything—outcomes of drills, times for runs, goals scores, and so forth. "We give women permission to compete," he says. "They get tired of seeing their names at the bottom of the list, and they say, 'To heck with this, I *am* going to compete."

Dorrance boasts of creating a team that is both nurturing and competitive, and in his books cites numerous and loving letters from former players who appreciate his leadership and his values. He is not without detractors: In 2003 he and the university settled a lawsuit brought by a former player who had accused Dorrance of sexual harassment and creating a hostile atmosphere for her. He admitted no wrongdoing, and terms of the settlement have not been made public.

When Dorrance and Summitt began coaching in the late 1970s, he was in the distinct minority. As colleges started or elevated women's varsity programs, they almost invariably hired female coaches. In 1972, more than 90 percent of women's teams had a woman as their coach, according to a longitudinal study of coaching trends by R. Vivian Acosta and Linda Jean Carpenter that is now in its twenty-seventh year.[8] As Summitt's, Rose's, and Hatchell's stories show, some women capitalized on the moment and built successful careers as college coaches and administrators.

The operative term, though, is "some." Particularly after the NCAA took over women's sports, male coaches began to find their way into the coaching ranks. By 1987, less than half of women's teams had a female head coach, and in 2004, only 44 percent of women's teams did. At the same time, women have never been welcomed as coaches of men's teams. Since the 1970s, less than 2 percent of men's teams have had a female head coach, and those teams have generally been in individual sports where men and women train and compete in identical events, such as golf, swimming, and track.[9]

This trend has two sets of implications. First, for female athletes, far fewer women are learning the ethos of fair play, sportsmanship, and personal development that the coaches of the AIAW tried to instill. (That said, over the years many women have said they prefer male coaches to females for an assortment of reasons.)

The other issue is for women coaches themselves. Coaches of women's teams make far less, on average, than coaches of men's teams, in many cases even when they have the same responsibilities—in 2002–3, head women's coaches in the NCAA's Division I-A made fifty-five thousand dollars on average, while head men's coaches made more than one hundred thousand. So women are locked out of the best-paying jobs, and increasingly are either choosing not to go into coaching or cannot get jobs coaching men.

The same trends are true for female athletics administrators. When Title IX was enacted, female administrators were in charge of more than 90 percent of women's sports programs. By 2000, that number had fallen to 17.9 percent. However, the number has since recovered slightly, to 18.5 percent. Female athletics directors are still few and far between, even as women have become a significant number of college presidents.[10]

Summitt and Dorrance have been the dominant coaches in their sports for the better part of three decades, but their hegemony has slipped as other universities have begun beefing up women's sports. Connecticut has dominated Tennessee and the rest of women's basketball since 2000, but new teams are popping up in the top ranks of the sport. The University of Oklahoma, which nearly dropped women's basketball in the mid-1980s due to a perceived lack of interest, made it to the national finals in 2002, losing to UConn 82-70 in a game that drew the highest ratings of any college basketball contest—men's or women's—ever broadcast by ESPN. In soccer, Santa Clara University and the University of Portland have challenged the Tar Heels in recent years, bringing an element of parity to the sport.

The upstarts are led by smart and hungry coaches. The athletes on those teams, though, can also thank a series of court decisions in the 1990s for forcing a broad range colleges to get serious about women's sports for the first time.

7

CHAPTER
•

A Watershed Moment

After Congress made it very clear with the Civil Rights Restoration Act of 1987 that Title IX did apply to sports, after all, athletes started finding their way to court to force colleges to abide by the law. Their numbers were small—athletes have only four years to compete in college sports, so finding plaintiffs who can stick with a case long enough to force change or see it become a class-action lawsuit is difficult. Finding both plaintiffs and lawyers got much easier in 1992, when the Supreme Court turned around and gave Title IX more teeth.

Christine Franklin was a sophomore at North Gwinnett High School, northeast of Atlanta, in 1986. A teacher and coach at the school, Andrew Hill, began harassing her that year, asking her about her sexual experiences with her boyfriend and calling her home to ask her for dates, according to court filings. The following year he had her excused from class three times and raped her in a private office. Although informed of the situation and of similar allegations against Hill made by other students, neither the school administration nor the county school system took any action against him.[1]

Title IX expressly forbids sexual harassment, and Franklin filed a complaint with the Office for Civil Rights in 1988. After an investigation, OCR determined that because Hill and North Gwinnett's principal, William Prescott, were no longer working at the school, the district was in compliance with the law. Franklin then sued the school district in federal court, demanding that she be awarded money to compensate her for her suffering. Both the district court and the appeals court ruled that Title IX did not authorize courts to levy monetary damages. On its way out of office, the Bush administration filed a friend-of-the-court brief arguing the same position.

The Supreme Court, however, saw it differently. Under long-standing legal tradition, Justice Lewis Powell wrote, if somebody has the right to sue under the Constitution or other laws, and Congress has not specified how penalties should be awarded, then the courts are free to assign penalties they believe to be appropriate. The Court had decided in Geraldine Cannon's case that individuals had the right to sue institutions for Title IX violations, so plaintiffs were entitled to whatever damages courts deemed fit.[2]

This decision immediately changed the significance of Title IX, particularly in sports. As noted earlier, NCAA officials began talking about expanding women's opportunities as a matter of moral principle, but the Franklin case meant that colleges ignoring the law could face serious penalties in the pocketbook. It also gave an incentive to scores of other plaintiffs to pursue Title IX cases, increasing the likelihood of lawsuits against athletics departments.

Among the women who began bringing lawsuits were athletes whose teams had been dropped for financial reasons, or those who thought their colleges needed to add new teams. One of the first cases was brought in 1992, just as the Supreme Court was issuing the Franklin decision, by a group of athletes at Indiana University of Pennsylvania led by Dawn Favia, a gymnast. The previous year, IUP faced a budget crunch, which it remedied by cutting women's gymnastics, women's field hockey, men's soccer, and men's tennis, leaving the university with seven teams for men and seven for women.[3]

However, one of the remaining men's teams was a football team. Before the cuts, Indiana had 313 male athletes and 190 females; afterwards, the Indians had 248 men and 149 women on sports teams. More men were cut, but on a percentage basis, the cuts were roughly equivalent, with the proportion of women on varsity teams remaining at 38 percent. The student body, on the other hand, was 55 percent female.

In his opinion, Judge Maurice B. Cohill declared that Frank Cignetti, Indiana's athletics director, "is a sensitive man, obviously between the proverbial rock and a hard place. His budget has been drastically cut; he must therefore make cuts in the athletic program, yet he is faced with the constraints of Title IX."[4]

Indiana had promised to start a women's soccer team, but, as Cohill wrote, "you can't replace programs with promises," despite OCR's stance in the 1980 investigators' manual that having a plan in place would mitigate disparities that violated its guidelines. The judge also noted that Indiana awarded only 21 percent of its scholarship budget to female athletes, which might have artificially depressed interest in sports among women considering attending the university.

Cohill's ruling mainly focused on the need for Indiana to raise participation numbers for female athletes. The university was failing all options under the three-part test, he ruled: it clearly had fewer female athletes, on a percentage basis, than female students; having dropped sports, it could not claim to have a history and continuing practice of expanding opportunities for women; and the university could not prove that it was meeting the interests and abilities of female athletes, despite honoring scholarship commitments to women whose teams had been dropped and promising to add the soccer team.

In working through each element of the three-part test, Cohill observed that the Education Department's set of Title IX guidelines—not just the 1975 regulations but also the 1979 policy interpretation— "deserves our great deference," thanks to the authority Congress had given the department to enforce the law. Even though Congress had not voted on the policy interpretation, Cohill wrote, courts had to defer to it. This set the three-part test up as the law of the land, despite previous efforts by the NCAA and future efforts by other lawyers to argue that the 1979 document was merely a set of suggestions for Title IX compliance. Cohill's ruling was the first brick in what became a very large wall of case law protecting Title IX against revision in the courts.

Another brick was laid the following year, when the U.S. Court of Appeals for the Tenth Circuit ruled in a similar case that Colorado State University had violated Title IX by dropping its women's softball team. Not only did the court rule the Education Department's rules deserved "great deference," but it also provided more commentary on the three-part test:

> In effect, "substantial proportionality" between athletic participation and undergraduate enrollment provides a safe harbor for recipients under Title IX. In the absence of such gender balance, the institution must show that it has expanded and is continuing to expand opportunities for athletic participation by the underrepresented gender, or else it must fully and effectively accommodate the interests and abilities among members of the underrepresented gender.[5]

Thus, the district court placed the three-part test squarely in the context of decades of civil rights laws, lawsuits, and enforcement actions, including the Philadelphia Plan. The numerical definition of fairness gives an institution a kind of supercompliance, a measure of assurance that it will not be sued. The second and third tests appear subordinate, and much more likely to be debated and litigated.

In both the Indiana and Colorado State cases, universities were ordered to reinstate the teams and restore their budgets for coaching, equipment, travel, and scholarships. "We do not believe that the defendants will be irreparably harmed if the field hockey and gymnastics teams are reinstated," Cohill wrote of Indiana. "The budget, while shrinking, has space for reallocation and cutbacks in other areas."

While these two cases made their way through the courts, Trial Lawyers for Public Justice was fighting a similar battle in Rhode Island against a far different opponent: Brown University.

In 1991, Ivy League universities faced the same budget crunches as Indiana, Colorado State, and other institutions across the country. Their athletics departments had to make cuts, as did many other departments across institutions. Yale elected to save more than half a million dollars by eliminating administrative positions and also by dropping men's varsity water polo and wrestling, as well as junior-varsity hockey.[6]

Brown's athletics department was one of the largest in the country, with thirty-one sports. In 1991, it announced it would drop men's golf and water polo and women's gymnastics and volleyball to save seventy-five thousand dollars per year.[7] Brown did not get rid of the sports altogether; it merely relegated them to club status, meaning that the university would allow students to compete against teams from other colleges but would not pay for coaches, travel, uniforms, or other expenses.

The Ivy League, officially formed in 1954, had long since abandoned the fields of big-time college football. The league banned the awarding of athletic scholarships upon its founding, placing its members at a recruiting disadvantage for elite players, but, by its account, affirming the proper place of sports in a student's education. Ivy League athletes are supposed to be students first, given that they are attending the most prestigious universities in the country.

However, ever since the days of Dudley Allen Sargent, sports have been very important at the Ancient Eight—Brown, Columbia, Cornell, Dartmouth, Harvard, Pennsylvania, Princeton, and Yale—and they have always maintained scores of varsity teams that attract a large portion of the student body. In 1951, 20 percent of male students at Ivy institutions were varsity athletes.[8]

Women had participated in physical-education programs at Ivy institutions and their coordinate women's colleges, such as Barnard in New York, Radcliffe in Cambridge, and Pembroke in Providence. Some of their teams competed on a limited basis against other members of the "Seven Sisters" colleges, which included Bryn Mawr, Smith, and Wellesley, in sports like basketball, fencing, riflery, rowing, and tennis. Brown started the first women's intercollegiate ice hockey team, the Pembroke Pandas, in 1965.[9]

In the 1970s, following the passage of Title IX, most Ivy League schools were going coeducational or absorbing the coordinate women's colleges. Despite, or perhaps because of, these changes, the move to formalize women's sports programs came quickly. The league held its first women's championship, in rowing, in 1974. Events for basketball and soccer soon followed, and by 1997 the league had a full slate of women's championships in cross-country, gymnastics, swimming, outdoor track, and volleyball. Fencing, field hockey, lacrosse, squash, tennis, and indoor track soon followed, giving the Ivies one of the most comprehensive women's sports programs available anywhere in the country.[10]

Not everything came easily. Yale rowers made headlines in 1976 when they stripped nude in the office of the women's athletics director to protest their lack of a locker room. They had written "Title IX" across their breasts and backs and read a statement to the director, Joni E. Barnett: "These are the bodies Yale is exploiting. On a day like today the ice freezes on the skin. Then we sit for half an hour as the ice melts and soaks through to meet the sweat that is soaking up from the inside."[11] Yale built an addition to its boathouse to accommodate them.

Brown's women's tennis team, in an effort to raise funds for a spring-break trip like the one the men's team took, showed movies in the university swimming pool in the mid-1970s. Porn flicks, to be precise. The money came in quickly.[12]

By the 1990s, though, Ivy League women's sports programs and certainly Brown's were among the best in the country. Brown's women's soccer team won nine out of ten league titles in the 1980s, advancing as far as the quarterfinals in the NCAA tournament. The Bears' coach, Phil Pinince, also led the softball team to the Ivy League title in 1990, and swimmer Jen Boyd won three All-America certificates the same year, earning a nineteenth-place finish in the NCAA team competition all by herself.

Gymnasts and volleyball players at Brown were not as concerned with those accomplishments as with the demise of their own teams. A group including gymnast Amy Cohen met with Lynette Labinger, a Providence attorney, who brought in Arthur Bryant of Trial Lawyers for Public Justice, who had argued *Temple v. Haffer*. In April 1992, they filed suit against Brown, accusing the university of discriminating against women by not offering sufficient sports opportunities for them and forcing gymnastics and volleyball players to be "student-fundraiser-athletes" instead of just "student-athletes," as Cohen, the lead plaintiff, put it.[13] They asked to certify the suit as a class action, meaning that all current and future Brown women athletes were included, and requested an injunction ordering Brown to restore the teams immediately and not to reduce any other women's program "unless the percentage of 'opportunities' to participate in intercollegiate athletics equals the percentage of women enrolled in the undergraduate program."[14]

Cohen's lawyers argued that Brown was not complying with any part of the three-part test. First, the proportion of women on varsity teams was far lower than the proportion of women in the student body, so Brown could not claim to be meeting part 1. Second, Brown had expanded its women's program dramatically in the 1970s, but had not added a women's sport since 1982, so it could not be in compliance with part 2. Third, the lawyers argued, not only did the campus have interested and capable gymnasts and volleyball players, it also had viable numbers of women athletes who wanted to compete in varsity fencing, rugby, sailing, and water polo, so Brown could not claim it was fully and effectively accommodating the interests and abilities of women on campus.[15]

Robert A. Reichley, Brown's vice president for public affairs, was quick to respond. He pointed out that Brown ranked second out of the 292 colleges in Division I in the number of sports it offered for women. While only 39 percent of varsity athletes were women, he said, that compared favorably with the rest of Division I; as a whole, only 31 percent of Division I athletes were female. And thirty-seven male athletes were affected by the team cuts, compared with only twenty-three women.[16]

"We feel we are in compliance" with Title IX, Reichley said at the time. "We feel our record is better than most schools in the country, and we are one of the leaders in offering sports opportunities to women."[17]

In their brief and during a hearing before Judge Raymond J. Pettine of the U.S. District Court for Rhode Island in October 1992, Brown officials made the rest of their case clear. Julius Michaelson, a lawyer for the university, told the judge that granting the injunction would result in a "loss of control of the budgeting process of Brown University." Further, he argued, the Title IX statute did not require the university to maintain gender proportionality between the athletics department and the student body. "Equal opportunity does not require proportional representation," he said.[18]

Moreover, he argued, violating Title IX requires much more than failing the three-part test. Both the 1979 policy interpretation and the 1980 investigator's manual require the Office for Civil Rights (and, presumably, the courts) to investigate all areas of an athletics program, such as coaching, scheduling, and equipment, to ascertain whether the law has been violated.

Finally, Brown denied it was in violation of the three-part test. Perhaps a smaller number of women than men were on varsity teams, even proportionate to their representation in the student body, but that was because proportionately fewer women were interested in sports. Brown offered the opportunity to participate in sports to many more women than actually took them up on the offer, lawyers argued, and the university should be judged on the basis of the number of opportunities provided, rather than on the actual number of women that went out for each team.

The hearing went on for three weeks, and Pettine confessed in court, "I flip-flop from one side to the another as days go along." Brown stuck to its position that the cuts were a financial decision well within the university's purview, autonomous from government interference, and that the university was meeting the third part of the three-part test, "fully and affectively accommodating the interests and abilities" of women on campus. Labinger, on the other side, told the court that "the harm is happening every day" for athletes denied a chance to compete.[19]

In late December, Pettine agreed with the plaintiffs almost right down the line. In a thirty-six-page opinion, he described the case as raising "novel issues concerning Title IX and intercollegiate athletics" and requiring a detailed examination of the 1979 policy interpretation as well as the facts surrounding Brown's case in particular.

First, he ruled, the court had to use the policy interpretation and the investigator's manual as "important guides in unraveling the requirements of the athletic regulation," especially given that the arguments between the two parties arose from different interpretations of the same documents.[20] Second, athletics programs at different colleges can vary so much that all of the components of the interpretation and the manual may not apply in the same way at different colleges, so Pettine found it appropriate to rule strictly on the question of participation.

Third, the language on how many athletes and particularly female athletes a college must have actually appears in a section dealing with "levels of competition" provided to male and female athletes in the policy interpretation, Pettine noted. He read this section as requiring two steps of analysis: applying the three-part test and then evaluating each sports program by two criteria:

> 1. Whether the competitive schedules for men's and women's teams, on a program-wide basis, afford proportionately similar numbers of male and female athletes equivalently advanced competitive opportunities; or
>
> 2. Whether the institution can demonstrate a history and continuing practice of upgrading the competitive opportunities available to the historically disadvantaged sex as warranted by developing abilities among athletes of that sex.[21]

Brown failed the three-part test as well as his two new criteria, Pettine ruled. Using figures from a 1990–91 gender-equity report, Pettine declared that Brown's athletics department needed to have the same proportion of women as the student body as a whole, even though sports teams at that moment were 37 percent female and the student body stood at 52 percent.[22]

Pettine did not specifically describe the first test as a safe harbor, as the Colorado State judge had, but he did refer to the second and third tests as "escape routes" for Brown. At least since 1980, the male-female ratio of Brown athletes had hovered at 61-39, while the student body's was 51-49. And even though Brown had upgraded its facilities, coaching, and other benefits for female athletes over the course of the decade, the second test had to do primarily with the number of athletes and teams, Pettine ruled, and given Brown's plans to eliminate two women's teams, the university could not claim compliance with the second test.

Finally, "Brown is cutting off varsity opportunities where there is great interest and talent, and where Brown still has an imbalance between men and women varsity athletes in relation to their undergraduate enrollments. . . . Testimony at the hearing showed that these two teams were viable varsity squads when they were demoted in May 1991," he wrote. Thus, Brown could not look to the third test for an escape.

This situation had nothing to do with institutional autonomy, Pettine ruled. Brown was free to downgrade its sports program or abolish it altogether. However, if it wanted to maintain its present varsity scheme, it had to increase the number of female athletes.

Thus, he ordered the university to restore the gymnastics and volleyball teams. He also found evidence of significant disparities between male and female teams in other areas covered by Title IX and declared that those issues could be resolved at trial.

Brown officials resolved to fight. In a press release responding to Pettine's injunction decision, the university laid out its own definition of gender equity: "Brown believes that the ratio of its male to female intercollegiate athletes mirrors the interests and abilities of its students. Plaintiffs in this suit offered no evidence of the interests and abilities of students to perform at the intercollegiate level."[23]

Brown's case rested on a point that comes up time and time again in debates over Title IX: Not as many women are interested in playing sports as men. This is a widely held assumption, and many people, including Brown officials, have used it to justify offering fewer teams or participation opportunities for women. There is some evidence to justify it: Coaches report having a much harder time recruiting large squads of women if not all of them will get to play, while men gladly show up to join a team even if it means they will sit on the bench. In *Leveling the Playing Field: School, Sports, Sex, and Title IX*, Jessica Gavora argues that biological and psychological reasons for the disparity in interests exist.[24] Furthermore, Brown pointed out, Title IX specifically states that it mandates no quotas, and that compliance with the law shall not require that any individual be denied an educational opportunity.

What role this should play in determining whether schools and colleges are offering enough sports opportunities for women was precisely the issue before Pettine and the Brown litigants. The plaintiffs—and the Clinton administration, in an appellate brief—argued that the question of interests and abilities was covered under the third part of the three-part test. Brown obviously was not in compliance with that part because it had interested and talented women on campus who wanted to play volleyball and compete in gymnastics, according to the plaintiffs. The university argued that it was satisfying the interests and abilities of women more than adequately, regardless of the test.

The U.S. Court of Appeals agreed in December 1992 to grant a temporary stay of Pettine's order. A hearing on the case took place the following February, and three months later, a three-judge panel of the appeals court lifted the stay and agreed to enforce Pettine's order to reinstate the teams to varsity status and fund them accordingly.

"Brown earnestly professes that it has done no more than slash women's and men's athletes by approximately the same degree," wrote Judge Bruce M. Selya in a forty-one-page opinion that described this as a watershed case. "But, Brown's claim overlooks the shortcomings that plagued its program before it took blade in hand. . . . Even balanced use of the budget-paring knife runs afoul of Title IX where, as here, the fruits of a university's athletic program remain ill-distributed after the trimming takes places."[25]

In less botanical language: If a college has proportionately fewer women on sports teams than in the student body, it is on extremely perilous ground if it tries to cut women's teams.

Selya also said that "equal opportunity to participate lies at the core of Title IX's purpose." Even if a college is meeting the scholarship and accommodation requirements of the law, it is still in violation if it offers women a smaller number of athletic opportunities than the law requires. Furthermore, he said, "a university which does not wish to engage in extensive compliance analysis may stay on the sunny side of Title IX simply by maintaining gender parity between its student body and its athletic lineup."[26]

This put the imprimatur of a federal district court on the primacy of the first test, the numbers-based standard of compliance. Selya went one step further by making the second and third tests a little harder to meet. The second test, he said, would inevitably lead a school into compliance by means of the first or third test. And the third test, he said, required *fully* accommodating the interests and abilities of women—not just accommodating them to the same extent as male students. "If there is sufficient interest and ability among members of the statistically underrepresented gender, not slaked by existing programs, an institution necessarily fails this part of the test," he wrote.[27] This suggests that if a college is trying to comply with the third part of the test and had a single female athlete who had the ability and interest in competing in, say, fencing, it would be required to offer her a team on which to compete.

Bryant, the plaintiffs' lawyer, declared that the decision meant that Title IX required colleges to meet the first part of the three-part test. "The ruling makes clear what we have said all along—women must be given opportunities to participate in intercollegiate athletics proportionate to their undergraduate enrollment," he said in a written statement. "If they aren't interested or don't have the ability, that's fine. Otherwise, they have to be accommodated. If a school wants to eliminate teams before women have their fair share, they have to eliminate men's teams."[28]

Even at this early phase of the lawsuit, the decision to enforce the temporary injunction fundamentally changed the way universities interpreted the law and their responsibilities. It made the third test at least as hard to meet as the first. Nominally, the first test requires schools to have more female athletes than the third test does—presuming, of course, that the assumption is true and that women really are less interested in sports than men. However, if a college is required to accommodate fully the interests of women, even if it is failing to do so for men, then it may very well have to keep adding sports until it meets the proportionality goal of the first test.

At Brown, the university reversed course and made plans to finance the women's teams for the 1993–94 season. The university also admitted two gymnasts and a volleyball player it had previously rejected for the incoming class of 1993. One of the benefits taken away from the demoted teams was Brown's willingness to give athletes an advantage in the admissions process over other students, a common practice among Ivy League universities and other colleges that admit only a small fraction of their applicants.[29]

However, this was only the first phase of the case. Brown elected to try its chances in a full trial before Judge Pettine at the federal district court in Providence instead of appealing the temporary injunction to the Supreme Court. The university sent out a press release on the eve of the trial declaring that it was actually complying with all three parts of the test. It was meeting the "stated interests and abilities" of women, according to an analysis of questionnaires submitted by high school students applying to Brown, statistics garnered from surveys handed out with the SAT, and an analysis of sports participation at high schools that sent students to Brown.[30]

Brown was preparing to field eighteen varsity teams for women that year, double the national average for Division I institutions, counting fifteen "funded" varsity teams, two unfunded teams, and one unfunded coed team, officials boasted, showing a strong history of expanding sports for women, even though much of that history had taken place in the 1970s, through "years of severe financial difficulty." During the 1980s, the percentage of female athletes in the varsity program had risen from 34 to 45 percent, and thus the university was complying with the second test. Finally, Brown women played sports at a rate nearly triple the national average, so the college must have been in compliance with the third test.

And, almost parenthetically, 45 percent of Brown athletes were female. That was well in excess of the national average, but it was short of the undergraduate population at Brown, which was 51 percent female. The university did not say if this affected their compliance with the first part of the three-part test, but its lawyers argued separately that the test itself was an illegal quota and thus should be thrown out—an argument that would be used repeatedly by other critics of the law. The plaintiffs, they argued, were engaged "in an attempt to transform Title IX into an affirmative action statute."[31]

Before any of these arguments could be tested in court, Brown and the plaintiffs announced a settlement of all the other issues in the case. Bryant and Labinger had accused Brown of deficiencies in coaching salaries, recruiting budgets, overall expenses, and other benefits for female athletes, but in the settlement, reached three days into the trial, they acknowledged that the university had made great strides in those areas.

"This agreement will establish Brown as a model for gender equity in the treatment and support of athletes," Labinger said.[32] As part of the agreement, the university said that it would maintain volleyball as a varsity sport for at least the next five years, through 1999–2000.[33] Brown also agreed to renovate locker rooms for the rowing and ice hockey teams and to elevate women's skiing from club to varsity status.[34]

Three months later, as the trial drew to a close, Brown offered a few new arguments to its defense. Noting that Pettine had questioned a number of witnesses about whether women were demonstrably less interested in sports than men, as well as about what constituted a "participation opportunity" in athletics, Brown's top lawyer, Beverly E. Ledbetter, pointed out that "every relevant data source, whether inside or outside the University, clearly shows that men and women have different levels of interest in participating in varsity athletics."[35]

A national survey of high school students showed that while participation levels for girls shot up during the 1970s, they leveled off during the

1980s. In 1993–94, 2.1-million girls played high school sports, 37 percent of all athletes. Another study, conducted by the National Center for
Education Statistics, found that among college-bound high school students, consistently more boys than girls "say sports [are] important
among friends" and "play ball with friends at least once per week." A
College Board survey found that roughly half of the male students who
took the SAT and asked that their scores be sent to Brown were interested in participating in varsity sports in college, while only about
30 percent of the girls with an interest in Brown did.[36]

Behind the barrage of statistics lay two questions, one philosophical
and one tactical. First, can raw participation numbers be used as an accurate measure of interest and ability? Many people say yes, but advocates for women disagree sharply. Whenever new opportunities have
been opened up for girls and women, they have filled them. The dramatic increase in the number of female athletes during the 1970s demonstrated that. If you build a women's team, players will come. If women
are not demonstrating the same level of interest in sports as men, then
there must be some other cause. Girls may not have gotten the same level
of coaching or as much encouragement from their parents as their brothers during childhood, for example. Labinger and Bryant brought a pha-
lanx of expert witnesses to argue these points.

Second, would the courts allow Brown to present all of these data as a
way of complying with the 1975 regulations, which called for colleges
simply to offer a "selection of sports and levels of competition" that
would "effectively accommodate the interests and abilities of members
of both sexes," skirting the three-part test in the 1979 policy interpretation? As Brown's lawyers argued, the policy interpretation did not have
the same legal status as the 1975 regulations, so would the courts give it
the same "great deference" that they would give the regulations?

Pettine's answer to both questions was no.

Brown could not use surveys of current, future, or prospective students, or students nationally, to ascertain levels of interest in sports to
argue that it was satisfying the interests of its own female students, not
when interested and able female athletes were already on campus—not
just volleyball players and gymnasts but skiers and water polo players,
he ruled. If Brown wanted to comply with the third test, it needed to
abide by the First Circuit's definition of it.

In addition, the policy interpretation was entitled to full deference, as it
was "a guideline designed to interpret a rule, regulation, or order, namely,
Education Department's own regulations." Brown had argued that the
interpretation contravened the statute's ban on quotas and the Javits
amendment's requirement that Title IX's be "reasonable . . . considering

the nature of particular sports," but Pettine ruled the flexibility inherent in the test accomplished both goals.[37]

Brown officials took this to mean that Pettine believed sports programs should meet the proportionality standard above all else, and it threatened to eliminate men's teams if the judge ruled the university had to reinstate the women's programs.

"Brown University continues to believe that strict numerical proportionality—that is, a conformance of gender ratios between the athletic and general undergraduate student bodies—is neither fair to the student body nor required by Title IX," the university said in a written statement. "We believe that any fully compliant athletic program must accommodate their interests and abilities of *all* students, regardless of gender. Title IX was never intended to be a quota bill for athletes. Its intent was to eliminate discrimination in education. Proportionality is not and shot not be a fair measure of compliance."[38]

The plaintiffs, of course, were elated. The decision, they claimed, "should serve as a wake-up call to universities around the country that they better start complying with the law or face a court order to do so."[39]

Pettine ordered the university to submit within 120 days a plan for complying with the law.[40] Brown did so, with a certain lack of enthusiasm.

> The plan has one goal: to make the gender ratio among University-funded teams at Brown substantially proportionate to the gender ratio of the undergraduate student body. To do so, the University must disregard the expressed athletic interests of one gender while providing advantages for others. The plan focuses only on University-funded sports, ignoring the long history of donor-funded [i.e., club] student teams.
>
> . . . [The plan] is inconsistent with Brown's philosophy to the extent that it grants advantages and enforces disadvantages upon student athletes solely because of their gender and curbs the historic role of coaches in determining the number of athletes which can be provided an opportunity to participate. Nevertheless, the University wishes to act in good faith with the order of the Court, notwithstanding issues of fact and law which are currently in dispute.[41]

Brown said it preferred to maintain its program as it was at the time, with gymnastics and volleyball teams at "donor-funded" status. To comply with the court order, however, addressing the "issue of proportionality while minimizing additional undue stress on already strained physical and fiscal resources," the university proposed to cap the rosters of men's teams, enforcing minimum roster sizes for women's sports, and adding women's junior varsity teams in basketball, field hockey, lacrosse, soccer, and tennis, which would be funded by the university even though the athletics department would not receive a budget increase to accomplish any of these plans. If Pettine rejected this plan, Brown officials said, the next step would be to cut men's teams.

Pettine did reject the plan, but he refused to let Brown drop any men. His objections were that the proposal did not make a distinction between university-funded and donor-funded squads, even thought the judge had ruled that there were substantial differences in the way the two types of teams operated. Second, the junior-varsity squads did not make a difference in the numbers for the proportionality count, because only members of varsity teams were supposed to be counted.

Pettine also noted that "an institution does not provide equal opportunity if it caps its men's teams after they are well-stocked with high-caliber recruits while requiring women's teams to boost numbers by accepting walk-ons. A university does not treat its men's and women's teams equally if it allows the coaches of men's teams to set their own maximum-capacity limits but overrides the judgment of coaches of women's teams on the same matter."[42] He concluded that "Brown's stated objectives will be best served if I design a remedy to meet the requirements of prong three rather than prong one."[43] Noting that Brown would have to cut 213 men to comply with the proportionality test, he ruled that the university could comply with the interests-and-abilities test by upgrading women's gymnastics, fencing, skiing, and water polo to university-funded varsity status. Surely Brown could find a way to do that without slashing a huge number of male athletes.

His order was stayed pending Brown's appeal to the First Circuit. In it, university lawyers brought out virtually every argument ever presented to critique the 1979 policy interpretation and applied it to Pettine's ruling:

OCR's three-prong standard, as applied by Pettine, violated Title IX's prohibition on preferential treatment and quotas.

Pettine equated "participation opportunities" with the actual number of athletes on varsity teams. Other athletes had the "opportunity" to participate, but did not choose to do so.

Pettine erred by using actual participation rates based on the previous year's initial squad lists, rather than using coaches' accounts of the actual number of players on teams throughout the year.

Assessing participation and enrollments rates should be done by using several years' worth of data, rather than just the previous year, as Pettine had.

Pettine failed to take into account Brown's rapid expansion of women's sports in the 1970s and 1980s, especially given that other universities waited until the 1990s to begin catching up.

Brown had a 25 percent increase in the representation of women in its
athletics program in the late 1980s, which Pettine failed to note.

Pettine erred by ruling that that the unmet interest of female athletes constituted intentional discrimination, even though there was even more
unmet interest among male athletes.

Pettine ignored findings of substantial difference in levels of interest in
athletics between male and female students.

Pettine argued that donor-funded teams were not as viable as university-
funded teams, but they should have been equated.

Pettine gave too much weight to the 1979 policy interpretation.[44]

Pettine had "palpably defied" Title IX by ordering the university "to
institute a gender-based quota system in its intercollegiate athletics
program contrary to the proven relative interests of its male and female
students," Brown officials argued, resulting in "extremely poor public
policy which violates the spirit and intent of Title IX."[45]

Brown's lawyers changed their definitions slightly in their appeals
brief. The university, they said, now had twenty-one intercollegiate teams
for women, including fifteen varsity teams, three "varsity teams entirely
donor-funded," and three "club teams that participate in intercollegiate
competition," rather than eighteen teams that were either university
funded or donor funded, as they had claimed previously. Pettine had
ruled that the complexity of these tiers did not help the university, particularly because more women's teams were donor funded than men's
teams.

Virtually every college and university in the country, as well as sports
organizations and higher-education associations, filed briefs supporting
Brown's position. All of them had woken up to the fact that the decision
could mean drastic inroads by the courts on the autonomy of academic
institutions and their athletic programs.

None of their arguments were persuasive to a new three-judge panel
of the First Circuit, which ruled two to one in April 1996 in favor of the
plaintiffs. The interpretation of Title IX in the previous appeals court
decision was the official law for the circuit, Judge Hugh Bownes wrote,
despite a suggestion from Brown that this panel could set aside the earlier panel's interpretation. Thus, Brown's array of challenges to the
court's analysis of the 1979 policy interpretation was moot.

The judges also rejected Brown's argument that the case was about affirmative action and quotas. Colleges did not have to adhere to the first
test, but nothing in the law banned the Education Department from offering it as an option, and a relatively simple option at that, Bownes
wrote. The flexibility of the three-part test meant that it could not be
construed as a quota system. "Brown's interpretation conflates prong

one and three and distorts the three-part test by reducing it to an abstract, mechanical determination of strict numerical proportionality," he wrote. "In short, Brown treats the three-part test for compliance as a one-part test for strict liability."[46]

The judges also overwhelmingly rejected Brown's argument that women are generally less interested in sports than men, both as an "untrustworthy avenue of reason" and irrelevant to the case:

> We view Brown's argument that women are less interested than men in participating in intercollegiate athletics, as well as its conclusion that institutions should be required to accommodate the interests and abilities of its female students only to the extent that it accommodates the interests and abilities of its male students, with great suspicion. To assert that Title IX permits institutions to provide fewer athletics participation opportunities for women than for men, based upon the premise that women are less interested in sports than men, is (among other things) to ignore the fact that Title IX was enacted in order to remedy discrimination that results from stereotyped notions of women's interests and abilities.
>
> Interest and ability rarely develop in a vacuum; they evolve as a function of opportunity and experience. The Policy Interpretation recognizes that women's lower rate of participation in athletics reflects women's historical lack of opportunities to participate in sports.
>
> . . . Moreover, the Supreme Court has repeatedly condemned gender-based discrimination based upon "archaic and overbroad generalizations" about women. The Court has been especially critical of the use of statistical evidence offered to prove generalized, stereotypical notions about men and women.
>
> . . . Thus, there exists the danger that, rather than providing a true measure of women's interest in sports, statistical evidence purporting to reflect women's interest instead provides only a measure of the very discrimination that is and has been the basis for women's lack of opportunity to participate in sports. . . . To use a numbers-based lack-of-interest defense to become the instrument of further discrimination against the underrepresented gender would pervert the remedial purpose of Title IX. We conclude that, even if it can be empirically demonstrated that, at a particular time, women have less interest in sports than do men, such evidence, standing alone, cannot justify providing fewer athletics opportunities for women than for men. Furthermore, such evidence is completely irrelevant where, as here, viable and successful women's varsity teams have been demoted or eliminated.[47]

The court did, however, nullify Pettine's specific order for Brown to upgrade the women's teams to university-funded varsity status. The university had the right to comply with the statute as it saw fit, and even though the judge's plan was an acceptable way of complying with the law, Brown was within its rights to chop its men's squads, Bownes wrote.

The decision was not unanimous, and the circuit's chief judge, Juan R. Torruella, dissented from Bownes and Judge Norman H. Stahl. According to Torruella, who is noted for his conservative interpretations, two Supreme Court cases, including one in 1996 in which the U.S. Supreme Court ruled that the Virginia Military Institute could no longer remain an all-male institution, offered precedents to indicate that the three-part test might violate the equal-protection provisions of the Fourteenth Amendment to the U.S. Constitution.

Torruella also thought that both Pettine and his colleagues had misread the three-part test. First, he argued, given that colleges were not required to provide contact sports for women, rosters of such teams should be excluded from the count of participants used to comply with the first part of the test. Next, cutting men's participants or teams as a means of complying with the first test ought to be considered relevant to the history of program expansion necessary for compliance with the second test. Finally, in addition to being impossible to meet, the majority's understanding of the third test necessarily caused a school to discriminate against male students because it required the school to meet women's interests to a higher degree than it did men simply because the women were women.

"Even a single person with a reasonable unmet interest defeats compliance," Torruella wrote in his dissent. "This standard, in fact, goes farther than the straightforward quota test of prong one. According to the district court, the unmet interests of the underrepresented sex must be completely accommodated before any of the interests of the overrepresented gender can be accommodated."

Torruella argued that all three tests required illegal quotas. The first test was, on its face, a quota; the second test required colleges to be moving in the direction of complying with the first test, necessitating a quota; as for the third test, "a quota with an exception for situation in which there are insufficient interested students to allow the school to meet it remains a quota."[48]

Even though three other appellate courts had imposed similar rulings, Brown decided to take its case to the Supreme Court. In its brief, the university argued the First Circuit had violated Supreme Court precedent in employment law cases by looking at the university's entire student body rather than at the pool of interest and capable potential athletes. This was an important case for the court to hear, Brown's lawyers wrote, because the First Circuit decision had ramifications for every college in the country with a sports program.[49]

Brown did not go alone. Lawyers filed nine friend-of-the-court briefs supporting the Brown side and representing sixty colleges and universities; eight collegiate coaching and athletic organizations; Caspar Weinberger; four higher-education associations; the State of Colorado; forty-eight representatives and one senator; USA Wrestling, USA Swimming, and United States Water Polo; and four conservative groups. All asked the Supreme Court to reverse the First Circuit's ruling.[50]

This grouping represented a new nexus forming to contest the law. The College Football Association was a professional group representing coaches and athletics officials, although it was less than a year away from dissolving. It urged the court to set aside the three-part test and exempt football from the Title IX equation because the 1975 regulations allowed universities to offer contact sports for men only, much as Torruella had suggested. The other sport associations represented men's teams being cut by colleges to reduce their numbers of male athletes, and they argued that these cuts harmed the country's ability to produce Olympic-caliber athletes. The four conservative groups opposed Title IX as an illegitimate government intervention. They had the backing of Republicans like R. Dennis Hastert, the future Speaker of the House, and Sen. Phil Gramm of Texas, as well as Weinberger, who argued that both the First Circuit's reading of the 1979 policy interpretation and the interpretation itself contravened the 1975 regulations he authorized.

The universities said that the First Circuit ruling had transformed Title IX "from a statute of equal opportunity into a statute of equal result," and the education association's argued that the ruling had given schools an "insurmountable burden." Colorado, whose conservative attorney general (and future secretary of the interior under George W. Bush) Gale A. Norton authored the brief, argued that the decision mandated the preferential treatment of women in violation of the Fourteenth Amendment.

Aside from arguing that Brown's appeal was flawed, Cohen's lawyers, Bryant and Labinger, pointed out in their response that during the long course of the lawsuit, the Third, Sixth, Seventh, and Tenth Circuit had all handed down rulings substantially the same as the First Circuit's.

Ultimately, the Court decided it did not need to hear any of these arguments firsthand. In March 1997, without comment, it declined to take the case, sending Brown all the way back down the judicial ladder to the federal district court in Rhode Island to resume arguing over a plan to comply with Title IX. Judge Ernesto Torres approved a new plan in 1998 for Brown to upgrade its women's water polo team to funded varsity status and guarantee money to the fencing, gymnastics, and skiing teams. Brown was required to maintain the proportion of female athletes

within 3.5 percentage points of the proportion of female undergraduates. It is hard to tell whether the university is actually complying with
this provision: According to filings with the Department of Education,
women were 53 percent of Brown students and 48 percent of Brown
athletes in 2002–3.

It is hard to overstate the impact of the Brown case. A cause for joy
among female athletes, coaches, and activists, it outraged many athletic
directors, who were convinced that they were already doing more than
enough for female athletes. Regardless, it propelled them into dramatically expanding their offerings for women. By one count, NCAA colleges added 1,162 new varsity teams for women between the time of the
lawsuit's filing and the Supreme Court's decision not to take the case.[51]

The decision also fueled a growing fire among Republican leaders and
libertarian activists, who were already outraged at the Clinton administration's efforts to enforce the law. Their crusade to revise Title IX made
headlines and generated debates consistently from 1998 to 2004.

Brown officials are still bitter over the court battle, which cost them
over $1 million in lawyers' fees awarded to the plaintiffs, not to mention
their own expenses. Testifying before a federal commission reviewing the
law in 2002, Brown's general counsel, Beverly Ledbetter, continued to
argue that the government ought to revise the 1979 policy interpretation
to focus on student interests and to preserve institutional autonomy.

"Of course colleges and universities can and should do better," she
told members of the commission. "They must adopt standards for setting
their priorities, and they must make those standards known. Whatever is
decided, neither colleges and universities nor their student athletes nor
their student bodies should be subject to the whims of shifting regulatory
schemes. The umbrella is large enough and should always be large
enough to allow threatened men's teams, including wrestling and swimming, emerging women's teams, and yes, even football, to coexist within
an athletic environment that is ethical, reasonable, rational, and flexible
and yet embraces institutional autonomy."[52]

Brown's lengthy court battle over Title IX and its application to athletics complicated more than it resolved, according to many of the groups
filing briefs in the case. If anything, the debate illustrated the formidable
differences in common understandings of the role and status of scholastic sports.

The regulation and the policy interpretation take no account of the
long history of men's sports, or of the fact that Brown and many of its
peers had decided long before Title IX was passed that their institutional
mission was best served by a broad and comprehensive sports program.
Instead, the rules and regulations offer a legal framework to equalize

men's and much-younger women's sports programs. If colleges want to have massive sports programs for men, then they must accommodate women on the same level. The First Circuit looked at Brown, which everyone agreed had an exemplary women's program, and found that in meaningful and measurable ways it did not measure up to an even more exemplary men's program.

Colleges' efforts at gender equity should not be judged in comparison to their peers, the First Circuit ruled. Instead, they should be compared to a college's men's program. Most men's programs are, by historical accident, much better developed than women's programs. Equalizing the two is going to be tough.

The ruling made participation numbers, rather than treatment of female athletes or the provision of athletic scholarships, the focal point of the debate over Title IX. It also consecrated the policy interpretation as the standard for compliance over howls of dismay from men's coaches, who had athletes lining up to play for them.

Does the policy interpretation and the First Circuit's understanding of it mandate quotas? By any measure it gives colleges powerful incentives to structure their athletes programs so that women get a high percentage of slots on varsity teams.

But if Brown officials were correct, and women truly are less interested in sports than men, then any college in the country ought to be able to accommodate the interests of female students by adding roster spots. And they should be able to stop long before they reach the proportionality standard.

If they cannot, that would prove Brown wrong at the outset, because it would demonstrate that women *are* as interested in sports as men.

8
CHAPTER
•

Clarifications amid Controversy

The Brown case was a wake-up call, and it came at precisely the right moment. More and more girls were getting interested in sports, especially after seeing the success and celebration of female athletes at the 1992 and 1996 Olympics. Professional sports leagues for women proliferated, giving girls even more heroes. The NCAA announced its policy would be to support expanding opportunities for women until all colleges were in compliance. The rich and powerful Southeastern Conference set its own rule requiring each of its twelve members to have two more sports for women than for men, to help colleges offset the one hundred–plus men each had on its football roster.

Of course, the SEC could afford to make such a move. In the middle 1990s, the money was especially good in college sports. The NCAA had signed its first billion-dollar contract to broadcast the men's "March Madness" basketball tournament with CBS in 1990, distributing most of the largess to its members.[1] In 1994, the SEC signed its own $100 million deal with CBS to broadcast football games.[2]

But that was not true for all of college sports. Colleges trying to compete with the SEC's members and other rich institutions found themselves struggling to find enough money to support coaches' salaries, facility improvements, and the rising tuition costs they had to pay through player scholarships. In 1992, the NCAA announced a series of cost reductions, including a measure to slash scholarship limits for Division I men's sports. Colleges were told they could award only eighty-five football grants, down from ninety-five, and scholarships for all other teams were cut by 10 percent.

Many athletics directors, faced with competing financial pressures, decided to limit men's roster spots and even to drop entire men's teams to avoid Title IX lawsuits—cutting men to comply with the first part of the test was a perfectly legal means of complying with the law. It was also odious, and not just to male athletes. The briefs submitted in the Brown case show that a coalition of the angry was forming. Coaches, athletes, and a variety of new players were enraged by what they saw as a law penalizing individual men as a means of appeasing a group of women.

Football coaches held to the Javits amendment, arguing that its statement that reasonable provisions must be made for different sports had been undermined by the three-part test. Louder were wrestling and swimming coaches, who saw colleges cutting their teams almost every month. They decried the three-part test as a quota system, particularly given the language in the Brown case describing the first test as a "safe harbor" on "the sunny side of Title IX." In addition, the inscrutability of Title IX compliance was becoming a frequent topic of complaint for university administrators, especially with the Education Department refusing to give a numerical value to define compliance with the first test, saying that measuring compliance with the law could be done only on a case-by-case basis.[3]

After the University of Illinois cut its men's swimming and fencing teams in 1992, male athletes struck back. A group of swimmers sued the university, trying to use the same arguments as the Brown and Indiana athletes but claiming reverse discrimination. The university had eliminated their team because it consisted of men, they said, thus discriminating against the male athletes on the basis of their sex—violating Title IX's express provision forbidding differences in the treatments of the sexes.

Their argument carried little weight with Joe B. McCade, a federal district judge:

> Men's interests and abilities are presumptively met when substantial proportionality [i.e., meeting the first test] exists, and this did not change following the cut.
>
> . . . Under the regulations and the case law, members of the men's swimming team have not been discriminated against, even though their program was eliminated, they have been excluded from varsity participation as individuals, and their individual interests will not be "fully and effectively accommodated," because the percentage of men participating in the varsity program is "substantially proportionate to the percentage of men represented by the undergraduate population."[4]

In other words, as long as men were equivalently represented in the classroom and in the locker room—or, as was more likely the case, overrepresented—individual men could not claim discrimination, even if their teams had been cut. That smacked of a quota, and that attracted the attention of conservative groups who previously had had nothing to do with sports.

One of them was the Independent Women's Forum, formed by Lynne V. Cheney and others in 1992 to argue against traditional feminist positions on affirmative action, the Equal Rights Amendment, and other social issues. Kimberly Schuld, director of the forum's Play Fair project on Title IX and sports before joining the U.S. Commission on Civil Rights in the second Bush administration, put the issue this way in 1999:

> Being a male in today's feminized society is something akin to being (in the words of one Southern gentleman) the bastard child at the family reunion. You can't help what you are, yet you are eyed with suspicion, treated as a second-class citizen and blamed for the sins of generations past. Women have achieved majority status in many facets of society, yet feminists still argue that women remain oppressed by the male "patriarchy."
>
> . . . Nowhere in schools is discrimination against males more predominant and accepted than in varsity athletics. Men's teams are being cut and capped at an alarming rate in an effort to show the federal government that women are not being shortchanged. In the meantime, new athletic opportunities for women are not developing, primarily due to lack of interest.
>
> . . . The original language of the law itself has never been changed. It simply guarantees equal opportunity in educational programs. However, federal bureaucrats and their feminist allies have created an environment of preferential treatment for women and girls at the expense of men and boys.
>
> The statute also clearly states that Title IX is not intended as a quota bill, and further, that it cannot be used to punish the over-represented sex (males) for past discrimination against the under-represented sex (females). Both of these tenets are being violated in current practice.[5]

Fanning the flames for conservatives, as on so many other issues, was Bill Clinton. Clinton had named Norma V. Cantù, a lawyer with the Mexican American Legal Defense and Educational Fund, as assistant secretary of education for civil rights in 1993. She came to Washington without much interest in athletics, intending instead to focus on expanding opportunities for females in science and mathematics. The proliferations of compliances and investigations of athletics programs in the early 1990s forced Cantù and the Education Department's Office for Civil Rights to make sports a priority. In 1994 she appointed Mary Frances O'Shea, an investigator in OCR's field office in Chicago, to be the national coordinator for Title IX policy, even though each region was still allowed to investigate institutions independently and offer advice without consulting with O'Shea or OCR headquarters in Washington.

Before Cantù's arrival, the civil rights office had been extraordinarily passive on Title IX issues in athletics, even after the passage of the Civil Rights Restoration Act, according to a scathing report published in 1993 by the Lyndon B. Johnson School of Public Affairs at the University of Texas at Austin. (The primary author of the report, Kenneth R. Tolo, was subsequently hired by the Education Department and worked with Cantù and her boss, Secretary of Education Richard B. Riley.) Researchers reviewed twenty "letters of finding" issued by OCR in Title IX cases in athletics, finding that investigations routinely lasted between seven and twenty-six months, despite the office's requirement that complaints be settled within 180 days.[6]

The report also condemned the office for contradictory and dilatory responses to Title IX complaints:

> OCR's underlying lack of commitment to ensuring civil rights and to making gender equity a reality is clearly evident in the area of intercollegiate athletics. For example, OCR performance standards do not direct or encourage its investigators to achieve fully the objectives of Title IX. OCR clearly appears to place too much emphasis on process and not enough on results. The agency seems more committed to processing complaints and meeting deadlines than to conducting rigorous investigations aimed at achieving gender equity in intercollegiate athletic programs. Furthermore, when violations are found, OCR does not have a strong record on monitoring institutions to ensure that infractions are corrected. Rather, the agency routinely finds universities in compliance based on the existence of a corrective action plan, without incorporating follow-up reviews.[7]

In particular, the report blamed OCR investigators for rarely checking to see if colleges had procedures for students or employees to follow in making complaints about gender equity, as the law requires. It also indicated that Terrel Bell's plan of proclaiming institutions in compliance with the law even if obvious violations existed, as long as they had a plan to address gender equity, had become routine.

For example, at Mercer University in Macon, Georgia, an investigation found that nearly 70 percent of the budget for coaches' salaries went to the coaches of men's teams. The civil rights office found the university in compliance after it promised to make the women's volleyball coach a full-time employee and pay her as such—even though doing so was only a tiny step toward addressing the salary inequities.[8]

In addition to blaming the office for its lax enforcement policy, the Texas report pointed out that OCR was understaffed and underfunded.

Michael Williams, assistant secretary for civil rights during the first Bush administration, had published a plan to beef up the enforcement staff in 1990 but had not followed through.[9]

Some of that changed after Clinton and Cantù took office. Between 1992 and 1996, the Education Department settled eighty complaints of sex discrimination in college sports, according to a 1996 report by the General Accounting Office. All of these involved participation claims, and of them, sixteen colleges either demonstrated compliance with, or agreed to take steps to comply with, the first test; four did so with the second test; and forty-two did with the third test. The department also hosted focus groups in 1994 and 1996 with college athletics officials and others, the results of which prompted the department to issue a clarification of the three-part test and the rest of the 1979 policy interpretation.[10]

A subsequent GAO study found that although Title IX complaints about athletics made up a tiny minority of all gender-equity complaints (136 of 1,455 received from 1994 to 1998), they were a large majority of the "compliance reviews" initiated by OCR staff—thirty out of forty-one.[11]

The wrestlers and their political allies found a friend in J. Dennis Hastert, a Republican congressman from Illinois. A former wrestler and coach who had led Yorkville High School to a state title, Hastert called hearings on Title IX in the spring of 1995 primarily for the purpose of lecturing Cantù. Title IX "is the only civil-rights law I know of where innocent bystanders are punished," he said. "The elimination of opportunities was never the intent of Title IX."[12]

During the hearing, Eastern Illinois University's president complained that OCR had insisted that his institution add four women's sports, including gymnastics and field hockey, which were not popular sports in the state or in the university's conference. Instead, he opted for dropping men's swimming and wrestling.[13]

Hastert asked Cantù to clarify the law, and in September she circulated a draft "letter of clarification" that adopted the safe-harbor language of the First Circuit to describe the first test, and detailed ways colleges could meet the other two tests. She received more than two hundred comments about it, many of which included calls for the department to abandon the three-part test altogether. "Your clarification falls short of reaching the goal I understood you to support," Hastert wrote to Cantù, who went on to argue that the 1979 interpretation and the draft clarification ran counter to both the original language of Title IX and the 1980 investigators' manual (which had been replaced by a new manual in 1990). "OCR must use the original intent of Congress as its guiding principle—to prohibit discrimination based on gender," Hastert added.[14]

Greg Waggoner, athletics director at Western State University of Colorado, said that the clarification "simply makes explicit what was implicit before. Prong one is the one prong that really counts, proportionality . . . there is no flexibility in complying when you get down to it. Because of this, there is no way to truly accommodate for all the mitigating circumstances."[15]

Coaches, students, and administrators also wrote to Cantù, most of them expressing similar sentiments. As they saw it, the first test was the *only* test, and the other two only waypoints on the path to proportionality. For many colleges, proportionality could be reached only by cutting men's sports. "The idea of destroying opportunities for the purpose of expanding female opportunities drives a stake in the heart of gender relations," wrote a high school teacher from Peoria, Illinois.[16]

Not all women and women's activists were happy with the clarification, either. Margaret J. Bradley-Doppes, then a senior associate athletics director at the University of Michigan, was among many who wrote to Cantù to say that OCR needed to enforce its current guidelines, not issue new ones. "It has been twenty-three years, and the loss has been almost six generations of [college] women that have been denied participation slots and athletic scholarships."[17]

Cantù stuck to her guns. In January 1996, she released the final letter of clarification (appendix H), which was substantially the same as the draft. In it, the assistant secretary accepted one proposed revision, made by the National Women's Law Center, which stated that a violation of the participation rules set down in the three-part test would be considered a violation of Title IX by itself, regardless of an athletics department's compliance with other sections of the law. An "institution's failure to provide nondiscriminatory participation opportunities usually amounts to a denial of equal athletic opportunity because these opportunities provide access to all other athletic benefits, treatment, and services."[18]

The clarification offers a sort of commentary on each part of the test. It specifies that, for the purposes of counting exactly how many athletes are on a team, colleges must include athletes who practice and compete regularly, those listed on rosters, and those who have been injured but continue to receive scholarship funds.

As for how close the percentage of female athletes has to be to the percentage of female students, the crucial question on everyone's minds, the clarification is agnostic. "OCR makes this determination on a case-by-case basis, rather than through use of a statistical test." A college would definitely be in compliance if the percentages matched, according to the document, but given that enrollments and squad lists fluctuate, colleges are given an unspecified amount of wiggle room. "It would be unreasonable to expect the institution to fine tune its program in response to this change in enrollment."

As for the second test, the clarification reminds colleges wanting to comply with it that they must be able not only to demonstrate a history of adding programs that have satisfied women's developing interests, but also to show that they have a plan for program expansion in response to the continued evolution of those interests. In addition, dropping men's teams is not enough to prove a history of expanding sports offerings for women.

To demonstrate compliance with the third test, the department pointed out, as the First Circuit did in the Brown case, that it required both full and effective accommodation of women's interests. If colleges could show that among female students there was no "a. unmet interest in a particular sport; b. sufficient ability to sustain a team in that sport; and c. a reasonable expectation of competition for that team," then they would be deemed in compliance. If colleges had recently eliminated viable teams for women, as Brown had done, "OCR will find that there is sufficient interest, ability, and available competition to sustain an intercollegiate team." In addition, if high schools and amateur sports leagues in areas from which institutions draw their students sponsor a given sport for women and the college does not, "OCR will ask the institution to provide a basis for any assertion that its students and admitted students are not interested in playing that sport."

In a letter to educators accompanying the clarification, Cantù adopted the First Circuit's language.

> The first part of the test—substantial proportionality—focuses on the participation rates of men and women at an institution and affords an institution a "safe harbor" for establishing that it provides nondiscriminatory participation opportunities. An institution that does not provide substantially proportional participation opportunities for men and women may comply with Title IX by satisfying either part two or part three of the test. The second part—history and continuing practice—is an examination of an institution's good faith expansion of athletic opportunities through its response to developing interests of the underrepresented sex at that institution. The third part—fully and effectively accommodating interests and abilities of the underrepresented sex—centers on the inquiry of whether there are concrete and viable interests among the underrepresented sex that should be accommodated by an institution.
>
> In addition, the Clarification does not provide strict numerical formulas or "cookie cutter" answers to the issues that are inherently case- and fact-specific. Such an effort not only would belie the meaning of Title IX, but would at the same time deprive institutions of the flexibility to which they are entitled when deciding how best to comply with the law.[19]

Like the 1979 policy interpretation, the clarification does not have the force of law. Also like the interpretation, however, courts have used it to make judgments in Title IX cases. In their filings with the First Circuit, Brown's lawyers accused Cantù of changing the department's rules for enforcing the law midstream, but she insisted that the clarification was a logical and uncontroversial reading of the statute. The judges agreed, commenting that the clarification "does not change the existing standards for compliance, but . . . does provide further information and guidelines for assessing compliance under the three-part test."[20]

With blood boiling among men's sports groups and others over the clarification and the Supreme Court's decision not to hear the Brown case, women celebrated the twenty-fifth anniversary of the law's passage in 1997. To mark the occasion, the National Women's Law Center triumphantly fired off complaints to twenty-five colleges, accusing them of violating Title IX's regulations on scholarships for female athletes.

"Given that the vast majority of our nation's colleges and universities continue to severely limit athletic opportunities for female students, it is not asking for much to expect schools to be fair to the young women who do get a chance to play," said Marcia Greenberger, the center's director, at a press conference.[21]

The twenty-five colleges that received the complaints were not the worst offenders. Instead, they represented a cross-section of Division I institutions. The center had chosen them using data obtained by the *Chronicle of Higher Education* under the Equity in Athletics Disclosure Act of 1994. The act, sponsored by Illinois Democratic congresswoman Cardiss Collins, required colleges to publish information on roster sizes for men's and women's teams, as well as budgets for recruiting, scholarships, coaches' salaries, and other expenses, annually.

The law had gone into effect for the 1995–96 academic year, and the NCAA created a standardized form for its members to use. The *Chronicle of Higher Education, USA Today*, the *Kansas City Star*, and a few other newspapers gathered the reports and published portions of them verbatim, finding that scholarship budgets lagged behind participation rates at many institutions.

The National Women's Law Center chose as its exemplars Bethune-Cookman, Boston, Coppin State, and Wofford Colleges; Boston, Bowling Green State, Brigham Young, Colorado State, Duke, Hampton, Liberty, Northeastern, South Carolina State, Utah State, Vanderbilt, and Wake Forest Universities; the College of William and Mary; and the Universities of Colorado at Boulder, Maine at Orono, New Hampshire, North Texas, Oregon, Texas at El Paso, and Tulsa.

The letters caused a stir, partly because the data they used were flawed. The NCAA forms and the National Women's Law Center had established the representation of female athletes on varsity teams by taking the roster count for each sport and adding them up, then dividing the total of female athletes by the total of all athletes. But those roster counts included athletes who participated in more than one sport, such as runners who compete in cross-country, indoor track, and outdoor track. At the time, female athletes were somewhat more likely to participate in multiple sports than male athletes, so counts were thrown off in a way that exaggerated the disparities between the percentage of women on varsity teams and the percentage of scholarship budgets allocated to female athletes.

The civil rights office investigated all twenty-five complaints, and during the course of its investigations, Cantù sent a letter to Bowling Green State's general counsel, Nancy S. Footer, providing what some people saw as a radical reinterpretation of what the law required. "If any unexplained disparity in the scholarship budget for athletes of either gender is 1% or less for the entire budget for athletic scholarships, there will be a strong presumption that such a disparity is reasonable and based on legitimate and nondiscriminatory factors. Conversely, there will be a strong presumption that an unexplained disparity of more than 1% is in violation of the 'substantially proportionate' requirements."[22]

Previous OCR documents, including the 1980 and 1990 investigators' manuals, had spelled out a more complicated process in which investigators would plug scholarship and participation rates into a formula to determine compliance. This was a much stricter standard, according to athletics officials, but Cantù said it was only a straightforward reading of the law and the regulations.

"We were measured, in participation versus scholarships, by a stick no one knew about," said Peter A. Liske, athletics director at the University of Toledo. "And the hardest part is that things change—[athletes] leave midyear or transfer or flunk out," making it difficult for a university to stay within the stricter boundaries of the 1 percent rule.

"It will be really interesting to see who litigates that point," Footer said. "It's clear than the agency's opinion about what 'substantial proportionality' means contradicts earlier issuances, and there's a very live and viable question about whether it could be made enforceable." Bowling Green, however, never tried to litigate the point.[23]

One example of the inaccuracies found was when the civil rights office investigated Texas–El Paso, or UTEP. According to the National Women's Law Center's complaint, 37 percent of the university's athletes during the 1995–96 academic year were women, but the university awarded just 31 percent of its scholarship budget to female athletes.

The Office for Civil Rights came up with a different count. It found that only 30.3 percent of UTEP athletes in 1995–96 were female on a head-count basis. Confirming that they received 31 percent of scholarship funds, OCR cleared the university of wrongdoing. "There is a strong presumption that a dollar disparity of 1 percent or less of the entire budgets for athletic scholarships is reasonable and nondiscriminatory, and OCR did not find any evidence contrary to this assumption," wrote Taylor D. August, director of the Dallas field office for OCR.[24]

Within a year and a half, the civil rights office quietly cleared eight of the institutions of wrongdoing: Bethune-Cookman, Brigham Young, Coppin State, Hampton, North Texas, UTEP, Vanderbilt, and Wofford. The office approved compliance agreements with the other seventeen, requiring them to increase funds for women's scholarships.[25]

In two of the resolved cases, college administrators said they had given OCR legitimate, nondiscriminatory reasons for their disparities. For example, Oregon had added a women's soccer team, but did not immediately award all twelve scholarships, preferring instead to parcel out grants over a four-year period so the team could continue to recruit new players every year.

Whether Cantù's letter to Footer added up to a shift in policy or not, it fueled suspicions about OCR among athletics officials and Republicans. Another point that infuriated both was a ruling by the Equal Employment Opportunity Commission, which employed Ellen Vargyas, formerly of the National Women's Law Center. In 1997, EEOC, published a guidance on the compensation of coaches, noting that coaches of men's teams had always been paid more than their counterparts for women's teams. That was permissible, the commission said, if the jobs were substantially different:

> At a large university, a man is head coach of football and a woman is head coach of women's volleyball. Both teams compete at the most competitive level and there are substantial pressures on both coaches to produce winning teams. The football coach has nine assistants and the team has a roster of 120 athletes. The volleyball head coach has a part time assistant and coaches 20 athletes. Sixty thousand spectators attend each football game, while 200 attend each volleyball game. The football games, but not the volleyball games, are televised. In comparing the man and woman, the man supervises a much larger staff and a much larger team. In addition, the football team's far greater spectator attendance and media demands create greater responsibility for the man. The football coach has more responsibility than the volleyball coach, and, as a result, the jobs are not substantially equal under the [Equal Pay Act].[26]

If the jobs were largely the same, such as a women's field hockey coach and men's lacrosse coach with similar numbers of athletes, assistants, and marketing responsibilities, then EEOC would look closely to ascertain whether differences in salary between men's and women's coaches were indeed justified. Revenue sports were not exempted: In one example, the commission said that a salary disparity between men's and women's basketball coaches was impermissible if justified simply on the grounds that the men's team brought in more money, particularly if the men's coach had the services of marketing staff, public-relations representatives, and an advertising budget. "Revenue is not a 'factor other than sex' that would justify the wage disparity since the woman is not given the equivalent support to enable her to raise revenue," the commission declared.[27]

As much fear and loathing as government regulation inspired among athletics administrators, it undoubtedly contributed to dramatic increases in women's sports and budgets during the 1990s. According to a General Accounting Office report in 2000, from 1989–90 to 1998–99, the number of women participating in college sports rose from about 122,000 to about 167,000.[28]

At the same time, despite negative headlines and the ire of male athletes and coaches across the country, some institutions continued to drop men's teams, often citing Title IX as a primary culprit. Athletes on those teams tried to take their fights to the courts; in addition to the Kelley plaintiffs from the University of Illinois, male athletes from Illinois State and Miami University in Ohio sued their institutions in the mid-1990s. However, district and appellate courts sided with the universities, and the Supreme Court declined to hear any of their cases. In the Illinois lawsuit, judges from the Seventh Circuit wrote, "Allowing a school to consider gender when determining which athletic programs to terminate ensures that in instances where the overall athletic opportunities decrease, the actual opportunities available to the underrepresented gender do not." Thus, they said, Title IX regulations do not violate the equal-protection provisions of the Fourteenth Amendment.[29]

Athletics directors found themselves stuck. At Miami, which had a broad-based program for both men and women that even included a "precision skating" team for the latter, a good number of women in the student body wanted to play varsity rugby and other sports. Miami competed (and continues to compete) in the Mid-American Conference, which offers very strong football programs but relatively little money from television contracts and bowl-game appearances, and could not afford to add any more women's teams, according to James C. Garland, the university's president. So in 1999, in an attempt to meet the first part of the test, Miami decided to drop men's soccer, tennis, and wrestling.

"We had overextended ourselves in recent years to meet gender-equity requirements, and we found we could not keep doing that," Garland said in a 1999 interview.[30] Even though the university had dramatically expanded its number of female athletes, in 1998 women were still only 44 percent of all athletes in 1998, compared with 55 percent of the undergraduate population. Without the wrestling, tennis, and soccer teams, Miami athletes would have been fifty-fifty male-female.

In February 1999, the board gave the four teams sixty days to raise money for a permanent endowment to support their sports. The golf team, which also had been facing elimination, came up with about $725,000, but the overall fund-raising effort raised only about $3.4 million out of a needed $13 million. The teams were dropped, athletes were given the option of transferring or retaining their scholarships for the remainder of their time in college, and the lawsuit was dismissed.

Wrestlers were by far the most outspoken and best organized of the athletes facing cuts in their sports. With coaches like Leo Kocher of the University of Chicago and J Robinson of the University of Minnesota eager to speak out, and legions of young men and their parents writing letters and making public appearances, the wrestlers put faces on an abstract debate. With supporters like Hastert and Minnesota Senator Paul Wellstone, who had wrestled in college at the University of North Carolina, the wrestling community succeeded in making the debate over Title IX a national issue.

While unsuccessful in Illinois and Ohio, they persisted in the courts as well. In 1998, wrestlers from California State University at Bakersfield got the first and so far only win in any case brought by male athletes under Title IX.

Bakersfield had decided to cap the number of men allowed on the wrestling team in 1995 after the Cal State system signed a consent decree with the state chapter of the National Organization for Women, which required each campus to maintain the gender ratio of the athletics department within ten percentage points of the gender ratio of the student body. Roster capping, or roster management, had become a popular way for colleges to reduce the number of male athletes on nonrevenue teams in an effort to comply with the first test. In 1997, Bakersfield decided to drop the team altogether.

The following year, a group of Bakersfield wrestlers represented by a former Stanford grappler, Mark Martel, and by the Washington-based Center for Individual Rights, sued the university in federal court, accusing it of treating the wrestlers differently because of their gender in violation of both Title IX and the Fourteenth Amendment. The lead plaintiff in the case was Stephen Neal, a heavyweight wrestler who won the

NCAA title in 1998. Losing teammates after the roster-capping plan went into effect was devastating, he said. "Sometimes in wrestling, it takes a couple of years for guys to develop," Neal said between bouts at a 1999 match. "But they're the ones who come into their junior or senior year and get really good. And those are the guys who were cut."[31]

A district court judge, Robert E. Coyle, agreed, granting the wrestlers a temporary injunction and forbidding Bakersfield to drop the team. In is ruling, Coyle said the wrestlers had demonstrated a likelihood of winning the case on its merits. "The court concludes that relying on proportionality to cap the men's athletic teams at CSUB in order to comply with the Consent Decree constitutes implementation of a quota based on gender in violation of Title IX."[32]

The victory was short-lived. Later that year, a panel of the Ninth Circuit Court of Appeals unanimously reversed Coyle's ruling in the strongest possible terms. The plaintiffs' interpretation of Title IX "would have allowed universities to do little or nothing to equalize men's and women's opportunities if they could point to data showing that women were less interested in sports," wrote Judge Cynthia Holcomb Hall in the court's opinion. But "a central aspect of Title IX's purpose was to encourage women to participate in sports."

Judge Hall closed her opinion with a strong statement defending Title IX. Noting the excitement caused by the U.S. victory in the Women's World Cup in 1999, she said that "Title IX has enhanced, and will continue to enhance, women's opportunities to enjoy the thrill of victory, the agony of defeat, and the many tangible benefits that flow from just being given a chance to participate in intercollegiate athletics."[33]

Martel, the Bakersfield lawyer, was furious. "The courts are stubbornly refusing to apply the law as it's written," he said. "The presumption underlying this thinking is that any time two different groups are participating in something at different rates, there is discrimination, and it has to be eliminated."[34]

A handful of judges has agreed with Martel — Coyle, Torruella, and in 1996, Judge Rebecca F. Doherty, a district judge in Louisiana. Ruling in a case involving softball and soccer players who said Louisiana State University had discriminated against them, Doherty criticized other judges for giving too much weight to the 1979 policy interpretation. She also argued that courts had misinterpreted the three-part test. The first part of the three-part test was predicated on a bald assumption that women were as interested in sports as men. "Without some basis for such a pivotal assumption, this Court is loath to join others in creating the 'safe harbor' or dispositive assumption for which defendants and plaintiffs argue," Doherty wrote. "Title IX does not mandate equal numbers of participants. Rather, it prohibits exclusion based on sex and requires equal opportunity to participate for both sexes."[35]

(Despite her criticism of the law, Doherty did not rule on anything that affected the legal standing of the three-part test. Instead, she was even more critical of LSU, which had, she said, failed to do anything to ascertain the interests of female students in deciding which teams to offer and what benefits to give them. The university, she said, violated the law "as a result of arrogant ignorance, confusion regarding the practical requirements of the law, and a remarkably outdated view of women and athletics.")[36]

Another woman to win a Title IX lawsuit against a university did so after trying to cross one of the most sacred gender barriers: joining a football team. After being named to the all–New York state team in high school, Heather Sue Mercer tried out for the football team at Duke University as a freshman in 1994. She did not make it, but participated in spring drills the following year and kicked the winning goal in the spring intrasquad game. Duke's coach, Fred Goldsmith, told reporters at the time she was on the team.[37]

That summer, however, Goldsmith refused to let Mercer attend preseason camp, and in a telephone conversation he suggested that she consider entering beauty pageants instead. The coach told Mercer's mother that putting the placekicker on the team was the "worst decision he had ever made in his life," and in September he refused to give her pads and issued a statement saying she was not on the "active roster" for the football team—a distinction he had never made for any other player.

In 1996, Goldsmith abandoned the "inactive player" category and simply kicked her off the team—making Mercer the first player dismissed from the Duke squad for allegedly not being good enough to play. The coach then chased her away from winter conditioning in 1997, and she contacted a lawyer the next spring. They requested a meeting with Duke officials, who refused.

Mercer then sued the university under Title IX. After a federal judge sided with Duke, the U.S. Court of Appeals for the Fourth Circuit ruled in 1999 that even though the law did not require colleges to allow women to go out for football, if a college freely chose to do so, the team was obligated to treat them fairly.

A separate district judge then reinstated Mercer's suit, which went to trial in October 2000. That month, a jury awarded her one dollar in compensatory damages and $2 million in punitive damages. At least three other women have since played in football games, all as placekickers—Ashley Martin at Jacksonville (Ala.) State University, Katie Hnida at the University of New Mexico, and Tonya Butler at the University of West Alabama.

Women playing football has not been much of an issue for most colleges, however. How to deal with male athletes in other sports has.

Over the course of the 1990s, many colleges cut back on men's sports drastically, particularly gymnastics and wrestling teams. Many more began capping rosters, as Bakersfield did. As Neal suggested, roster capping is particularly cruel because it eliminates walk-ons—athletes who either do not receive athletic scholarships or are not heavily recruited out of high school. Not only does this cut down on available athletes for teams with small scholarship allotments, but it also deprives athletes who compete for the love of the sport to play.

"We're losing our men at the walk-on level," said Dale Anderson, a lawyer who won a national title wrestling for Michigan State University and founded a group called Americans Against Quotas in the run-up to the 2000 presidential election. "These are kids who basically pay their own room and board and bring their own jockstraps. Their parents can't understand why these kids are being dropped for the sole reason that a university can meet a quota."[38]

For all the wrestlers' protestations, whether the total number of male college athletes has actually dropped remains a subject of bitter dispute. A General Accounting Office study found that the number of male athletes actually *increased* significantly during the 1990s, from 225,000 in 1989–90 to 237,000 in 1998–99.[39] These numbers have been affected by numerous schools switching from the National Association of Intercollegiate Athletics (NAIA) to the NCAA, which publishes far more information. The NCAA's own data show the total number of athletes increasing from 177,166 to 210,989 over that period, but the average number of male athletes per institution decreased from 232.8 to 208.69 over the course of the decade—a drop of nearly 10 percent.

Looking a little more closely, one sees that the vast majority of dropped teams and dropped athletes are in Division I. Between 1991–92 and 2001–2, NCAA members dropped slightly over fifteen male athletes apiece. However, Division I members dropped more than twenty athletes apiece, with colleges in Divisions II and III dropping less than one male each. While some sports, notably wrestling and men's gymnastics, suffered drastic cuts, the number of football and basketball players grew or remained constant throughout all divisions, even after controlling for colleges joining and leaving the NCAA.

Budget woes account may account for some of the decreases, but the 1990s were a fairly prosperous time for most colleges. Given that the number of female athletes increased by roughly the same amount as the number of male athletes decreased, Title IX undoubtedly played a pivotal role in many athletics directors' decisions to cut teams.

One such decision became a cause célèbre at Marquette University, which cut funds for its wrestling team in 1993 in part to support the addition of women's soccer.[40] Alumni and fans of the team raised more than sixty thousand to finance the team after that, but in 2001 the team was dropped altogether to balance the university's numbers of male and female athletes. For Title IX opponents, Marquette became a flashpoint because the university has not had a football team for decades; thus, the sport cannot be blamed for putting the numbers of out balance.

Marquette has been successful in meeting its Title IX goals. In 1997–98, only 40 percent of Golden Eagles athletes were female; in 2001–2, 52 percent were, just three percentage points lower than the proportion of students who were female. The university has not increased the number of female athletics appreciably since 1997, choosing instead to cut roughly forty men.

Another common complaint among athletics officials and Title IX opponents has been the way colleges choose to add women's sports. Rowing has exploded in popularity at the college level, growing almost as fast as soccer, because colleges can put a huge number of women on a rowing squad. Crews have one and often several eight-oared shells (calling them "boats" usually earns a lecture from a crew), as well as several four-oared and occasionally a few one- or two-person shells. Crews also race in "lightweight" and "novice" divisions, the former reserved for women weighing less than 130 pounds and the latter for first-year rowers. In calculating compliance with the first test, female crews can go a long way toward offsetting the number of men required for a football team.

Rowing, however, is nonexistent at the high school level, except in pockets in the Northeast, Mid-Atlantic, and Pacific Northwest. Coaches instead recruit high school volleyball and basketball players for the squads, along with any other tall, vaguely athletic women who show up.

This aggravates a common complaint among Title IX opponents. Wrestlers, swimmers, and other male athletes train for their sports starting in elementary school and even earlier, yet are excluded from college teams. Women with little sports experience are allowed and even wooed with scholarship funds to go out for varsity crews—or equestrian teams or even bowling squads, both of which have become popular among colleges desperate to attract more female athletes.

Far fewer male athletes have a chance to earn athletic scholarships, given the pressure on schools to increase women's rosters and the larger number of men competing for smaller numbers of grants. Division I women's track teams may grant up to 15 scholarships, while men's teams are limited to 12.6, for example. (In sports other than Division I-A football and Division I basketball, colleges divide scholarship funds as they see fit, even into half- and quarter-grants or even just pittances for books. Football and basketball teams must give full scholarships to each participant.)

These arguments by opponents of Title IX have not found much sympathy with the general public. According to a poll commissioned in 2000 by the *Wall Street Journal* and NBC News, 79 percent of American adults said they approved of Title IX, and 76 percent said they approved of "cutting back on men's athletics to ensure equivalent athletic opportunities for women." The results did not vary much by political party or demographic group. Even 73 percent of men said they approved of cutting men's sports to create opportunities for women.[41]

"There's not a parent I speak to, especially dads, who isn't incredibly enthusiastic about what sport is doing for girls," said Donna Lopiano, the Women's Sports Foundation's director. "They also don't like the elitist direction of men's sport. They don't want all their dollars going to a select few, and they intensely dislike the arrogance, selfishness, and misbehavior of the professional athlete or the spoiled college athlete."

Schuld, of the Independent Women's Forum, said she thought the survey's questions were too broad to get an accurate reaction. "The larger and grander, the more innocuous the questions are, the higher or more-favorable the results are going to be," she says. "It's not that they're unfair—they're just too basic to really give people information."

One anecdotal defense employed by Brown and many other institutions to attacks about low numbers of women on sports teams is the question of opportunity—they give women many opportunities to participate in sports, but not enough women come out, or decide they want to stay on a team if they are not going to get playing time. But the same may be true of male athletes cut from Division I teams. Nobody has documented the success or failure those athletes have had finding places to play at other colleges, but men who want them can usually find other teams ready to take them.

9

C H A P T E R

•

Sports before College

The reams of policies and regulations issued under Title IX are written to apply to college sports. More specifically, they apply to the big-time college sports of Division I as they existed in the 1970s—hence the lengthy discussion of athletic scholarships, academic tutors, athletic dormitories, among other topics. This orientation makes it difficult to apply large sections of the law to high school sports, even though the law applies to high schools just as it does to colleges.

High school sports for girls have evolved alongside college sports for women. In some cases, high schools have added sports because colleges have; in others, public demand has led high schools to start girls' soccer, lacrosse, and other teams. In 2002–3, nearly 42 percent of the 6.8 million athletes at American high schools were girls, roughly the same percentage as at the nation's colleges.[1]

Those trends have held true since the passage of Title IX. In 1970–71, schools reported having 3.7 million boys (93 percent) and 294,000 girls (7 percent) on varsity teams. By 1980–81, the number of boys had shrunk slightly, to 3.5 million (65 percent) while the number of girls had exploded to 1.9 million (35 percent).[2] The 65-35 split remained constant through the 1980s, as did the total number of boys and girls playing high school sports. In the 1990s, both numbers began to climb, especially for girls. By 2000–1, the participation gap had narrowed to 58-42.

In *Tilting the Playing Field*, Jessica Gavora argues that the slow growth of girls' sports in the 1980s and 1990s demonstrates that girls' interest in sports had largely been satisfied by the rapid expansion during the 1970s, most of which took place before the 1975 regulations and 1979 policy interpretation went into effect, meaning that schools were starting teams without any federal guidelines.[3] In court cases like Brown's, universities have argued that high school participation rates are an accurate measure of "real" student interest in athletics.

Advocates for women's sports, on the other hand, point out that in many parts of the country, schoolgirls still face far greater inequities than college women in sports. Presented with second-class status (the first class being football players), their participation rates and thus their chances to express an interest and learn the skills needed to compete in sports remain artificially depressed. The same applies to recreational sports, such as YMCA leagues and city parks-and-recreation programs, although those are largely exempt from Title IX scrutiny.

In any case, participation rates have not been a major issue at the high school level. That could be because high schools have not dropped many boys' sports, or because the Office for Civil Rights has not pressed the issue of the three-part test on high schools. Or it could be because few parents realize the law requires high schools provide equitable opportunities for male and female athletes.

Instead, the major lawsuits and public debates have focused on issues of treatment—whether girls should be allowed to try out for boys' teams (and vice versa), whether girls' teams have inferior fields and equipment, or whether practices and games are scheduled in an equitable manner.

One of the most persistent issues in Title IX lawsuits at all levels is whether the offending entity is indeed responsible for complying with the law. If a college, school system, or other institution is a direct recipient of federal funds, then it is clearly required to meet all of Title IX's obligations. For other organizations, like athletic associations, the question is whether the organization is acting on behalf of a state or federal agency.

This is important because high schools and colleges generally only sponsor sports sanctioned by a governing body. To convince high schools to expand sports for women, parents and advocates have had to force state associations to recognize those sports, and they needed to establish some legal leverage.

For example, until 1992 the Kentucky High School Athletic Association had a rule on its books stating that for it to recognize a new sport and offer a championship, 25 percent of the 290 schools under its jurisdiction needed to express interest in sponsoring it. For the preceding ten years, the association (like its counterparts in most other states) sponsored "slow-pitch" softball for girls but not "fast pitch," a distinctly different game that requires stronger pitching, batting, and fielding skills. Fast-pitch softball is much closer to boys' baseball than to slow-pitch softball.

In 1988, the KHSAA surveyed its schools, and twenty-six, or about 9 percent, said they would be interested in fielding fast-pitch teams. Individual girls were not surveyed. In 1992, a second survey showed that interest had doubled—fifty schools were interested in starting teams, but still short of the 25 percent threshold.[4]

Colleges play fast-pitch softball, and Lorie Ann Horner and a group of other students were worried that they would have no shot at earning college scholarships if they were limited to slow pitch. They sued the KHSAA and the Kentucky Board of Elementary and Secondary Education in 1992 in federal court, claiming that their rights under Title IX and the Fourteenth Amendment were being violated. The association and the board countered, among other things, that they were not covered by title IX because they did not receive federal funds. A district judge did not consider that question, ruling in the favor of the defendants on other grounds, but a panel of the U.S. Court of Appeals for the Sixth Circuit took up the question and in 1994 ruled that both the association and the board were indeed recipients of federal funds.

The Kentucky Department of Education had gotten $396 million from the government to support school lunches and other mandates, and the appeals court ruled that the department had delegated authority in certain instances to the board, which in turn had put the KHSAA in charge of scholastic sports programs. Since state law gave both organizations the right to govern sports, both were subject to Title IX, the court ruled.[5]

Other courts have used the Sixth Circuit's logic in cases involving state high school athletic associations in Florida, Ohio, Pennsylvania, and Virginia. (Thus far, however, the NCAA has been exempted by the law. The college association has argued that while it voluntarily complies with the law, it is under no legal obligation to do so. Renee M. Smith, a volleyball player at Saint Bonaventure University from 1991 to 1993, sued the association when it refused to waive a rule allowing her to compete as a graduate student. She alleged more men than women were granted such waivers, violating Title IX, but the Supreme Court ruled that the NCAA had no Title IX obligations. "At most, the association's receipt of dues demonstrates that it indirectly benefits from the federal assistance afforded its members. This showing, without more, is insufficient to trigger Title IX coverage," wrote Justice Ruth Bader Ginsburg.)[6]

Once it had asserted that the KHSAA had to abide by Title IX, the Sixth Circuit judges found other faults with the association's regulations. In 1992, when the Horner lawsuit was filed, Kentucky sponsored ten sports for boys—basketball, baseball, cross-country, football, golf, soccer, swimming, tennis, track, and wrestling—and only eight sports for girls: basketball, cross-country, golf, slow-pitch softball, swimming, tennis, track, and volleyball. In noncontact sports (all but basketball, football, and wrestling), the association allowed girls to try out and play for boys' teams if their school did not field a girls' team in a given sport.

That, the KHSAA had argued, was plenty to accommodate girls' interests in sports, and besides that, the 25 percent rule was a good way to save schools money.[7]

The district court rejected the KHSAA's arguments, ruling that the 25 percent rule had nothing to do with Title IX. Whether school administrators wanted to sponsor a sport or not was irrelevant, Judge Charles W. Joiner wrote. "The interests of the member schools is not necessarily identical with that of the students," he said. "While reliance on the interest of the member *schools* in adding a sanctioned sport may appear to be gender-neutral, it is a method which has great potential for perpetuating gender-based discrimination."[8]

While schools (and associations) would not be required to field fast-pitch teams if only one player was interested in participating, the fact that fifty schools indicated they could and would field teams meant there was an unmet interest that KHSAA had to accommodate, Joiner concluded.

During the litigation the Kentucky state legislature passed a law requiring the KHSAA to offer sports that were closely parallel to sports offered at state colleges. That spelled the death of slow-pitch softball in Kentucky, and the district court and the Sixth Circuit ruled that the Horner case was moot.[9]

As more and more girls were drawn to sports, they and their parents noticed—and began to complain vociferously about—inequities between their teams and boys' teams. Softball players had to make do with rutted fields, often at city parks far from their schools, while booster clubs provided minor-league quality baseball diamonds. Boys' teams played in prime time, while girls played at off hours or as a pregame warm-up of sorts. Girls got the leftovers for uniforms and equipment. Weight rooms were reserved for football teams.

Softball has continued to be a flashpoint for these controversies, mostly because it is such a close parallel to boys' baseball. Debates over slow pitch versus fast pitch grew heated in many places, and softball parents became vigorous advocates and litigants when their daughters had to play on fields inferior to boys' baseball fields. (They cannot share them: Fast-pitch softball is played on a dirt infield with no mound, and the pitcher stands 45 feet from home plate. Baseball diamonds have grass on the infields, and the pitcher stands on a mound 60.5 feet from the batter.)

In December 2000, for example, state judge Anne C. Conway ruled that the Brevard County, Florida, school board had violated Title IX and a state gender-equity law by relegating softball teams at Titusville and Astronaut High Schools to shabby fields far away from the schools, after building new fields for the baseball teams on the school campuses.[10] The judge required the county to spend six hundred thousand dollars on new softball fields, which came equipped with dugouts with refrigerated water, electronic scoreboards, batting cages, and bleachers along the first- and third-base lines.[11]

In many states, particularly in the South, girls have struggled to make inroads—even though a few girls' basketball teams have been phenomenally successful, such as at high schools in Shelbyville, Tennessee, and Hart County, Georgia. Much of this has to do with a communities that live and die with high school football teams and are reluctant to put much money into other sports, except perhaps baseball and occasionally basketball. Booster clubs have long supported these sports, but girls' sports are still a relatively new phenomenon. Participation rates still lag in rural states like North Carolina, South Carolina, Nevada, Utah, Tennessee, Mississippi, Louisiana, and Alabama, and girls' sports are supported best only at affluent, suburban high schools.[12]

"It's the good ol' boy system," Linda Schrenko, Georgia's superintendent of education, told the *Atlanta Journal-Constitution* in 1999, saying that most, if not all, high schools in the state were in violation of Title IX. "And good ol' boys have traditional roles for girls that don't include athletics."[13]

More than half the state's high school principals did not know if their districts had a Title IX coordinator, a requirement of the 1975 regulations, according to a special report in the newspaper. Three-quarters of the budget used to supplement salaries of teachers with coaching duties went to the coaches of boys' sports. More than $12 million in additional pay went to boys' coaches as well. Only about a third of the state's high schools had volleyball teams, the third most popular sport in the country. And 86 percent of the state grants that went to sports went to support projects for boys' teams. Macon High School received one hundred thousand dollars to help build a new football stadium. According to the Atlanta paper, that the funds did not benefit girls was not an issue for the school's athletics director and assistant principal, Tommy Moore. "Gender equity," Moore said. "We got girls in the band. The cheerleaders are girls. Half the people in the stands are girls. We hold graduation in the stadium, and half the graduates are girls. Our managers are girls; our statisticians are girls."[14]

The *Atlanta Journal-Constitution* contrasted Georgia's schools with Florida's. The Sunshine State had had its own gender-equity law on the books since 1984, and amended it in 1994 specifically to cover high school sports. High schools were required to file annual reports on spending and participation rates by gender, and schools were required to meet a state proportionality standard: The proportion of female athletes had to be within 5 percentage points of the proportion of students who were female.[15] That portion of the law went into effect in 1997–98, but so far no schools have faced punishments for failing to meet the standard.

Nonetheless, the law seems to have propelled Florida far beyond Georgia in providing participation opportunities for girls. The Atlanta newspaper found that the number of Florida girls participating in sports increased 24 percent in 1997–98 from the previously year, and by 1998–99, 41 percent of Florida high school athletes were girls, while only 36 percent of Georgia athletes were female.[16]

The following year, the Georgia State Assembly passed the Georgia Equity in Sports Act, a watered-down version of the Florida legislation. It had no percentage-point mandate for girls' participation numbers, and it did not reorganize the state athletic association to promote more positions for women, as Florida's did. But it did require school systems to report participation levels and expenditures and to designate gender-equity coordinators.

By 2001–2, the percentage of Georgia athletes who were girls was up to 40.1 percent, not far off Florida, at 40.9 percent.[17]

Inequities, of course, persist in Georgia, Florida, and around the country. More than a few of them have been chronicled and attacked by Herb Dempsey, a retired teacher in Seattle who has begun a Title IX crusade. After he left teaching, he said, his wife told him to find a hobby. "So I went to one of Darcy Lees' [a state education official] classes in Title IX and began ripping chunks out of my local school district where my daughter was one of those athletes being treated disparately or is that desperately and since I have a background in uniformed law enforcement and public education I knew both bureaucracies quite well," he wrote in a 2003 e-mail. "Since then it has cost districts millions and I still get to kick butt, so it has worked out very nicely."

A sample Dempsey complaint:

November 25, 2002

James Hammond, Principal
Bethel High School
22215 38th Avenue East
Spanaway, WA 98387

Dear Principal Hammond:
Several years ago I filed a complaint a part of which alleged that Bethel High School operated a competitive interscholastic athletic program that was sexist in that the opportunities for participation in athletics were

substantially disproportionate to the gender ratio in the student body generally. Today those numbers are no less discouraging. In 1997, 59% of the athletes were male and last year, 60%. For comparative purposes we are using the Student Body proportions of 54.5% male and 45.4% female as a baseline for the 2001–2002 School Year.

Washington State said such inequality is a breach of Article XXXI, section 1, Amendment 61, of the Washington state Constitution, which requires equal treatment of all citizens regardless of sex. (RCW 28A.640.010) In a simplified version of what happened the Bethel High School Girls' Bowling Team just cut 21 girls. This established an unmet interest and a failure to maintain a practice historical pattern of program expansion for the underrepresented gender and, when coupled with the substantial disproportionality clearly constitutes discrimination against the female students of Bethel High School.

Of course there are other numbers that will surface as we step through the hoops established by the Bethel School Board of Directors in the policy which protects the district's callous indifference to the needs of this minority group. But in a district environment that maintains rigid and inflexible attendance boundaries this seems to be as good a place to start as any as we start these first steps in our dance to the top. Bethel High School students are just that. They are prohibited from trying to find any school which may be less sexist and more accommodating.

As the superintendent has pointed out, this may be one of those issues that are handled at the individual building level so I decided to start at the building level. On the other hand, this may be, as the Administrative Law Judge pointed out in 1998, one of those cases where, "This is not an insignificant numerical disparity." For that matter both observations may be accurate and as you are the site administrator, I decided to start with you. So I file this complaint that: BETHEL HIGH SCHOOL IN THE BETHEL SCHOOL DISTRICT, A QUASI-MUNICIPAL CORPORATION IN PIERCE COUNTY IN WASHINGTON STATE, PROVIDES SUBSTANTIALLY DISPROPORTIONATE ACCESS TO OPPORTUNITIES TO PARTICIPATION IN INTERSCHOLASTIC COMPETITIVE ATHLETICS FOR MEMBERS OF THE UNDERREPRESENTED GENDER AT BETHEL HIGH SCHOOL.

I assume we will enjoy an informal conference on this matter before it proceeds further.

Yours truly,

Herb Dempsey

The Office for Civil Rights "is a joke," Dempsey said, who showers the agency in requests for information under the Freedom of Information Act. In 2002, he said, it did not investigate about half the complaints it received about high school sports. In the rest of the cases, it initiated an investigation but school districts quickly negotiated an "agreement to resolve" perceived violations. Those agreements are typically short-lived, he said:

> I have a case-in-point with my local school district. As soon as monitoring of the prime time in scheduling disappears the boys are getting, once again, nearly 60 percent of the varsity Friday contests. For the few years of the monitoring the girls actually has [sic] a few volleyball games in the fall on Fridays. Now Friday is, once again, for football. In another case-in-point at a local high school the disproportionality numbers improved during the monitoring and now are only one point better than when I started in 1997 with an OCR complaint of substantial disproportionality. In one Junior High the numbers are actually worse than in 1997. OCR isn't the answer but money really works for a short time in the courts and then we get the creep as the "good 'ole boys" again offer programs for boys.[18]

The issue of scheduling is a persistent one. Dempsey and parents complain that nobody attends girls' games because they are relegated to afternoons and other inconvenient times, while boys usually play football and basketball on Friday nights to full houses. Countless OCR agreements have required schools to move girls' contests into prime time, but Dempsey argues that such pacts have a short shelf life.

Seasonal schedules also have been a major issue in some locations. In Michigan, for example, high school girls played volleyball in the winter and basketball in the fall, even though in the rest of the country, volleyball is a fall sport and girls' basketball, like boys', is played in the winter.

A group of parents sued the Michigan High School Athletic Association over the peculiarity in seasons and other issues in 1998, touching off a lengthy court battle. After other charges were settled at the district court level, the question of seasons came to trial in 2001. Parents pointed out that in addition to volleyball and basketball, girls' soccer and golf were played in the spring and swimming and tennis in the fall, disadvantaging Michigan girls in general and specifically those seeking college scholarships. College coaches typically travel across the country during competitive seasons to watch promising players, and do not like having to make exceptions for strange seasons, such as Michigan's.[19]

In July 2004, the U.S. Court of Appeals for the Sixth Circuit sided with the parents, ruling that the MHSAA's schedule violated the constitutional rights of female athletes and ordered the association to change the season. An appeal was pending in August 2004.[20]

Michigan officials said they had legitimate reasons for boys' and girls' teams in the same sport playing in different seasons, most of them logistical. Gym space only goes so far, after all. Even though most other states played more traditional schedules, the MHSAA said there was nothing discriminatory about their own practices.

Judge Richard Alan Enslen ruled that, in fact, the scheduling arrangements were extremely discriminatory. Girls playing basketball in the fall did not get to participate in "March Madness" events, which had proved popular for boys' state-tournament games. They also did not get to play games in conjunction with professional events, such as Detroit Pistons games. Volleyball players could not compete in private club tournaments scheduled in the spring by USA Volleyball, which are prime recruiting events.

Given these issues, Judge Enslen ordered the MHSAA to come up with a new scheduling plan that would not disadvantage female athletes. The association's first proposal would have tinkered with golf, tennis, and swimming schedules, leaving the basketball, soccer, and volleyball in "disadvantageous" seasons.[21]

The local U.S. attorney filed a brief on the plaintiffs' side, arguing that both the original scheduling scheme and the new plan discriminated against girls. Enslen agreed, ruling that because basketball and volleyball were the two most popular sports in Michigan high schools, a third of the state's female athletes would remain disadvantaged under the plan. "It is simply impossible for any plan to achieve equity without switching the girls' basketball and volleyball seasons," he wrote. "This conclusion also seems particularly warranted considering the qualitative harms found to exist when those two sports are scheduled as they are currently."[22]

The case is pending before the U.S. Court of Appeals for the Sixth Circuit. As of the 2003–4 school year, Michigan girls were still playing fall basketball and spring volleyball.

As these battles have raged, girls' sports have made progress where Title IX is not a concern: At private schools, where the law does not apply, and small-town public schools like those mentioned earlier and on Native American reservations. In *Counting Coup*, Larry Colton recounts the intense interest surrounding the Hardin High School girls' basketball team on the Crow reservation in Montana. He tells the story of four hundred families following the team to a game at Glendive, two hundred miles away. The scene is reminiscent of the movie *Hoosiers*, in which a long line of car headlights follow a school bus from town to town across rural Indiana.[23]

Back in Georgia, the authors of the *Atlanta Journal-Constitution*'s series noted with some surprise that private-school teams dominated most girls' sports in state competition.[24] Unlike private colleges, private high schools generally are not subject to Title IX and other federal laws because they do not receive other financial assistance. However, many Georgia private schools require students, both boys and girls, to participate in some sort of sport for at least two seasons during high school.

In 2002–3, out of forty-nine state titles awarded in thirteen girls' sports, private schools won eighteen—a number far out of proportion to their representation among Georgia high schools. In Florida, private schools won eighteen out of forty-one girls' state titles. (High schools in both states and most others are divided into classifications based on enrollment, so there are multiple state champions in each sport.)[25]

The Atlanta newspaper noted that the Westminster Schools in Atlanta had fifty-eight junior high, junior varsity, and varsity teams, thirty of which were for girls. In 1998–99, the gender breakdown of those teams was 56 percent male, 44 percent female. One of Westminster's top rivals on most playing fields is the Marist School, which had sixty-four sports teams, thirty-three of them for girls, and the participation breakdown was nearly even—388 boys, 386 girls.

"We want kids involved in something," Marist's athletics director, Tommy Marshall, told the newspaper. "That should be part of high school. It's something good for the kids. And I don't know if they have that push in the public schools. It depends, school to school."[26]

Private schools like Westminster (the author's alma mater) and Marist certainly fund sports better than most public schools in the Atlanta area. They also have parents who insist their children success, and would not tolerate lesser opportunities for their daughters than their sons. And many students of both sexes participate in sports as a way of improving their high school records to impress college admissions officers. Both schools are often accused of recruiting athletes from the public schools and luring them with scholarships to offset tuition, but such charges have never been proven.

Across the country, the push to increase participation opportunities for girls has resulted in some high schools making surprising choices in sports. Georgia has been prodded into offering fast-pitch softball alongside soft pitch; although the latter is dying out, many schools continue to field teams in both sports. Florida now has weightlifting for girls, having held the first state championship in 2004. Cheerleading—not sis-boom-bah on the sidelines, but featuring squads competing against each other on stage—is now one of the most popular "sports" for high-schoolers.

High school sports for girls are at a pivotal moment, though. Just as they are becoming popular on a widespread basis, they are becoming less important for the very best athletes, like the Potomac Mischief soccer team mentioned in the introduction. For them, sport is a year-round activity, and they practice and compete with their club team in virtually every month of the year. High school soccer is something they do for fun, a time to socialize with their friends. Club soccer is their real sport.

This is true for boys as well as girls. In most sports, like basketball and soccer, there are far more club teams and opportunities for boys to receive instruction from expert coaches. Thus, girls have fewer chances to develop the skills needed to be competitive at an elite level. Club sports also suck both boys and girls past a tipping point, at which sport becomes an obsession as an end in itself, rather than a means of enjoyment and learning a set of skills and lessons that help players in later life.

10
CHAPTER
·

The Wrestlers' Response

W hen the 2000 election rolled around, wrestlers saw their best chance to place their plight on the country's political agenda. Groups like Iowans Against Quotas and Americans Against Quotas organized to get their message in front of the candidates and, thus, the public. They tried to get presidential hopefuls to sign a pledge to eliminate the three-part test as a quota system, and three agreed—Gary L. Bauer, Steve Forbes, and Alan L. Keyes.[1]

"We're trying to educate the public and achieve our purpose through influencing the next president," said Eric A. LeSher, president of Iowans Against Quotas. "We've definitely educated some of the other candidates, and we're now on their radar screen."

In response, the National Association of Collegiate Women Athletic Administrators circulated letters supporting the current interpretation of Title IX for its members to send to elected officials, and the NCAA's Committee on Women's Athletics called for a two-year promotional campaign to educate the public on the positive aspects of Title IX.

The Clinton administration, on its way out, was furious about the wrestlers' effort. Mary Frances O'Shea, coordinator of Title IX for the Office for Civil Rights, condemned the wrestling groups and others for spreading misinformation about the law. "This is a well-organized attempt to promote a misguided premise," she said. "The fact that some men's minor sports have been dropped in no way should be attributed to the growth of women's sports. Schools have identified a number of reasons for dropping sports or capping opportunities, which range from budgetary concerns—Division I-A football and basketball budgets consume 73 percent of the average total men's operating budget—to lack of interest, to having a mediocre team."[2]

The campaign was not expected to be successful—even from supposed allies. "This has been a political hot handle on a pan that not many folks want to put their hands on," said Grant Teaff, longtime director of the American Football Coaches Association. "I'd be surprised if they can get it to become an issue."

In a campaign feature, the *Chronicle of Higher Education* asked the presidential candidates: "Has the federal government gone too far in enforcing Title IX, the federal gender-bias law, in college sports? Should federal law assume that colleges must have an equal proportion of male and female students playing on sports teams?" Notwithstanding the inaccuracy in the second question, the candidates answered as follows:

BILL BRADLEY: I am a long-time supporter of Title IX and women's sports. In 1990, legislation I proposed asked colleges to reveal the graduation rates of student-athletes compared to all students, and one of the most interesting statistics to come out of that legislation was that women athletes were much more likely to graduate than nonathletes. I believe that this demonstrates the educational value of a balanced athletic program. I am disturbed that many colleges have chosen to meet Title IX by cutting nonrevenue sports for men rather than expanding opportunities for women, and would encourage colleges to focus on expanding opportunities for all students.

GEORGE W. BUSH: I support Title IX. Title IX has opened up opportunities for young women in both academics and sports, and I think that's terrific. I do not support a system of quotas or strict proportionality that pits one group against another. We should support a reasonable approach to Title IX that seeks to expand opportunities for women rather than destroy existing men's teams.

AL GORE: It is important that schools provide women with the same variety and quality of sports that men are now provided with. The intention of the law is to increase access and variety [for] women, and not to take opportunity away from men. However, some schools have chosen to cut men's teams to meet this requirement. It must be left up to the individual colleges to decide how they wish to handle compliance with the law. While some institutions may elect to cut men's sports to comply with the substantial-proportionality provision of the law, numerous other factors may contribute to this decision, such as financial viability, a team's likelihood of staying competitive, changes in athletic-conference priorities, to name a few. I continue to support the intent of Title IX. As a father of three daughters and one son, I would like to think that all of my children will have equal opportunity as they go through college, and beyond.

ALAN KEYES: Common sense, which acknowledges different interests and talents between the sexes, should rule here. The federal government is more likely to act rigidly and ideologically than to do good; it should leave institutions alone in this area.

JOHN MCCAIN: In 1972, when Title IX was enacted, women were at a great disadvantage in many facets of our society. It was designed to provide equal opportunities to women in both academics and athletics through a balanced combination of access and funding.

The difficult decisions that are currently facing educational institutions stem mainly from the courts' often-contradictory interpretations of Title IX. Some courts have ruled that equal access to athletic programs requires equal funding for men's and women's athletics. As a result, many schools have adopted policies of strictly equal funding for male and female athletic programs. Unfortunately, many popular athletic programs must then be cut, because the overall amount of funding available for athletics programs will not sustain identical men's and women's programs in every sport.

I support the law's intent of promoting equal opportunities to all students in a manner that does not unfairly penalize or limit opportunities for any students. I am hopeful that we can work together to find ways to make Title IX work to accomplish its original intent without causing the elimination of athletic programs.[3]

The message was clear, and dramatically changed from the early years of Title IX. All of the candidates, with the possible exception of Keyes, supported the idea of equal opportunity for women. The Republicans were open to the idea of some form of wiggle room to preserve men's opportunities, though, a position that was included in one plank of the party platform when it was approved in August at the Republican National Convention: "We also support a reasonable approach to Title IX that seeks to expand opportunities for women without adversely affecting men's teams."[4] The topic did not make it into any of the candidate debates, but this small eddy in the flow of the political dialogue was the first time Title IX had become a campaign issue. When Bush was elected, wrestlers and others were hopeful that change was on the way.

His first steps appeared to support that optimism. His choice for education secretary, Roderick R. Paige, was a football coach who had become dean of education at Texas Southern University and then superintendent of the Houston school district. Paige's doctoral dissertation at Indiana University was about the response time of football linemen.[5]

The Bush administration then chose two young conservative men as Paige's top two aides: Brian Jones and Gerald Reynolds. Jones, the department's general counsel, had been an employment lawyer in San Francisco and spoke and wrote for the Washington-based Center for New Black Leadership, a think tank whose members oppose affirmative action, back school choice, and take other relatively conservative positions. Reynolds, who succeeded Cantù as assistant secretary for civil rights, had been a lawyer for Kansas City Power and Light after serving as president of the Center for New Black Leadership. Unnoticed by the public, another lawyer joined the Education Department's civil rights team: Lou Goldstein, a Chicago lawyer with the firm of Goldstein and Fluxgold who had represented male athletes in lawsuits against Illinois State and Miami.

Of these, only Reynolds faced a tough nomination hearing, which took place more than a year after the actual nomination, in February 2002.[6] Leading the Senate Health, Education, Labor, and Pensions Committee, Sen. Ted Kennedy, the Massachusetts Democrat, asked Reynolds if a corporate lawyer "deserved" to be in charge of civil rights in education. Reynolds responded that he had spent half his time at New Black Leadership working on education issues.

Two Democrats on the panel, Patty Murray of Washington and Paul Wellstone of Minnesota, queried Reynolds about his views on Title IX. Reynolds hedged, saying that "on its face, it does not require a quota."[7]

Meanwhile, the wrestlers turned up the heat on their own. A consortium of coaching associations and groups of wrestlers whose teams had been cut filed suit in federal court in Washington against the Education Department itself, claiming that the 1979 policy interpretation and Cantù's 1996 policy clarification violated Title IX and the Fourteenth Amendment because of their use of the three-part test, and that both documents had been published improperly under the Administrative Procedures Act, and thus should not be considered official Education Department policy.

Lawrence J. Joseph, the plaintiffs' lawyer, said his case was different from the eight previous challenges to Title IX in sports, all of which had failed at the appellate level, because his clients were challenging how the regulations themselves came about. No president or attorney general approved the three-part test, much less the first test, and he said that colleges were using the first test to guarantee they would not be sued.

Women's groups feared the lawsuit would give the Bush administration an opportunity to throw Title IX to the courts without any defenses, as the Reagan administration had done in the *Grove City College v. Bell* case. But the Justice Department mounted a vigorous defense of the Education Department's rules-making process, asking Judge Emmet G. Sullivan to dismiss the lawsuit.[8]

Asking for a summary judgment to dismiss the case, the department argued that the plaintiffs could not prove that changing the regulations governing Title IX would solve their problem. The department did not deal with the merits of the plaintiffs' claims about the three-part test, but instead challenged the case on procedural grounds.

"The administration strongly supports Title IX," Jones said in a written statement. "Title IX has opened up opportunities for young women in both academics and sports. We believe we should strive to expand opportunities for women in a way that does not diminish existing men's teams."

The government's brief argued that the groups should not be allowed to sue because the remedy they wanted—declaring the three-part test void and forcing the Education Department to craft new gender-equity guidelines—would not make colleges restore men's teams, or even stop cutting them. The wrestlers should be suing colleges for their decisions to cut men's teams (not withstanding the fact that all such lawsuits had failed), not the Education Department for giving them the option to do that in the regulations. Furthermore, the department argued, the wrestlers should not be allowed to sue, because the statute of limitations expired in 1985, six years after the 1979 policy interpretation was published. The plaintiffs had argued that the 1996 clarification constituted a new regulation, but the Justice Department disagreed.

"It would have turned the whole government inside out if a brief hadn't been filed like the one the government filed," said Marcia Greenberger of the National Women's Law Center. But women's advocates were not entirely pleased by the Justice Department's brief or the Education Department's response, saying that the government had not gone far enough in defending Title IX. "We couldn't help but notice and comment on the fact that what was missing, which was certainly unusual, was even a passing reference to underlying support for the regulations and policies."

Neither the Justice Department's brief nor the Education Department's statement did much to stanch speculation that the Bush administration might reopen the discussion over Title IX regulations. "We did hear concerns from some within the administration that such an effort was and is under way," Greenberger said. "There is nothing about this filing that undercuts those rumors or would give anyone cause for comfort that this administration is committed to Title IX policies and regulations that have been in effect since the 1970s."[9]

Sure enough, a few months later, on the thirtieth anniversary of the law's passage, Paige announced the formation of the Secretary's Commission on Opportunity in Athletics. Stumbling through a prepared statement before Kennedy's committee, Paige said the committee would be charged with "strengthening enforcement" of Title IX and "expanding opportunities to ensure fairness for all athletes."[10]

This did not sit well with Greenberger and her allies. Representatives of the National Women's Law Center were scattered around the Senate hearing room where Paige was testifying before the Committee on Health, Education, Labor, and Pensions, distributing news releases with the headline, "NWLC to Bush Administration: 'Hands Off Title IX.'"

The very existence of the commission, the release said, was evidence of the administration's lack of commitment to upholding the law. Meanwhile, the College Sports Council, the umbrella group for the plaintiffs in the case against the Education Department, issued its own news release complaining about its lack of representation on the commission.

The commission consisted mainly of athletics administrators who had held high-profile positions either in the NCAA or the National Association of Collegiate Directors of Athletics, as well as a few athletes and coaches, a professor with no ties to college sports, and, in an ex-officio capacity, several Education Department officials: Cynthia Cooper, an Olympic and professional basketball star; Ted Leland, athletics director at Stanford; Percy Bates, faculty athletics representative at Michigan; Bob Bowlsby, athletics director at Iowa; Gene DeFilippo, athletics director at Boston College; Donna de Varona, an Olympic swimmer and former president of the Women's Sports Foundation; Julie Foudy, a professional soccer player and current president of the Women's Sports Foundation; Tom Griffith, general counsel for Brigham Young; Cary Groth, athletics director at Northern Illinois; Jones; Lisa Graham Keegan, chief executive officer of the Education Leadership Council; Muffet McGraw, head women's basketball coach at Notre Dame; Rita Simon, a professor of law and politics at American University; Reynolds; Mike Slive, commissioner of the Southeastern Conference; Graham Spanier, president of Penn State, Sally Stroup, assistant secretary for postsecondary education; and Debbie Yow, athletics director at Maryland.[11]

At first glance, the commission appears unbalanced in favor of women's groups, considering de Varona's and Foudy's ties to the most vocal and visible of them. However, Bowlsby and Leland were collegiate wrestlers, and Simon, director of the Women's Freedom Network, described herself as a libertarian who is "a strong believer in equality but not particularly in affirmative action."[12] Griffith had been a longtime Senate committee lawyer before arriving at BYU a year earlier. And throughout the commission's meetings, Jones, Reynolds, and Stroup were regular participants.

Rather than referring to specific regulations or even the three-part test, Paige used plain language to charge the commission with answering eight questions:

1. Are Title IX standards for assessing equal opportunity in athletics working to promote opportunities for male and female athletes?

2. Is there adequate Title IX guidance that enables colleges and school districts to know what is expected of them and to plan for an athletic program that effectively meets the needs and interests of their students?

3. Is further guidance or other steps needed at the junior- and senior-high-school levels, where the availability or absence of opportunities will critically affect the prospective interests and abilities of student athletes when they reach college age?

4. How should activities such as cheerleading or bowling factor into the analysis of equitable opportunities?

5. The [Education] Department has heard from some parties that whereas some men athletes will "walk on" to intercollegiate teams—without athletic financial aid and without having been recruited—women rarely do this. Is this accurate and, if so, what are its implications for Title IX analysis?

6. How do revenue-producing and large-roster teams affect the provision of equal athletic opportunities?

7. In what ways do opportunities in other sports venues, such as the Olympics, professional leagues, and community recreation programs, interact with the obligations of colleges and school districts to provide equal athletic opportunity? What are the implications for Title IX?

8. Apart from Title IX enforcement, are there other efforts to promote athletic opportunities for male and female students that the department might support, such as public-private partnerships to support the efforts of schools and colleges in this area?[13]

This was a curious approach. The simplicity of the language was attractive, particularly to reporters and others unfamiliar with the law, but the phrasing of each question raises related issues:

1. The framework of Title IX guidelines have nothing to do with "promoting opportunities for male" athletes. The law and its component parts are designed to increase opportunities for the underrepresented sex, that is, women, to a position of parity with those for men.

2. By 2002, the Education Department had put forth a regulation, an interpretation, a clarification, and two investigators' manuals, all strictly dealing with Title IX and sports. Were they all so bad that more guidance was needed?

3. Primary- and secondary-school athletics were indeed critically important, and the department had a strong argument that more needed to be done.

4. The Office for Civil Rights had already ruled that cheerleading was an activity and not a sport. In addition, many colleges and the NCAA itself had recognized bowling as a sport.

5. The question of whether men are more likely to be "walk-ons" has been a perennial debate in college sports. But walk-ons are a phenomenon unique to Division I and Division II of the NCAA, and most men's and women's teams alike mix scholarship athletes and walk-ons. The 1979 policy interpretation and the 1996 clarification refer to both.

6. Similarly, the 1975 regulations, the 1979 policy interpretation, and the 1996 clarification all spell out the meaning of the Javits amendment, which allowed for reasonable variances in the treatment of teams because of legitimate differences in the nature of sports. Given the numerous failures of amendments to exempt revenue-producing sports in Congress, the question of how to treat revenue-producing teams had long since been asked and answered.

7. This is an interesting question to ask, but it has little bearing on the legal responsibilities of schools under the law.

8. This is a vague and possibly loaded question. Colleges and schools already have numerous corporate partnerships, including sponsorship arrangements for their sports teams, but are required to use available funds to treat teams equitably, regardless of the source of those funds. One of the controversies involving both wrestlers and high school teams has been whether private donors can help out a male team without incurring additional obligations for the institution to help women's teams. Time and again, the Office for Civil Rights and the courts have ruled in the negative.[14]

Paige could have charged the commission with reviewing the Education Department's Title IX guidelines, as the wrestlers would have wanted, or he could have told its members to assess whether colleges were complying with them. Brian Snow, a veteran of both court cases and OCR investigations as general counsel at Colorado State University, said the commission could do much to simplify the Education Department's rules for Title IX. "So many regulations haven't really been adopted formally but just invented through letters or other communications, and it's happened during various times" and administrations, Snow said. "Title IX is a wonderful statute, but when you start getting into interpretations, . . . you have to say, How much are we in accordance with the statute, how much do the regulations reflect the purposes of the law, and are we adopting policies that truly provide for the lack of discrimination?"[15]

Instead, Paige chose to lay out the commission's responsibilities in a vague document that at many points failed to connect with the law and the public's understanding of it. As it turned out, the members of the commission spent little time assessing any of the eight questions, instead hearing hours upon hours' worth of witnesses argue, and arguing themselves, about the requirements of the three-part test.

Indeed, at the group's first meeting, Jones said that the practical questions, "how do we apply the three-part test, and whether we're properly guiding institutions on how to assess the interests of women, are what we have to discuss."[16]

At that meeting, in August 2002 in a hotel conference room in downtown Atlanta, the commission did not talk much among themselves, choosing instead to hear from a few expert witnesses and then issuing an open invitation to a parade of coaches, parents, and advocates who told them that Title IX is the best thing that ever happened to some athletes and the worst thing that ever happened to others.

Christa Leahy, a former Princeton University lacrosse player who was then a law clerk in Chicago, pointed out that courts had treated the first test as a "safe harbor" for colleges trying to comply with Title IX, causing athletics directors to cut male athletes and men's sports to reach the goal of substantial proportionality. Members of the commission, including Education Department officials, asked if there might be ways to de-emphasize substantial proportionality, either by making the third test simpler to meet or by measuring a population other than the student body to gauge whether colleges are offering enough opportunities to women.

Throughout the two-day meeting, members of the commission heard athletics directors, coaches, and others complain that they could not find enough women for varsity teams. The commission also heard from wrestlers and fans of the sport arguing that Title IX regulations needed to be substantially revised. Female coaches and athletes, however, argued that the law should be more vigorously enforced, not changed.[17]

The commission held three very similar meetings through the fall, in Chicago, Colorado Springs, and San Diego. In December, the group gathered in Philadelphia for the first of two sessions to debate what it might recommend to Paige. It was an interesting way to make policy: Athletics officials, lawyers, and academics flinging ideas at each other around a circle of tables in a dim hotel conference room, while an audience of advocates, reporters, and more lawyers looked on from the peanut gallery.

Members took turns round-robin style, offering their personal recommendations for changes in the U.S. Education Department's rules and regulations governing Title IX. Two general approaches quickly emerged: rewriting rules to give more weight to women's demonstrated interest in sports in assessing Title IX compliance, and clarifying the law to make it easier for athletics administrators to prove that their programs are treating women equitably. "Being in athletics, I want to know what the target is," Yow said. "Show me the target, the basket, the goal."[18]

The real problem with Title IX enforcement, she said, was a lack of specificity. She suggested getting rid of the three-part test and instead making a new rule that every athletics program in the country has to be half male and half female, with the ability to swing five or seven percentage points to allow officials "wiggle room" to accommodate fluctuations in rosters. With a seven-percentage-point swing, that would mean that at least 43 percent of every college's athletes would have to be women.

According to a *Chronicle of Higher Education* analysis, 180 of the 321 colleges in Division I of the National Collegiate Athletic Association in 2000-2001 would have met that standard. Among the 117 that played Division I-A football, 65 would have qualified.

"We need to have a standard that is easily measurable, enforceable, objective, and beneficial to those who don't want to get bogged down in periodic surveys because the target changes," Yow said. "With this, there's no need for survey documents, no need to use female-enrollment numbers. It stops the bleeding for men, and vastly improves the situation for women."

Getting away from the first test was a popular theme among the commissioners. Many of them said it was inappropriate to use gender breakdowns of undergraduate populations as models for the composition of athletics programs.

"At some point, we need to get to the bottom of the flawed assumption that the undergraduate population has anything to do with athletic interest" and abilities, said Bowlsby. He proposed basing requirements for participation rates at a particular university on similar rates at feeder institutions, such as high schools and junior colleges in the university's region.

Reynolds had a number of thoughts. Basing the first part of the three-part test on something other than the undergraduate population might be worth discussing, he said. He also suggested reviewing the second part of the test. "If a school has done a bad job in the past of complying with Title IX, should successor ADs be penalized for the discriminatory conduct of previous ADs?" he asked. He also said that the Office for Civil Rights needed to educate athletics officials and serve as the "official repository of knowledge" about the law. "There's been a vacuum. I think OCR needs to do a better job of getting out there," he said. "Throughout the town-hall meetings, people have been critical of OCR, and some of that criticism is grounded in fact. We have to do a better job, and hopefully, after we come up with our recommendations, those recommendations can help guide the process. The process is under way in terms of articulating policy and disseminating information, and I hope we get additional recommendations."[19]

Several other commissioners called for the Education Department to rewrite its rules to make them clearer and easier to understand. Griffith, a former Senate committee lawyer, suggested that the government's Title IX rules be turned either into laws passed by Congress or, at a minimum, regulations subject to public review.

Dick Aronson, executive director of the College Gymnastics Association, said he was optimistic that the changes being discussed would give colleges enough flexibility to find ways to comply without cutting male athletes. "Debbie's proposal is credible," Aronson, in an e-mail message, said of Yow's call for a fifty-fifty split of athletes. "Her plan seems to approach a workable 'quota.' The only problem that I foresee is that 50-50 may not give enough room for [Division I] football programs, therefore, less 'wiggle room' " for other sports.[20]

However, Mike Moyer, director of the wrestling coaches' association, asked during a break in the meeting why quotas should be used at all. "Where else in colleges do we see this?" he said.

Leland of Stanford said that people condemn Title IX as a quota system because they think the second and third prongs do not work. "Let's make 2 and 3 more usable, more operational, definable, and understandable," he said.

Rarely in the commission's debates, though, was much concern expressed for the inequities women still face. "They were talking about how they heard from men's wrestlers and gymnasts about how their sports were being dropped," said Jocelyn Samuels, vice president of the National Women's Law Center. "The question is, where's the concern for the women who never got the opportunity to play?"

Other observers also said they were troubled by the commission's membership: All of its members were associated with Division I sports programs or the Education Department. Yet the suggestions they make would have affected colleges at all levels, as well as high schools.

Beyond that, some of the commissioners noted, colleges drop teams for many reasons besides pure gender-equity numbers. The cost of running big-time football and basketball programs is rising much faster than the cost of women's sports programs. However, many of the panel's members demurred when Foudy suggested that the Education Department study ways to curb excessive spending. Such a move would raise antitrust issues, Griffith said.

Leland said he was surprised that the group's proposals were as controversial as they were. "These were sweeping changes," he said. "If they were adopted by the Department of Education, they would change the way the department and individual institutions do business."[21]

Each commissioner was invited to submit one proposal to recommend to Paige:

> Modify the first prong so an institution would not count actual athletes, but instead a set number of athletes per sport, such as twenty athletes each for men's and women's soccer. If the men's soccer coach wanted to keep thirty athletes on the team and the women's soccer coach wanted only eighteen, they could do so. This would allow men's coaches to keep walk-on athletes who now are often cut to meet gender-equity targets. (Leland)
>
> Call on the Education Department's Office for Civil Rights to conduct periodic surveys of male and female students to determine how many have an interest in college sports. This could be used as the basis for the first prong, instead of using the undergraduate-student population. The office should create programs to encourage girls to participate in high-school sports. (Cooper)
>
> Publish a new policy statement to clarify exactly what all three prongs mean. (DeFilippo)
>
> Abandon the emphasis on "substantial proportionality" as the "safe harbor" that ensures compliance with Title IX and replace it with a test that puts all prongs on the same footing, and find additional ways of demonstrating equity. A sports department's compliance with Title IX should be evaluated by looking at all of the tests in aggregate, instead of allowing colleges to meet only one. (Spanier)
>
> Redefine the first prong to require all colleges to have a fifty-fifty ratio of male to female athletes, with a certain variance, such as three to seven percentage points. This would provide "wiggle room" in case colleges have nondiscriminatory circumstances that affect the ratio. The second prong should be abolished. (Yow)
>
> Call for consistent education and enforcement by the Office for Civil Rights. Look at the three tests equally, and redesign federal gender-equity reports to account for the second and third parts of the test. The commission should call for a review of whether National Collegiate Athletic Association scholarship limitations are hampering Title IX. (Groth)
>
> Repeal the Equity in Athletics Disclosure Act, which mandates that each institution publish a report on its staffing, participation, and budgeting for men's and women's teams. The Education Department does not use the report and cannot verify the data that colleges publish under it. (Stroup)

Clarify the three-part test and create a clear set of penalties for institutions that do not comply. In addition, the Office for Civil Rights needs to work on having consistent decisions across its various regions. (Bates)

Issue a strong recommendation that colleges consider finding ways to curb excessive expenditures, especially in revenue-producing sports. (Foudy)

Better define substantial proportionality, permitting a five- or seven-percentage-point gap between the proportion of female athletes and that of female undergraduates. Issue new regulations to be considered under the normal federal rules-making process or to be considered as new laws by Congress. (Griffith)

Strengthen the third prong by performing regular surveys of the student body. Issue a statement that the commissioners strongly believe in equal opportunity but that it is not tantamount to equal results, because gender balance in athletics at individual campuses is affected by such factors as student interest. (Simon)

In gauging the interest and abilities of students at an institution, use the population of traditional-age students instead of the entire full-time, undergraduate female population, since NCAA rules forbid most older students from competing in Division I sports. (McGraw)

Find ways to add incentives to compliance with the second and third prongs, or add an additional "prong 1a": Allow a college to comply if its proportion of female athletes is at least three percentage points higher than the proportion of female athletes at high schools in the college's region. (Bowlsby)

Reconsider rules regarding private financing of sports teams, possibly allowing private support for men's sports. Reconsider the second prong and find ways to make it a better option for compliance. (Reynolds)[22]

The vagueness of these suggestions and the superficiality of the discussion created the perfect springboard for both sides to turn the commission's last meeting, in January 2003 in downtown Washington, into a circus.

Before the meeting even began, both the wrestlers and the women's groups held press conferences to complain about the commission. Donna Lopiano of the Women's Sports Foundation said that most of the recommendations could result in freezing women's participation statistics at current levels, even in cutting women's teams at some colleges. The commission was telling women that they were "entitled to equality only if no boy loses the chances to play any sport, and if there are budget problems, preserving boys' sports is more important than equality for girls," Lopiano told a roomful of reporters and advocates at the National Press Club. "All they're doing now is rewriting the definition of equality to mean 'less than equal.' "[23]

A block away, a separate press conference featured representatives of the College Sports Council, who said the commission offered a chance to apply some "common sense" to the enforcement of Title IX. "We're pleased the commission was created to finally provide a forum for open dialogue," said Eric Pearson, chairman of the Sports Council. "The only people fighting change or any discussion of change are lawyers with a vested interest in keeping quotas in place." Added Jessica Gavora, "As long as there is a proportionality standard, a quota measure, that's going to be the reigning standard, the compliance standard judges go to. It's an easy safe harbor. I share the opinion that the notion of quota is a logically-flawed test of interest. It's not a test of fairness we use in any other area of higher education, in dance classes, in engineering, even in other single-sex operations like housing."[24]

As college students summoned by the Feminist Majority and NOW marched outside in the rain, chanting "Save Title IX," the commission itself was left to squabble over its findings and recommendations. The group appeared to agree on a broad range of findings, including the following statements:

> After 30 years of Title IX, great progress has been made, but more needs to be done to create opportunities for women and girls and retain opportunities for men and boys.
>
> Escalating operational costs in intercollegiate athletics may threaten the effort to end discrimination in athletics and to preserve athletic opportunities.
>
> The Education Department's Office for Civil Rights has consistently failed to offer clear guidance about Title IX's requirements, has not enforced the law strongly enough, and has not followed federal regulatory policy to make new rules to carry out the law.
>
> Capping the number of male athletes to meet the first part of the three-part test, as colleges sometimes do, does not benefit male or female students.[25]

They agreed on the following recommendations:

> Any changes to Title IX rules should be made through the federal regulatory process—either as laws passed by Congress or as proposed rules published in the Federal Register and subject to public comment—instead of issued carte blanche by "unelected, perhaps nonresponsive bureaucrats" in the Education Department, in Griffith's words.
>
> The Office for Civil Rights should make clear that cutting teams in order to demonstrate compliance with Title IX is a "disfavored practice." Therefore, educational institutions should pursue all other alternatives

before cutting or capping any team when Title IX compliance is a factor in that decision. If teams have to be cut, athletes should be given justification and adequate notice.

The Department of Education should encourage the redesign of reports published under the Equity in Athletics Disclosure Act so that they provide the public with a relevant and simplified tool to evaluate the status of compliance with Title IX on college campuses.

The Office for Civil Rights should educate colleges about its standards governing the use of private funds to prevent sports from being dropped or to allow specific teams to be added.

The panel's discussions featured a great deal of sparring between the college administrators on one side and de Varona and Foudy on the other. The two representatives of the Women's Sports Foundation argued about nearly every point, such as excluding a paragraph about the level of interest in sports at women's colleges and encouraging the Office for Civil Rights not to undermine current interpretations of the law. They found themselves on the losing end of several votes by the commission, prompting mutterings about the possibility of a minority report.

After the first day of the meeting, de Varona said she was not encouraged that what they had discussed dealt adequately with the gender-equity problems women still faced in college sports. "We have to keep reminding the commission that there are still inequalities," she said. "The numbers being given out are all about men's opportunities that have been dropped, but we're still in a box. There are needs in this country that aren't being met, and we need to express that."[26]

The discussion got even more heated the second day, when the panel began voting on its members' personal recommendations, without receiving any legal advice or discussion of how the recommendations jibed with Title IX, the 1975 regulations, or the 1979 policy interpretation. On Yow's fifty-fifty proposal, the commission deadlocked seven to seven, with one member not voting, so the group agreed to include the measure without endorsing it in its final report.

Other commissioners, included Cooper and Simon, argued for measures that would cut the ties between participation in athletics and undergraduate enrollment. Both suggested offering sports opportunities in proportion instead to the number of female students who actually expressed an interest in playing sports. This would have flown in the face of several court rulings, in which judges said basing participation levels on such surveys "would freeze progress at the status quo" for women, according to Valerie Bonnette, a former Office for Civil Rights investigator who now runs Good Sports Inc., a consultancy for colleges on gender equity and athletics issues.

The commission did endorse a recommendation that read, "The Office for Civil Rights should allow institutions to conduct interest surveys as a way of demonstrating compliance with the three-part test. The office should specify the criteria conducting such a survey in a way that is clear and understandable."[27] Of course, colleges complying with the third part of the three-part test already use such surveys, so it was unclear what this proposal would actually do were it made part of Title IX law.

More controversially, the commission agreed to Leland's proposal that the civil rights office measure participation *opportunities* rather than the actual number of participants on teams. The number of opportunities would be set by designating a set number of roster spots for each team. Colleges would be able to count those roster spots and establish budgets for each of those teams based on the designated numbers, but would be allowed to keep as many or as few actual athletes as they liked. Stanford, Leland said, already used that system.

Lamar Daniel, the Title IX consultant, was amazed when told of Leland's suggestion. "I think that's the height of absurdity," he said. "The OCR office in San Francisco is derelict for not pointing that out. If I was there, I'd eat their lunch."[28]

The commission approved several other ideas that would have had major impact on Title IX compliance. One was to leave walk-ons, athletes who do not receive scholarships or are not heavily recruited, out of the count for the three-part test. Another was to remove "nontraditional" students, that is, those over the age of twenty-five, from counts of undergraduates. The commission never discussed the fact that at most institutions, the majority of nontraditional students are women, which would result in skewing enrollments at many colleges in favor of men. Apart from these, the panel approved fifteen statements of finding and other less controversial suggestions for changes in Title IX policy.

Secretary Paige issued a statement saying the Education Department was strongly committed to equal opportunity for male and female athletes in all contexts and that the three parts of the participation test should be given equal weight, making clear that cutting men's teams to comply with Title IX is a "disfavored practice."

Many representatives of women's groups were furious with the commission's work for many reasons, but the biggest was the commissioners' lack of knowledge of Title IX regulations and case law. "If I gave them a test on the 1996 clarification, they would all fail—F's," said Christine A. Grant, retired women's athletics director at the University of Iowa. "This is just about predetermining the amount of discrimination we're going to practice. If this goes through, in perpetuity women are going to be underrepresented, underprivileged, and I can never support that."[29]

Moyer, of the National Wrestling Coaches Association, was more optimistic. "I'm most encouraged by the fact that everyone recognizes the need for change," he said. "We've had six months of debate, and everyone recognizes the most important concern—that enrollment is not the appropriate measure of interest."

In the wake of the two-day meeting, confusion reigned supreme. In addition to not examining the proposals in light of existing Title IX law, the commissioners had not looked at what the proposals would actually mean for colleges, as Cary Groth told fellow members of the commission. "In looking at all these proposals, I'd feel irresponsible if we were to vote on any of them without looking at the numbers," she said.[30]

At the University of Missouri, the athletics department was meeting the interests-and-abilities part of the three-part test, according to Sarah Reesman, senior woman administrator at the university, who had brought Bonnette in to help address gender-equity concerns.[31] The university offers all the women's sports available at Missouri high schools, and assessing club and intramural programs as well as regional competition, appeared to be offering all the sports it could.

Missouri would be in trouble if it were found not to be in compliance with the third part of the test. The athletics department was way off the first part, thanks to a massive football program that had 119 players in 2001–2. Missouri would have had to add at least 99 female athletes or drop at least 71 men from its teams to be able to argue that it met the substantial-proportionality guideline.

The second part did not work, either: The last time the Tigers expanded their sports offerings for women was 1997, when the women's soccer team took the field.

Under Yow's proposal, the proportionality measure would be replaced by a rule saying that colleges must have a fifty-fifty split of athletes, with three percentage points of "wiggle room." If Missouri chose to comply with the standard under such a scenario, the university would have needed to "fix" its athletics offerings so that at least 47 percent of varsity athletes would be women. That could have been achieved by adding 39 female athletes or dropping 44 men.

Under the proposal to eliminate walk-ons and count only scholarship athletes toward totals for the first test, the gap between Missouri's athletics and undergraduate populations would have shrunk substantially—perhaps not enough to bring the university into compliance with the test, at least as it is currently used, but much closer. The university had 520 scholarship athletes, including 247 women, or 47.5 percent of the total.

Under McGraw's suggestion to count only "traditional" full-time students toward totals to determine the gap between the proportion of female athletes and the proportion of female students, Missouri would not benefit appreciably. Of 17,968 undergraduates aged twenty-four or under, 52.5 percent were female.

Leland's "slots" strategy makes Missouri's gap much larger than under the current measure because the university has comparatively fewer women and more men than national averages for Division I-A. Based on the NCAA's participation survey, Missouri would be allocated 316 male athletes, nearly 60 percent, and 213 female athletes—putting the university farther from compliance with the first test than it currently is.

Foremost, though, this exercise showed just how frustrating the recommendations were. Were they supposed to replace the entire three-part test? Were the commissioners trying to rewrite elements of the first test? Did even they know?

Old Washington hands say that this is a common strategy for administrations that want to change a particular policy—appoint a blue-ribbon panel, get a report that points to the direction that the party in power wants to pursue, and move on. The commission did its part, and in late February, the Education Department published a report making a fairly strong statement that Title IX guidelines should be changed to stop colleges from cutting men's teams and male athletes, offering little discussion of the problems facing female athletes.[32] "While everyone benefits from increased athletic participation by girls and women, no one benefits from artificial limitations on athletic opportunities for others," the report stated. "Title IX needs to be strengthened toward the goal of ending discrimination against girls and women in athletics, and updated to that athletic opportunities for boys and men are preserved."[33]

The report said that "all agree that there has been a troubling decrease in athletic opportunities for boys and men." It cited a study by Jerome Kravitz, a Howard University professor who estimated that from 1981 to 2001, colleges had dropped between 1,290 and 1,434 men's teams, cutting roughly fifty-seven thousand men out of college sports.[34]

The draft's twenty-three recommendations, rephrased slightly from the panels, are grouped into four themes: "commitment, clarity, fairness, and enforcement." In a press conference to present the report to Paige, Leland and Cooper did agree that more needed to be done for women. "We heard a lot of arguments that after 30 years, we're still not there," Leland said. "Most of the commissioners would say that we still have much to do to ensure that women have equal opportunities."[35]

However, he said, a majority of the panel's members agreed that Title IX was in need of an in-depth review and that the Office for Civil Rights' enforcement of the law needed some "adjusting."

Those themes prompted a swirl of controversy. The wrestlers said they were pleased, but that the recommendations did not go far enough. Advocates for women's sports said the proposals would deal women a terrible setback in scholastic and collegiate athletics departments.

Paige immediately issued a press release saying the department would "move forward" only on the fifteen recommendations that received unanimous approval from the commissioners. But that did not stay critics of the panel, like Marcia Greenberger of the National Women's Law Center, who said any uncertainty in the law would prompt colleges to delay plans for new women's teams while new regulations were debated in the Education Department and even in the courts.

At a press conference on Capitol Hill, de Varona and Foudy released a minority report saying that the commission did not "compile all the evidence necessary to fully address the state of gender equity in our nation's schools, and did not allow sufficient time for commissioners to conduct either a careful review of the evidence that *was* compiled or an assessment of the potential impact of the various recommendations."[36]

They also published their own set of seven recommendations, many of which parallel the more general recommendations in the main part of the commission's report. For example, they said the Education Department should do more to educate schools and colleges about Title IX's requirements and to make clear that cutting men's teams is not a favored option.

Also at the news conference, the actors Geena Davis and Holly Hunter announced a national campaign to educate the public about Title IX and the commission's recommendations, while four Democratic senators—Tom Daschle of South Dakota, Edward M. Kennedy of Massachusetts, Patty Murray of Washington, and Harry Reid of Nevada—criticized the report as flawed. Daschle, the Senate minority leader, said the commission's recommendations would "slacken our efforts for equal opportunity." "This would be a terrible step backwards," he said.[37]

Murray said she would call on the Senate's Health, Education, Labor, and Pensions Committee to hold hearings on the commission and its findings. Sen. Olympia Snowe, a Republican from Maine, also released a statement criticizing the majority report.

Groth said that she had declined to sign the minority report, but that she thought the full commission's report could have better incorporated the concerns de Varona and Foudy raised. "I think we could have done a better job capturing the conversation and debate regarding the recommendations, and that's what I'm concerned about," she said, pointing out that the commissioners did not vote on the final report as a whole. "I couldn't tell you, if we were to vote on it, who would be in favor of the report."[38]

Furthermore, Groth said, the commission's eight-month term made its members feel rushed from the outset. "I know we're under a time constraint, but I couldn't help thinking, This is a 30-year-old law, and we're in a hurry?" she said. "Not that anyone on the commission would have wanted to go for five more months, but getting down to nuts and bolts, and really spending more time on the guts of it, might have been helpful."

Representatives of men's sports said they were mostly pleased with the majority report. "There's an acknowledgment that there is a problem, and that's a huge step," said Leo Kocher, head wrestling coach at the University of Chicago. "I think that what they're recommending falls short of what's going to be fair to males and females, and there's a lot more work to be done, but I'm grateful they listened."[39]

Arthur L. Coleman, who worked in the Education Department under Cantù, said the report dealt with many criticisms that have long been leveled against the Office for Civil Rights. What happens next, he said, largely depends on what form any new policies take. "If what the department ultimately puts out is really and truly a clarification, some further explanation or technical assistance that proves to be a very practical guidance of implications of this law, and it's consistent with prior standards, my supposition is that it would be unlikely to have to go through the formal rule-making process with notice and comments," said Coleman. "If the standards are changed, there's an obligation that they actually engage in that process."[40]

The press conference and the minority report, which received at least as much press as the actual report, appeared to have a galvanizing effect on defenders of Title IX, even those in unlikely spots. At his first NCAA convention in January 2003, the association's new president, Myles Brand, offered a qualified endorsement of the law. "We should move forward in fully implementing Title IX in a timely and aggressive manner, despite the discomfort of some individuals or institutions," said Brand, who had just been hired from Indiana University. One of his vice presidents, Judy Sweet, told a packed conference hall that the commission's ideas could cost women 10 to 33 percent of the participatory opportunities they enjoyed at a typical Division I institutions, as well as millions of dollars in athletics scholarships.

Their concerns were amplified by Robert Hemenway, chancellor of the University of Kansas and chairman of the Division I board of directors. "The board expressed a strong belief that Title IX has been exceptionally successful," he said. "If any change is going to be made, it's important that it not have the effect of restricting opportunities for women."[41]

When the commission published its final report, Brand criticized it in stronger terms. "Title IX is not broken, and it does not need to be fixed," he said during a speech at the National Press Club. "It needs to remain in place in its current form for it to be fully successful."[42] The secretary of education ought to reject any new interpretation of Title IX that could freeze women's participation rates at current levels, Brand said. He called himself an "advocate for gender equity," which he defined as having the number of female athletes at a college be proportional to the number of female undergraduates there.

Then, in June, Judge Emmet G. Sullivan resoundingly turned down the wrestlers' lawsuit. He ruled that the groups could not prove that overturning the rules would help their cause or that they had the appropriate legal standing to bring a lawsuit.[43] In his opinion, Sullivan wrote that the groups had "failed to meet their burden of persuasion on the question of whether they are the proper parties to be asserting the claims they raise against" the Education Department.[44]

Second, he wrote, even if they did have standing to sue the department, they had not proved that discarding the 1979 and 1996 policies would cause colleges to reinstate dropped teams. A "multiplicity of factors" plays into institutional decisions to drop sports, he said, and Title IX is one of them. Individuals and organizations are free to sue educational institutions for their actions under the law, but not the Education Department, he said.

A month later, the commission's report died a relatively quiet death. In July, Reynolds sent out a letter to college and high school officials saying the department would enforce Title IX rules as they stood. Reynolds—not Paige—said he was accepting only four recommendations:

> The department stated that "nothing in Title IX requires the cutting or reduction of men's teams in order to demonstrate compliance with Title IX, and the elimination of teams is a disfavored practice."
>
> The department's Office for Civil Rights "will aggressively enforce Title IX standards, including implementing sanctions for institutions that do not comply."
>
> The office will "ensure that its enforcement practices do not vary from region to region."
>
> Reynolds also noted that "private sponsorship of athletic teams would continue to be allowed," but that having private sponsors did not change an institution's obligations under Title IX.

Reynolds did have some harsh words for Cantù's 1996 clarification. "This led many schools to believe, erroneously, that they must take measures to ensure strict proportionality between the sexes," Reynolds wrote. "In fact each of the three prongs of the test is an equally sufficient means of complying with Title IX, and no one prong is favored."

Reynolds said that henceforth, the first test would not be given any more weight than the other two.[45]

The move infuriated coaches of wrestling and other men's teams that had been dropped by colleges. Jim McCarthy, a spokesman for the College Sports Council, said the White House and the Education Department had caved in to pressure from women's groups. "It's apparent that the Bush administration has sold out college kids across the country," McCarthy said, arguing that male athletes, especially walk-ons, would suffer most.[46]

Women's advocates, of course, were delighted. "I think it's great," said Grant. "Over all, the Department of Education is backing off entirely, and we've got to be really pleased."

Did the commission or Bush's first administration affect how the public, as well as schools and colleges, view Title IX and its requirements? Not really. Five colleges announced in 2003 they were dropping men's teams. A handful of others announced they were starting women's teams.

But the commission's work demonstrated how far Title IX has come politically. The fear of alienating the parents of soccer- and softball-playing daughters drove the Bush administration to punt on any changes to the law. The NCAA emerged as a force calling for strong enforcement of the law. And in law as well as the courts, the complaints of wrestlers and other male athletes were publicly shoved to the side.

Title IX, it seems, is here to stay.

CHAPTER

The Tragedy

Participating in sports is a tremendously valuable experience for anybody. The physical and social benefits are obvious. The educational benefits are a little harder to spot, but they are there. Sport can teach normative lessons on teamwork, respect for the rules of the game, and respect for one's opponents. Competition teaches courage, practice teaches perseverance, and playing for a championship requires an athlete to reach inside to summon abilities she may not have known she had. The heat of the game is a beautiful, passionate, captivating moment.

Dudley Allen Sargent knew that. Senda Berenson knew that. Teddy Roosevelt knew that. The coaches and athletes of the AIAW knew that. So do Pat Summitt, Leo Kocher, Julie Foudy, and all the other athletes, coaches, and professionals mentioned in these pages.

Americans cherish high school and college sports for the lessons taught on the field and court. Sport's value, in an educational setting, is as a means to an end, not as an end in itself.

But college sports for men, particularly at the country's largest colleges, has always been about other ends. Winning on the football field and basketball court, and occasionally in the hockey rink or baseball diamond, have always been a way for colleges to build goodwill among fans, alumni, state legislators, donors, and present and future students. Colleges have always tolerated recruiting students because of their athletic prowess and, even at the country's most prestigious institutions, have been willing to bend academic standards to bring in the best players. College sport has become a nakedly commercial enterprise, whether it is to bring in millions of dollars at Miami or Michigan or to attract new students to MacMurray College or Mount Union College.

The tragedy of Title IX's passage is that female athletes have been sucked into this mess.

Even beyond elite programs like Lady Vols basketball and Tar Heels soccer, the volume has been turned up on women's sports. Recruiting and winning are becoming all-encompassing goals, as they have been in men's programs for generations. More female athletes than ever have the chance to play and learn valuable lessons from sports, but they are becoming subject to the same pressures.

Recall the creed of the National Amateur Athletic Federation's Women's Division from chapter 1, and consider the state of women's sports in the early twenty-first century:

> College athletes, even those at small colleges, train and compete for years at schools and private clubs to earn the opportunity to compete in college. They are recruited extensively by coaches, compete in tryouts merely to earn a spot on the practice squad, and train for their sports year-round. This is true not just of football players, but of male and female athletes in all sports.
>
> Athletes' exploits are supposed to reflect well upon their colleges and schools. College presidents speak freely about the publicity their teams generate, and the fact that colleges are expected to compete in big-time sports if they are to be judged big-time institutions by fans and donors.
>
> Coaches at all levels are expected to train and prepare teams to compete for regional and national titles. In Division I of the NCAA, coaches' contracts typically include bonuses for conference and national titles. Division III colleges have rapidly expanded fields for championship tournaments in recent years, and colleges compete avidly for the National Directors' Cup, awarded to the institution with the best record in national championships in all sports.
>
> All-American awards are cherished for individual athletes, and while prevented from earning monetary prizes, athletes are given valuable souvenirs and favors for qualifying for postseason contests.
>
> Colleges employ entire departments to market and publicize their athletes and teams.
>
> Women now constitute a minority of the coaches of women's teams, and are a tiny minority of athletic administrators.
>
> Gate receipts, as well as television contracts and other moneymaking opportunities, dictate game times and schedules for both men's and women's sports.
>
> Teams compete in widely spread conferences, as well as in national competitions that send them across the country.
>
> Individual accomplishment and winning are the purpose of sport, while sportsmanship is widely perceived to be in decline.

In short, the lessons of the women's sports establishment have been subsumed by the male model of college sports. This is playing out in troubling ways: Female athletes suffer from particular physiological and emotional programs that rarely trouble male athletes, such as eating disorders and damage to knee ligaments. Female athletes' graduation rates are still far higher than those of male athletes and even of women who do not play sports, but researchers are finding evidence that female athletes are not performing up to their capabilities in the classroom. While white women have experienced a boom in participation opportunities, those from other ethnic backgrounds have not joined teams at the same rate. And the intensity of sport at all levels, from peewee to professional, has ratcheted up to troublesome levels.

Nowhere is this more prevalent than in college recruiting. The NCAA has rigid rules defining periods when and how often its coaches can contact prospective athletes. However, those athletes often attend high-level summer camps at colleges they are considering, getting personal coaching and interaction from the college's staff. Coaches are pressuring athletes to make a decision earlier and earlier in order to nail down their rosters.

In most girls' sports, athletes play on travel teams, private clubs in which parents hire well-qualified coaches to work with their children year-round. As the name implies, the teams travel across the country throughout the spring, summer, and fall, competing in a variety of showcase events and national tourneys that bill themselves as championships.

Parents spend two hundred dollars a month or more on coaches, uniforms, travel, and other expenses for children who are highly involved in club sports. A handful of these kids on the very best teams will have a chance to win scholarships to the top colleges in Division I in the NCAA. The rest play to fill out their brag sheets, to try to earn a spot on lower-level teams in any of the NCAA's three divisions, or because they cannot get enough of the game or their friends on the team.

They all play high school sports, too, but with just a touch of contempt, at least on their parents' part. High school coaching is a hit-or-miss prospect for elite players—many coaches are teachers who volunteer because they enjoy or have a little background in the sport, not the licensed, experienced coaches who take club jobs.

The competition for athletic scholarships is worrisome in itself. The joke on the field is that if a parent saved all the money she spent on soccer for her daughter, she'd be able to pay the daughter's way to college. But the intensity of that competition leads players to specialize in one sport at earlier ages, increasing the chances that players will burn out and stop enjoying sports and ruining the experience for all but the best athletes.

This is even an issue for young children, according to Bob Sterken, a soccer dad in Tyler, Texas. His daughter plays for the Ladybugs, an under-eight team coached by his wife, Alison. He describes a game played against their big rivals:

> The coaches on the other team had asked my wife and her assistant to lunch the day of the game. They wanted to talk about the North Texas Soccer Association playing rules. In particular, they wanted to discuss required playing time. They understood the rules on playing time to be that they were required to play a player for only one quarter of the game. At lunch these two coaches said that their U8 players have to "earn their playing time."
>
> Alison told him that the rules at U8 require each player to play for at least half of the game. That night at the game, the Ladybugs started strong and dominated play for the first quarter. And then Alison started playing her bench. They only play seven on the field including the keeper. She has four girls who do not yet have the speed, skills, nor the understanding to really play with the girls who are stronger and faster.
>
> After Alison started playing her weaker players the [other team] started scoring. I watched [their] bench closely. He did not play his weaker girls at all until well into the fourth quarter. With the game in hand and his weaker players still sitting on the bench in the cold night air, I walked over to him and politely suggested that it was time to let his bench have a little time on the field. He did not take this well.
>
> This coach asked me if I expected him "to just quit trying to win." I quietly told him that this game is about player fun and development not winning. He laughed and asked me what planet I was from. I fully expect those girls who sit the bench for his team to quit the game . . . soon . . . probably for good and they are only eight.[1]

This kind of specialization is not confined to girls' teams. Little boys have been concentrating on year-round sports for many years, but the trend for both sexes has gotten far more pronounced in recent years. Teenaged players in most sports attend college camps during the summer, hoping to catch the eye of coaches who will begin recruiting them in their junior and senior years. Many take private lessons with coaches who played in college or professional leagues. Football players compete in seven-on-seven leagues in the summers with their high school teammates, and both male and female basketball players participate in a complex schedule of camps and tournaments sponsored by the Amateur Athletic Union throughout the spring and summer.

Coaches and outside critics of college sports see two dangerous trends in the rush to specialization: the prioritization of skill development at the expense of academic and social development, and the steady whitening of the sports population. Because their parents can afford to live in areas with athletic fields and to ship them hither and yon for club teams and private lessons, middle-class children and especially white ones have been the direct beneficiaries of the professionalization of amateur sports.

One of the more prominent outside critics has been William G. Bowen, president of the Andrew W. Mellon Foundation and coauthor of *The Game of Life* and *Reclaiming the Game*. In essence, Bowen and coauthors James L. Shulman (*The Game of Life*) and Sarah A. Levin (*Reclaiming the Game*) argue that the country's most elite colleges, including the Ivy Leagues and the small New England liberal-arts colleges, are placing too much emphasis on athletics as they assemble their freshman classes every year. As a result they admit a large number of athletes whose academic credentials lag behind those of other students. The middle-class students who make up the majority of the applicants to these schools and their parents are not stupid, so they work hard on becoming elite, recruitable athletes in order to attend these institutions.

The Game of Life traces what the authors called a divide between athletes and other students that manifests itself in a variety of areas: high school academic credentials, grades in college, choice of major, and so forth. The divide is visible at all kinds of institutions, from big state universities like Michigan to small private women's colleges like Bryn Mawr.

"The first book [*The Game of Life*] suggested a lot of things, including the idea that the divide was widening," Bowen points out.[2] Presidents of institutions in the New England Small College Athletic Conference (NESCAC) asked for a look at more recent groups of students, he adds, "and what we found was that there is indeed evidence of widening. We got a better fix on the trends [in *Reclaiming the Game*]."

By analyzing the credentials and experiences of students who started college in 1995 and 1999, and by tracking blue-chip athletes who were highly sought by coaches, Bowen and Levin reached the conclusion that recruited athletes, who often constitute as much as 25 percent of the incoming classes at these institutions, receive a substantial advantage in admissions.

Harvard, Swarthmore, and other elite institutions admit only a tiny portion of their applicants, but athletes on coaches' lists have a much better chance of getting in than other students with comparable SAT scores and high school grades.

Athletes do not have the worst academic profiles of all admitted students, Bowen and Levin hasten to point out. However, there are more athletes toward the lower end of the class. Male nonathletes who applied to Ivy League universities in 1999 with SAT scores between 1100 and

1199 had almost no chance of getting in, while the odds for male athletes with those scores were fifty-fifty.

Once in college, the majority of recruited athletes end up toward the bottom of their classes. One might expect as much, given their lower credentials coming out of high school, but Bowen and Levin found that both male and female recruits underperform in college course work even relative to their test scores and high school grades.

Men who were recruited to play the high-profile sports of football, basketball, and ice hockey at NESCAC colleges in 1995 ranked, on average, in the nineteenth percentile of their graduating class, for example. Football players underperformed by nearly twenty percentile points—meaning that athletes whose high school credentials suggested that they would be around the fiftieth percentile of their college classes, instead were around the thirtieth percentile.

Of the class that entered Ivy League colleges in 1995, 45 percent of female recruited athletes finished college in the bottom third, as ranked by grade-point average. At NESCAC colleges in the New England, 34 percent of female recruits finished college in the bottom third of their classes, compared to only 21 percent of female students as a whole. (To be fair, critics point out that both the Ivies and the NESCAC colleges have gotten so competitive in recent years that there is very little difference in class rank, suggesting that rank-in-class may be more a matter of coincidence or a single bad grade.)

A 2004 study of Rice University athletics documented similar trends. Female athletes admitted to the prestigious Houston university in 2003 had SAT scores 16 percent below other female students, and on average, female athletes graduated with lower grade-point averages (2.91) than female students as a whole (3.35).[3]

The second consequence of specialization, the economic stratification of women's sports, is especially clear when looking at minority students. Asian-American and Hispanic students participate in college sports in tiny numbers. Black men represent more than half of all scholarship basketball, football and track athletes, according to NCAA track statistics. But women do not play football, and a much smaller proportion of black women participate in college sports.

Nearly a third of the women shooting hoops in Division I of the National Collegiate Athletic Association are black, as are nearly a quarter of female track athletes. But only 2.7 percent of the women receiving scholarships to play all other sports at predominantly white colleges in Division I are black. Yet those are precisely the sports—golf, lacrosse, and soccer, as well as rowing—that colleges have been adding to comply with Title IX.

Some experts blame the NCAA and the (white) women's sports establishment for promoting sports in which minority athletes are unlikely to participate. But the problem lies deeper than that: Coaches cannot be blamed for failing to recruit women of color, when so few of them show up in the clubs and tournaments that help top athletes develop. Colleges cannot really be lambasted for their choices of sports, when those sports simply do not draw minority women the way track and basketball do.

Brannon Johnson is one of the exceptions. A native of Philadelphia, she said in a 2001 interview that "we had family basketball games growing up," and in the neighborhood, "the height of competition was to see who could beat each other down to the corner store."[4] Now, though, Johnson is a rower on the varsity crew at the University of Texas at Austin. In 2001 she was adjusting to college life and college rowing. She is the first in her family to attend college. "People may look at you twice" at regattas, she says, because a black woman in a boat is still a rarity. But her teammates have made her welcome.

She got into rowing through a program for inner-city kids run by Vespers, one of the oldest rowing clubs on Philadelphia's Schuylkill River. By the time she finished high school, she was among the area's top rowers, and people along the banks of the river would yell, "Go, black girl!" as she raced by, much to her embarrassment.

Since 1987, when Congress passed the Civil Rights Restoration Act, the fastest-growing sports in the NCAA have been women's soccer, rowing, golf, and lacrosse. The numbers of teams and of athletes have doubled and in some cases tripled in all four sports.

However, the number of women's basketball and track teams has risen only about 26 percent, despite the scores of colleges that have migrated into the NCAA from the National Association of Intercollegiate Athletics over that time. (Of course, black women in basketball and track have benefited from Title IX in other ways, as colleges have spent money on those programs to improve their facilities, their coaching, and their visibility.)

College fields, courts, and rivers are now teeming with equestriennes, female soccer players, rowers, and other athletes, but almost all of them, close to 70 percent, are white.

Women from other minority groups are similarly underrepresented in college sports: Only 1.8 percent of all female athletes are Asian, and only 3 percent are Hispanic. Coaches are happy to look further afield, though: More than 7 percent of female athletes are from other countries.

And members of all minority groups except black women have been going out for Division I sports in increased numbers since 1990–91, according to NCAA statistics. The proportions of American Indian, Asian, Hispanic, and foreign athletes on women's teams have skyrocketed, while the proportion of black women has remained steady between 13.9 and 15.6 percent over the past decade. Even so, black women continue to outnumber women of all other races except white.

Researchers, coaches, and athletes themselves offer a number of reasons for the dearth of black women in sports, including economics, culture, and psychology. For Tina Sloan Green, though, they all revolve around access.

Green, the director of the Black Women in Sport Foundation and a professor of physical education at Temple University, points out that most urban high schools do not have the "green space," or open fields, needed for sports such as soccer, lacrosse, and especially golf. They do not have coaches for those sports. There is nothing to suggest to a girl that she might be successful at them.

"When you have access to a sport, either you have success, or someone else sees that they might be successful," said Green. "But the cities are so jammed up."

Green, who is African-American, has some experience in this area. As a student at Philadelphia's Girls' High School, for gifted students, she found herself with a variety of sports to play, and excelled at field hockey. At West Chester University of Pennsylvania, the lacrosse coach persuaded her to add that sport to her repertoire.

Green then coached both those sports at Temple, winning three national lacrosse titles in the 1980s with the Owls before leaving coaching in 1991 to concentrate on teaching and foundation work. Her daughter, Traci, played tennis at the University of Florida.

The Greens had access to good coaching and the junior tennis circuit, the costs of which are far out of reach for many families. Having a top-ranked junior tennis player can cost up to thirty thousand dollars a year, Green estimates.

Because virtually all of the good players go through the club system in most sports, all the coaches offering college scholarships do, too. Access to the rich talent on the playing fields of Dallas and Houston was part of what prompted Chris Petrucelli to leave a job as coach of the University of Notre Dame's women's soccer team for the same job at Texas in 1999.

"Soccer in the U.S. is a suburban sport with a lot of little white girls running around," said Petrucelli. "There are [African-American] kids out there, but the pool we look at is very selective and relatively small. There are usually one or two minorities in it. We recruit them, but we haven't gotten them yet."

Beyond the economic hurdles, black women who do find their way into sports such as soccer or crew often face problems because the vast majority of their teammates are white, according to Teresa P. Stratta, a sociologist at the University of Tennessee at Knoxville. "There's a high correlation between the number of African-Americans on a team and their cultural expression," says Stratta, who is white. She recently conducted a two-year ethnographic study of women's teams at Temple. "A low representation of black athletes leads to more cultural inhibitions, having to put up with listening to country [music] and things like that." If two or fewer players on a squad are black or from another minority group, they find that coaches stereotype them into certain positions, and teammates will not bond with them. It is an isolating experience, Stratta says. "Even if you get just three or four black athletes on a team, there's a dramatic difference," she argues. "And if it gets to 30 percent to 40 percent, you have the really dynamic environment where there's an interchange, a very healthy model."

Many historically black colleges and universities offer the sports that women of color shun at predominantly white institutions. But those colleges do not necessarily give students the best chances to compete.

Colleges in the Mid-Eastern and in the Southwestern Athletic Conferences—which together include all of the historically black colleges in Division I—tend to allocate less money for women's sports than other comparably sized predominantly white institutions in their regions. They also offer fewer playing opportunities for women, especially given the far greater proportion of women at those colleges.

Most colleges in the Mid-Eastern Conference (MEAC), for example, average about 60 percent female, while only 40.5 percent of the athletes at those institutions are women, for a difference of nearly twenty percentage points. In the Southern Conference, which consists of colleges in roughly the same region as the MEAC, the difference in proportions is only 12.7 points.

Colleges in the Southwestern Conference (SWAC) each spent an average of $607,452 on women's sports in 2000–2001, or 29 percent of their total operating budgets for sports. Colleges in the Southland Conference, by comparison, spent just over $1 million apiece on women's sports, or 40 percent of their overall operating budgets.

Part of the reason has to do with economics: Most historically black institutions sponsor football teams, which require many male athletes and a lot of money, but do not make profits that athletics departments could use for women's sports.

However, the same is true of many predominantly white colleges at the lower levels of Division I, yet more of them do a better job of accommodating female athletes than do most historically black colleges.

In the MEAC and the SWAC, the main concession athletics directors have made to women is adding bowling teams, which are cheap to support and do not require much training or any new facilities. The NCAA has named bowling an "emerging sport" for women, and by 1999–2000 there were twenty-one teams in Division I, more than any other added sport except water polo.

"Part of what we have found is that the sports at major institutions don't necessarily have strong support from our constituents at the high-school level, so there is no natural feeder system," said Charles S. Harris, former commissioner of the MEAC and chairman of the NCAA's Division I Management Council.

Harris adds that the population of elementary and high school students is growing increasingly diverse, and that the association might face a problem if nonwhite children continue to avoid the sports that are popular right now.

In the past, college coaches often would introduce themselves to women on campus who might make good athletes. Anita L. DeFrantz remembers walking to class at Connecticut College and seeing a long, skinny boat in front of a classroom building. "I went over to inquire, and there was a man standing there," recalls DeFrantz, who is African-American. "I didn't know he was the coach, but he said, 'This is rowing, and you'd be perfect for it.' Since I'd never been perfect at anything, I thought I'd give it a go."

That encounter led her to an outstanding career in rowing. She was named to the U.S. Olympic teams in 1976 and 1980, winning a bronze medal in the former (and earning a certain measure of notoriety for trying to sue President Carter for boycotting the latter). She is now president of the Amateur Athletic Foundation of Los Angeles and a member of the International Olympic Committee.

But her story is a little outdated, for most sports, thanks to the specialization trend. The chances of someone walking on to a Division I soccer team today, without being recruited or having years of experience, the way DeFrantz picked up rowing in the early 1970s, are somewhere between slim and none.

Is the largely white sports establishment to blame for the lack of black women in those sports? No and yes, according to administrators and advocates.

Coaches can't be blamed for recruiting only the most skilled athletes they can find, or at least that they can get into their institutions. They are paid to win, not to provide growth opportunities for athletes who cannot contribute.

Some advocates for female athletes blame the women's movement. According to Green of Temple, feminists, and particularly advocates for women's sports, have overlooked the needs of minority women. "When you increase scholarships in these sports, you're not going to help people of color," she said. "But that's not in their line of interest. Title IX was for white women. I'm not going to say black women haven't benefited, but they have been left out."

Donna Lopiano of the Women's Sports Foundation said Green has a point. "The women's movement is so focused on so many gender issues that the plight of women of color, who are in double jeopardy, is often-times on the back burner," Lopiano said.

Moreover, the NCAA's rules requiring athletes to meet minimum standards for scores on standardized tests to be eligible to play college sports have further restricted opportunities for black women, Green said.

Programs to encourage kids in urban areas to play nontraditional sports have been started by most of the national governing bodies of various sports, including the U.S. Tennis Association, the U.S. Soccer Federation, and others. They have not borne much fruit, but college coaches are hoping for a parallel to the "Tiger Woods effect"—kids from unusual backgrounds getting interested in their sports, much as they did in golf when Woods emerged as a star in the late 1990s.

The NCAA and its member colleges also have encouraged these kinds of efforts through the National Youth Sports Program, a college-based effort that involves coaches and athletes in putting on clinics and organizing games for children throughout the country.

The final, and in some cases most troubling, trend arising from the rapid increase in women's sports participation is the set of health consequences that affect female athletes at much higher rates than male athletes. One of these starts at the knee: Women suffer from debilitating tears of the anterior cruciate ligament, or ACL, in outsized numbers. The *Chronicle of Higher Education*'s Jennifer Jacobson recounts the story of two soccer players suffering the exact same injury within minutes of each other:

> Heather Terry, a junior on the University of Virginia's women's soccer team, was playing defense against two teammates when she planted her right foot and turned to the left. Her right shoe got stuck in the damp grass, and her right knee twisted. She heard it pop. She fell, then screamed. And immediately, she knew what she had done.
>
> She knew in part because she had seen her teammate, Brooke Stastny, a sophomore, limp off the field 10 minutes earlier. Both players had torn their anterior cruciate ligaments, and entered ACL hell.[5]

The ACL is one of four ligaments stabilizing the knee and the upper tibia, or shinbone. It tears, as Terry discovered, when an athlete twists his or her knee or lands on the ground at an angle that puts an enormous amount of stress on it. It can take surgery and up to six months of difficult and painful rehabilitation to get the knee back to normal after an ACL tear.

Women are between four and six times more likely to tear their ACLs during athletic activity than male athletes, according to most studies. Professionals disagree about reasons for the disparity. Some blame women's hormonal cycles, arguing that estrogen levels can weaken ligaments like the ACL. Others suggest that women's wider hips and lower centers of gravity place more stress on ACLs. Still others argue that ACL injuries should not be regarded as an anatomical flaw, but rather as a result of persistent inequities in girls' sports opportunities: Boys grow up running and jumping around more than girls, training their knees to stiffen and strengthening them so that when they begin playing organized sports, rupturing an ACL is less likely.

As women's sports programs have grown, though, so have the number of sports-medicine and strength-and-conditioning specialists with an expertise in women's sports. Many colleges have developed specific strength programs for female athletes to cut down on ACL tears.

An even more profound health problem is what has become known as the "female athlete triad": amenorrhea, eating disorders, and early-onset osteoporosis. Thanks to social mores, women are often more worried about their weight than men are, and in athletes, weight concerns are exacerbated by the obvious fact that women who weigh less may be able to run faster, jump higher, or throw themselves into more somersaults. This leads female athletes into eating less. This can disrupt menstrual cycles and lead to inadequate dietary intake of essential nutrients like iron and calcium. Because women athletes burn so many calories, they are at a much higher risk of becoming anorexic.

Coaches are often a part of the problem rather than part of the solution. Many coaches hold weigh-ins, monitoring their athletes' weight very closely. One woman who had run track at an Ivy League university told me her coach had required athletes to weigh themselves before and after every practice as a way of making sure they did not get too dehydrated. An appropriate goal, but as she put it, she and her teammates were already obsessed about their weight, and the weigh-ins only made things worse.

Another runner at a respected college told me that during her freshman year, she and her roommate were amazed to see their older teammates hold unspoken contests to see who could eat the least. By the end of the year, though, she found herself restricting herself to salads, just like the upperclassmen on the team.

The growing intensity of girls' sports also may be contributing to another trend: teenage obesity. First, girls who have been identified as "talented" at an early age compete year-round in clubs, camps, and private sessions. By dint of repetition, they develop skills that other children, who may be "late bloomers" or may possess less obvious physical talents, do not. Thus, club players come to dominate middle-school teams and varsity clubs, leaving the late bloomers with no place to play. At the same time, "unstructured" time to run around and play with kids in the neighborhood is losing out to the constant round of practices and games.

Experts on youth sports also fear that increased expectations and year-round competition ruin sports for children. Due to injuries, stress, or simple boredom, participating in sports loses its charm for a great many. A study in *U.S. News & World Report* found that the most popular team sports for kids—basketball, soccer, softball, and baseball—all lost participants between 1998 and 2002.[6]

At the same time, school funding crises have pushed physical-education classes far down on the priority list for most middle and high schools. In Boston, requirements for physical-education classes dropped from ninety minutes per week to thirty-five minutes per week between 1998 and 2004.[7] In Florida, more than half of high school students did not participate in any form of PE in 2003.[8]

The danger is that sports for both sexes could be confined to those identified as "athletes" very early in life. With fewer educational and recreational opportunities, the vast majority of children are losing chances to receive the benefits of participation in sports—not just the health benefits, but also the chances to learn self-discipline, teamwork, perseverance, and the other values that sport can teach. This would be the ultimate repudiation of the ideals of Senda Berenson, Mabel Lee, Constance Appleby, and the other figures who developed a philosophy and practice of women's sports.

Chronicling these problems is not supposed to be an indictment of women's sports, or a suggestion that women should not be participating in athletics. Instead, in adapting to the highly competitive, often ethically questionable world of men's scholastic sports, women face certain challenges that they did not during the era when women's sports were controlled by physical-education departments. Does that mean something is wrong with women, or with the men's system?

12
CHAPTER
•

Triumph?

Title IX and its application to sports have certainly evolved since 1972, thanks to the many challenges, lawsuits, and controversies that have confronted it. In the main, it has been extraordinarily but not completely successful: It has created opportunities for thousands of female athletes, and it has forced the American public to recognize the value of women's sports, but women's teams still lack the deep cultural significance that athletics departments ascribe to men's sports. As a result, women still lag behind men in participation and funding in both high school and college sports.

These lags are more noticeable because Title IX has been so successful outside sports. Nearly 60 percent of college undergraduates are women nationwide, and at many colleges and universities that percentage is pushing 70 percent. More than half of law students in 2003 were women, and female students have made significant inroads in medical schools and even engineering schools. As a result, women are rapidly becoming a majority population in many professional settings, and it is not unreasonable to think that women could dominate law, politics, government, and much of the rest of society within the next ten to twenty-five years.

On campus, sports have become men's last bastion. In 2002–3, men were 59.1 percent of the roughly 500,000 athletes on varsity teams.[1] While a record 2.8 million girls played high school sports that year, they represented only 41.7 percent of all athletes.[2]

These numbers may not change much in the future for a simple reason: football. A quarter of all male athletes play the sport in college, nearly 75,000 in all in 2002–3. On average, teams had 90 players apiece, and eighty-seven had 120 or more. These huge numbers are necessary, coaches say, because since the 1940s colleges have played platoon football, with separate groups of players taking the field for offensive, defensive, kickoff, receiving, and field-goal plays. Players usually graduate high school already specializing in a particular area of the field, such as the defensive backfield or the offensive line, and even in particular positions, like running back or free safety.

The Javits amendment allows for reasonable "provisions considering the nature of particular sports" in determining how colleges fund and populate their sports teams, so spending larger sums of money on the sport and having many more male participants than female does not necessarily violate Title IX. But it places a tremendous amount of stress on athletics departments, particularly when university lawyers decide to comply with the first part of the three-part test and athletics directors see rivals building new facilities primarily for football and paying coaches more and more money. Many Division I-A coaches make more than a million dollars a year now, and several make more than $2 million.

So the number of male athletes continues to fall. Division I-A institutions outside the six most lucrative athletics conferences cut an average of twenty-seven men apiece between 2002 and 2003.[3] The population of female athletes may continue to drop as well—several colleges have threatened to drop women's teams as a cost-saving measure in the early part of the twenty-first century, and at least one, the University of Massachusetts at Amherst, has.

Football at all levels gathers a community like no other sport. Part of the attraction is the short and well-defined length of the season: Teams play between eight and sixteen games through the fall, mostly on Fridays (high school), Saturdays (college), and Sundays (professional). Another reason for this country's obsession with the sport is the brutality. And a third is the spectacle—the bands, the cheerleaders, the thousands of fans in the stands for the most popular contests.

In addition, smaller colleges in Divisions II and III of the NCAA as well as two-year colleges and other institutions are using football to boost their male enrollments. The general consensus is that having a team will attract not only the men on the team but also their friends and other male students who want to go to a "football school." Many colleges started the sport in the late 1990s and 2000s, even those with relatively small numbers of female athletes. The Education Department has never rendered an opinion on whether creating a gender imbalance in athletics to ameliorate one elsewhere in an institution is appropriate.

For all of these reasons, football is not going away any time soon, nor are the huge numbers of male athletes on squads.

Neither, though, is Title IX. Nine appeals courts have now ruled on the validity of the law and its rules applying to athletics, and all of them have upheld both. In 2004, the federal Court of Appeals for the District of Columbia denied an appeal from the National Wrestling Coaches' Association in its lawsuit against the Education Department, ruling that the coaches could not prove that changing the regulations would bring their teams back. (A senior judge on the circuit, Stephen Williams, thought otherwise, arguing in a dissent that the coaches' claim would have merit if they could prove that the Title IX policies were a substantial factor in coaches losing their jobs. He joined Torruella and Coyle as the only judges to rule against Title IX regulations or to dissent from a ruling upholding them.)[4]

It is possible that the second Bush administration might revisit the regulations. But it is likely that Congress would have to pass or at least review any revision. A Republican-controlled Congress might be willing to take up the issue, led by J. Dennis Hastert, the Illinois Republican who has been Speaker of the House since 1994. Congress could pass any law it chose, although voting to preserve men's sports or rolling back protection for women's sports would give women's groups a chance to demonize individual congressmen who voted for it. Observers thought Congress might put Title IX revisions into the reauthorization of the Higher Education Act following the 2004 election, but nothing happened during initial deliberations over the bill in May 2004.

A simpler process would be to issue a new policy interpretation, essentially overriding the 1979 interpretation. If the department erased the three-part test and issued a simpler guideline—for example, a statement that colleges ought to offer sports to men and women in response to demonstrated interest and ability—colleges would have an easier time complying. However, women's groups would undoubtedly take the department to court over the reversal, given Congress's explicit support of the law in the 1987 Civil Rights Restoration Act and the wealth of case law supporting the current interpretation of the rules.

The essence of the debate over Title IX comes down to the fact that Americans have not decided what "fair" means when it comes to opening up opportunities to people previously excluded. Conservatives hold that fairness has nothing to do with the numbers of people involved in a certain activity, and that if colleges (or any other organization) try to fix the proportion of female participants to match the proportion of the overall female population, they are imposing a quota system.

But satisfying a demonstrated interest is not necessarily "fair," either. If girls were given the coaching, encouragement, and exposure to sports that boys are, differences in participation levels might well disappear, according to proponents of women's sports. They clearly are not disappearing, so shouldn't the law encourage the institutions it covers to create the conditions to bring about better circumstances for women? That, after all, seems to be its mandate.

The larger point, though, is Title IX does not require schools and colleges to make everything fair for everybody. Instead, it requires schools and colleges not to discriminate on the basis of sex. Because these schools and colleges have chosen to offer sports opportunities, and to do so in a way that male and female students are separated, then they need to find a way to prove that they are offering equitable opportunities. And nobody has come up with a better means of allowing colleges to define "equitable" for themselves than the three-part test.

But the controversy over participation standards and the three-part test has overshadowed the still-dramatic inequities in how male and female athletes are treated. Sometimes it is as simple as men's teams getting new uniforms every season. Sometimes it is as much as a university like Oregon treating its football team to a brand-new, $3.2 million locker room with plasma-screen televisions and Internet access at every locker, when female athletes get no such amenities.[5]

The reason, of course, is that big-time college sports are a business, and men's basketball and football teams are treated like precious commodities. Even though they added roughly sixty women athletes apiece over the previous eight years, Division I institutions spent twice as much on men's sports ($6.1 million, on average) in 2002–3 as they did on women's sports ($3.1 million). The head coaches of women's teams made $55,000 apiece, on average, while head men's coaches made $101,000. Colleges spent $200,000 on recruiting budgets for male athletes, but only $97,000 on recruiting women.[6]

Also putting pressure on this equation is the diversity of Division I. Its members range from small liberal-arts colleges like Davidson and Lafayette to flagship state universities like Michigan and Texas. From both a numerical and budgetary standpoint, the gap between the biggest athletics programs and their smaller rivals appears to be growing. Along with lucrative television contracts and bowl-game arrangements, colleges in the elite Bowl Championship Series leagues (the Atlantic Coast, Big East, Big Ten, Big 12, Pacific-10, and Southeastern Conferences) reported average annual revenues of $41 million in 2002–3, while Division I-A teams outside the BCS had revenues of $15 million.

Exacerbating the disparities are state budget cutbacks, which are forcing colleges to cut sports budgets as well. State universities in Tennessee have dropped numerous sports—East Tennessee State even got rid of football in 2003—and many more may be on the chopping block.

Yet smaller Division I institutions are desperate for the imprimatur of membership in "the big time," however that is defined, and so they keep paying the fixed costs of football and men's basketball so that they may continue rubbing shoulders with the Michigans and Texases in the rankings.

As a result, the small fry are getting pummeled—even in women's sports. In 2001–2, the only non-BCS institutions to win national women's championships in Division I were those with a particular specialty: Brigham Young University (cross-country), the University of Minnesota at Duluth (ice hockey), Princeton University (lacrosse), Harvard University (rowing), and the University of Portland (soccer). The rest were dominated by teams from the major conferences, like the University of Florida and the University of California at Los Angeles.[7]

Meanwhile, ignoring the disparities in spending, college officials complain that they cannot find enough women to fill the spots they have available. Teams may "bloat up the number of women on their roster the first day knowing that in the end, those student-athletes don't have access to coaching, [and] might not have access to facilities," said Ted Leland, Stanford's athletics director, during the Education Department's hearings on Title IX and sports.[8]

Many colleges try to boost their numbers of female athletes to look closer to Title IX compliance than they may be, Leland said. At Indiana State University, every women's team except basketball had rosters much larger than the averages in 2001–2. The Sycamores' soccer team had thirty athletes, while NCAA colleges average twenty, and only eleven play at a time. The softball team carried twenty-three athletes, compared to a national average of seventeen, and the tennis team had fourteen. Only six tennis players compete in a match.

"We expect coaches of our women's sports to actively recruit, and to recruit walk-ons," said Andrea Myers, Indiana State's athletics director at the time. But her roster numbers were taken from the first day of practice, as is the case for most colleges reporting gender-equity statistics. Women's teams suffer more attrition than men's over the course of the season because, Myers said, female athletes generally will not stay on a team unless they are getting playing time and having a good experience. Many athletics officials across the country report similar experiences.

"I always say women have more to their lives than sports," Myers said. "Guys want to be part of a team—the smell of the locker room, I don't know. Women like sports, and if they're given the opportunity to play and compete, they're going to stay. But if they're not out there playing on a pretty regular basis, they find other things to do with their time."[9]

Athletics directors at universities like Indiana State have an unenviable task: keeping their teams competitive and treating male and female athletes equitably without access to the revenue that flows from stadiums and arenas at places like Indiana University and Notre Dame. Colleges can solve the equity part—the vast majority of Division I institutions without football teams have essentially the same number of female athletes as males—but being competitive is harder.

So the question is whether men's nonrevenue sports and, farther down the line, women's sports will be able to thrive in the hypercompetitive environment of college sports, regardless of the fate of the 1979 policy interpretation and the 1996 clarification. At the moment, many athletics directors seem to treat women's sports as a kind of regulatory burden, something they have to maintain in order to preserve their status. Hence the growth of sports that are at the very least unusual, such as rowing in the Midwest, equestrian (a noun, not an adjective, in the NCAA) in the South, bowling among historically black colleges, and any other sport where coaches can carry a large number of women on the roster. The University of Maryland, for example, redefined women's cheerleading as a competitive sport in 2003, in part to avoid having to cut men's teams.[10] Maryland has one of the few wrestling teams left in the Atlantic Coast Conference.

It is quite possible that more colleges will begin cutting women's teams as well, as costs continue to rise. The University of Washington tried to drop men's and women's swimming in 2001, and the University of Northern Iowa tried to drop men's tennis in 2002, but public pressure and the threat of lawsuits forced officials to change their minds.

No major changes in the way college sports work are on the horizon. Officials have been talking about ways to reform athletics for a hundred years, and no move has yet succeeded. The only radical solution that appears possible is if colleges were required to professionalize the revenue sports, paying players a salary and not forcing them to attend college. This could happen if a player won a lawsuit that forced a college to declare him an employee of the university, entitling him to market-driven pay, workmen's-compensation benefits, and other legal rights not afforded to "amateur" athletes.

Were this to happen, colleges might operate a two-tier system—professional sports teams and truly amateur teams as recreational pursuits for students. A small fraction of universities might choose to professionalize women's sports, but the main point is that there would be no incentive to treat male and female athletes in amateur sports differently. The professional teams would no longer function as educational programs, so they would be exempt from Title IX considerations.

Regardless of whether that happens down the road, women's sports do have a future as business enterprises. Although professional women's teams have not succeeded in capturing America's imagination, collegiate women's teams will continue to attract local and regional audiences as more generations grow up with women's sports surrounding them. It make take another twenty years, but in some sections of the country, women's soccer and volleyball could come to occupy as prominent a place in local culture as Lady Vols basketball or Tar Heels soccer does now. After all, that is how men's college and professional sports evolved, beginning as local attractions before becoming national phenomena.

But what does the marketability of women's sports have to do with the ethos of athletics as education, of "a girl for every sport, and a sport for every girl"? Senda Berenson and Mabel Lee would be horrified by the way women's sports are governed today, and would probably argue that the problems detailed in the previous chapter are a direct result of the evolution toward high-stakes, hypercompetitive sport. Should women's sports be even more commercialized, the academic problems that have plagued men's sports since the beginning may well find their way into women's sports, completing the demolition of the ideals of the AIAW and previous generations of physical educators.

The officials trying to keep men's sports in line with university ideals have had a hard time, stretching back to the early days of the NCAA. The association has steadily raised academic standards for athletes in stages since 1986, but coaches and athletes have just as steadily found ways around them. Professors have suggested disclosing athletes' grades to show whether they are getting by with the least amount of work. College presidents and conference commissioners have suggested making freshmen ineligible, thereby creating an incentive for athletes with professional ambitions to skip college entirely and go directly into professional sports. None of these solutions has mustered enough support to be attempted.

In Division III, Bowen has suggested a series of steps to reduce the intensity and value placed on sports by top liberal-arts colleges. Among them: making sure that athletes are recruiting athletes with the same credentials and academic outcomes as other students; creating more opportunities for students who are not highly recruited out of high school; and reducing the emphasis on national championships. Some Division III institutions are also pushing the NCAA to reduce the length of seasons and to find other ways of de-emphasizing sports.

All of these are controversial at all kinds of colleges. College presidents and athletics directors argue that athletes and events contribute immeasurably to the life of a college, in ways that do not translate directly to academic outcomes. Football and basketball games rally an entire community, creating something for fans, students, and alumni to take joy and pride in. Even if athletes are not doing as well as other students in the classroom, by having some exposure to college life, they benefit from an experience they might not have had otherwise.

The NCAA is trying to send a stronger message about the importance of the educational goals of college sports, as evidenced by the elevation of academic standards. However, colleges send a powerful message to parents by rewarding them for allowing their children to play a single sport year-round, to the exclusion of other activities. If sport offers a stronger guarantee of college admission than study—and Bowen's work indicates that is true not just at big-time sports powerhouses, but also at the country's most prestigious colleges—who can blame a student or parent from diving into sports?

The future of women's athletics is bound up in how colleges grapple with these issues. However, American society has embraced Title IX. Female athletes are part of the mainstream now at all levels, from tiny-tot soccer to professional basketball and even college football. Women's wrestling is an Olympic sport, starting with the 2004 Olympics.

Women now have a wealth of opportunities to find sports that best suit them and offer all the benefits of an athletic lifestyle. With only a modicum of talent, a female athlete can play soccer in recreational leagues as a child, compete on varsity teams in high school and college, and find adult leagues in most cities for the rest of her life. The same holds true for many other sports.

This is the triumph of Title IX. Parents now have the same expectations of their daughters as they do of their sons. In most cases, little girls have the chance to learn the same lessons, dream the same dreams, and shoot for the same goals as little boys.

And any girl who expresses a desire to play college sports, and shows the willingness to work hard to be an athlete, will find herself a place on a team.

ACKNOWLEDGMENTS

•

This book is a work of journalism. I do not believe anyone, much less a reporter, is capable of being completely objective, but he should do everything in his power to be fair and accurate. That is what I have striven to do here.

I was born about two months after Congress passed Title IX. I grew up in a place (Decatur, Georgia) where girls were expected to do everything boys were—math, music, sports, and so on. My high school, the Westminster Schools, was the same way. I did not realize that male and female sports could be treated differently until I arrived at the University of Missouri for graduate school and watched forty thousand people come to a meaningless football game against the University of North Texas. Even though I had grown up in the Deep South and ran cross-country (and complained bitterly about the favoritism shown football players), I had not realized how great the gap is between major and minor sports at all institutions except the very richest.

In studying and writing about college sports for the past decade, I have observed time and time again that the economics of college sports are responsible for the demise of men's gymnastics and wrestling. No athletics director wants to drop sports, but that is what he or she does when money is tight. Nobody ever freezes coaches' salaries or cuts back or tells the football team to use uniforms for a second year.

Furthermore, after talking to people like Birch Bayh, it has become clear to me that the law was intended to end discrimination against women in education, not to require colleges to cater to men's or women's interests in any particular measure.

Some people will consider these themes throughout the book to be my personal opinions and will accuse me of slanting my findings to fit them. Regardless of what anyone thinks, I arrived at them after years of believing Title IX to be a silly and superfluous law, and yelling at Education Department officials when they tried to tell me otherwise. As a track and cross-country runner, I am watching my sport vanish, too, and the obvious temptation is to blame a federal law for overregulating college athletics.

My task here is to contextualize Title IX and explain how the law and the court decisions following it have shaped sports and our larger culture. I hope that doing so will help people understand a little more about scholastic sports in this country and the culture wars that have played out in the gymnasiums and fields of American educational institutions.

I would not have been in a position to do any of this without having worked for the *Chronicle of Higher Education*. Doug Lederman and Scott Jaschik brought me to Washington in 1998 and trusted me to set the newspaper's agenda for covering college sports, particularly the Title IX debate, and my current editors, Phil Semas and Bill Horne, have continued that trust.

Bill Bowen and James Shulman at the Andrew W. Mellon Foundation pushed me deeper into the issues of Title IX and were kind enough to introduce me to Tim Sullivan and Peter Dougherty at Princeton University Press. Tim deserves all of the credit (and none of the blame) for making this into a real book.

The people who have fought the war for and against Title IX have been generous with their time and opinions. They include Donna Lopiano of the Women's Sports Foundation, Christine Grant of the University of Iowa, Marcia Greenberger of the National Women's Law Center, and Bernice "Bunny" Sandler of the Women's Research and Education Institute. Others who have shaped my thinking include Kenneth R. Tolo of the National Association of Schools of Public Administration; Leo Kocher of the University of Chicago; J Robinson of the University of Minnesota; Eric Pearson of the College Sports Council; and Dick Aronson of the Collegiate Gymnastic Association. The two true experts in this country on Title IX and sports are Val Bonnette of Good Sports and Lamar Daniel. Over the years, it has been a privilege to learn the ins and outs of the law from them. The players, parents, and coaches of the Potomac Mischief of the Washington Area Girls Soccer league have been generous with their time and thoughts.

A multitude of other friends and sources have shaped my understanding of the law and college sports: Myles Brand, my "agent" Jason Carmel, Joe Castiglione, Cedric Dempsey, Maureen Devlin, Jessica Gavora, Lou Goldstein, Jamie Hagerbaumer, Teha Kennard, Bob Lipsyte, Priscilla McChristian, Elaine Michaelis, Jean Lenti Ponsetto, Wally Renfro, Eleanor Smeal, Shelley Steinbach, Lu Wallace, Sarah Warren, and Steve Wieberg. Elsa Kircher Cole was kind enough to critique the manuscript, and Murray Sperber was a font of inspiration, wisdom, encouragement, and criticism all the way through the process. Jeff Orleans, possibly the wisest person in college sports, spent far too much of his time walking me through the history, legal theory, and implications of Title IX.

Special thanks to the staff of Lauinger Library at Georgetown University, especially the staff of the Federal Documents and Microforms section; and to the staff of the Theodore R. McKeldin and Hornbake Libraries at the University of Maryland, including Lauren Brown.

Finally, I would not have understood what sport is and ought to be without my coaches, Robert Shankman and Joe Tribble, or without my parents, David and Susan Suggs, who always encouraged my sister and me to do whatever we wanted and do it excellently. And especially my sister, Darby Armont, who showed me what it really means to be an athlete.

All quotations from individuals are from interviews conducted in 2003, unless otherwise noted. All citations from rulings or other legal documents are taken from documents in Lexis-Nexis, unless otherwise noted.

APPENDIX A

•

TITLE IX OF THE EDUCATION AMENDMENTS OF 1972

Full text of Title IX taken from Senate Conference Report 92-798, contained in 12971-3, *Senate Miscellaneous Reports on Public Bills* III, 148–50.

Sex Discrimination Prohibited

Sec. 901

(a) No person in the United States shall, on the basis of sex, be excluded from participation in, be denied the benefits of, or be subjected to discrimination under any education program or activity receiving Federal financial assistance, except that:

(1) in regard to admissions to educational institutions, this section shall apply only to institutions of vocational education, professional education, and graduate higher education, and to public institutions of undergraduate higher education;

(2) in regard to admissions to educational institutions, this section shall not apply (A) for one year from the date of enactment of the Act, nor for six years after such date in the case of an educational institution which has begun the process of changing from being an institution which admits only students of one sex to being an institution which admits students of both sexes, but only if it is carrying out a plan for such change which is approved by the Commissioner of Education or (B) for seven years from the date an educational institution begins the process of changing from being an institution which admits only students of one sex to being an institution which admits students of both sexes, but only if it is carrying out a plan for such change which is approved by the Commissioner of Education, whichever is the later;

(3) this section shall not apply to an educational institution which is controlled by a religious organization if the application of this subsection would not be consistent with the religious tenets of such organization;

(4) this section shall not apply to an educational institution whose primary purpose is the training of individuals for the military services of the United States, or the merchant marine; and

(5) in regard to admissions this section shall not apply to any public institution of undergraduate higher education which is an institution that traditionally and continually from its establishment has had a policy of admitting only members of one sex.

(b) Nothing contained in subsection (a) of this section shall be interpreted to require any educational institution to grant preferential or disparate treatment to the members of one sex on account of an imbalance which may exist with respect to the total number or percentage of persons of that sex participating in or receiving the benefits of any federally supported program or activity, in comparison with the total percentage of persons of that sex in any community, state, section, or other area: Provided, That this subsection shall not be construed to prevent the consideration in any hearing or proceeding under this title of statistical evidence tending to show that such an imbalance exists with respect to the participation in, or receipt of the benefits of, any such program or activity by the members of one sex.

(c) For purposes of this title, an educational institution means any public or private preschool, elementary, or secondary school, or any institution of vocational, professional, or higher education, except that in the case of an educational institution composed of more than one school, college, or department which are administratively separate units, such terms means each such school, college, or department.

Federal Administrative Enforcement

Sec. 902. Each Federal department and agency which is empowered to extend Federal financial assistance to any education program or activity, by way of grant, loan, or contract other than a contract of insurance or guaranty, is authorized and directed to effectuate the provisions of section 901 with respect to such program or activity by issuing rules, regulations, or orders of general applicability which shall be consistent with achievement of the objectives of the statute authorizing the financial assistance in connection with which the action is taken. No such rule, regulation, or order shall become effective unless and until approved by the President. Compliance with any requirement adopted pursuant to this section may be effected (1) by the termination of or refusal to grant or to continue assistance under such program or activity to any recipient as to whom there has been an express finding on the record, after opportunity for hearing, of a failure to comply with such requirement, but such termination or refusal shall be limited to the particular political entity, or part thereof, or other recipient as to whom such a finding has been made, and shall be limited in its effect to the particular program, or part thereof, in which such noncompliance has been found, or (2) by any other means authorized by law: Provided, however, That no such action shall be taken until the department or agency concerned has advised the appropriate person or persons of failure to comply with the requirement and has determined that such compliance cannot be secured by voluntary means. In the event of any action terminating, or refusing to grant or continue, assistance because of failure to comply with a requirement imposed pursuant to this section, the head of the Federal department or agency shall file with the committees of the House and Senate having legislative jurisdiction over the program or activity involved a full written report of the circumstances and the grounds for such action. No such action shall become effective until thirty days have elapsed after the filing of such report.

Judicial Review

Sec. 903. Any department or agency action taken pursuant to section 902 shall be subject to such judicial review as may otherwise be provided by law for similar action taken by such department or agency on other grounds. In the case of action, not otherwise subject to judicial review, terminating or refusing to grant or to continue financial assistance upon a finding of failure to comply with any requirement imposed pursuant to section 902, any person aggrieved (including any State or political subdivision thereof and any agency of either) may obtain judicial review of such action in accordance with chapter 7 of title 5, United States Code, and such action shall not be deemed committed to unreviewable agency discretion within the meaning of section 701 of that title.

Prohibition against Discrimination against the Blind

Sec. 904. No person in the United States shall, on the ground of blindness or severely impaired vision, be denied admission in any course of study by a recipient of Federal financial assistance for any educational program or activity, but nothing herein shall be construed to require any such institution to provide special services to such person because of his blindness or visual impairment.

Effect on Other Laws

Sec. 905. Nothing in this title shall add to or detract from any existing authority with respect to any program or activity under which Federal financial assistance is extended by way of a contract of insurance or guaranty.

Amendments to Other Laws

Sec. 906. (a) Sections 401(b), 407(a)(2), 410, and 902 of the Civil Rights Act of 1964 (42 U.S.C. 2000c(b), 2000c-6(a)(2), 2000c-9, and 2000h-2) are each amended by inserting the word "sex" after the word "religion."

(b)

(1) Section 13(a) of the Fair Labor Standards Act of 1938 (29 U.S.C. 213(a)) is amended by inserting after the words "the provisions of section 6" the following: "(except 6(d) in the case of paragraph (1) of this subjection)."

(2) Paragraph (1) of subsection 3(r) of such Act (29 U.S.C. 203(r)(1)) is amended by deleting "an elementary or secondary school" and inserting in lieu thereof "a preschool, elementary or secondary school."

(3) Section 3(s)(4) of such Act (29 U.S.C.(s)(4)) is amended by deleting "an elementary or secondary school" and inserting in lieu thereof "a preschool, elementary or secondary school."

Interpretation with Respect to Living Facilities

Sec. 907. Notwithstanding anything to the contrary contained in this title, nothing contained herein shall be construed to prohibit any educational institution receiving funds under this Act, from maintaining separate living facilities for the different sexes.

•

FOUNDING MEMBERS OF THE ASSOCIATION FOR INTERCOLLEGIATE ATHLETICS FOR WOMEN

Appalachian State College
Arizona State University
Arkansas Poly College
Ashland College
Auburn Community College
Averett College
Ball State University
Bates College
Bemidji State College
Berea College
Bergen Community College
Berkshire Community College
Bloomsburg State College
Brandeis University
Brown University
Butler University
Brigham Young University
College of Mt. Joseph
College of William & Mary
College of Wooster
California State University at Fresno
California State University at Long Beach
California State University at Los Angeles
California Polytechnic State University at Pomona

California Lutheran College
Castleton State College
Catonsville Community College
Central Michigan University
Central Missouri State College
Central State University (Okla.)
Central Washington State College
Chicago State University
Colby College
Colby Junior College
College of Idaho
Colorado State University
Cornell University
East Stroudsberg State College
Eastern Kentucky University
Eastern Washington State College
East Carolina University
Federal City College
Ferrum College
Fitchburg State College
Flathead Valley Community College
Florida Presbyterian College
Franklin College
Georgetown University
Goshen College
Goucher College
Grand Valley State College

Greenville College (Ill)
Grossmont College
Hartwick College
Haskell Indian Junior College
Herbert H. Lehman College
Hollins College
Illinois State University
Indiana State University
Iowa State University
Iowa Wesleyan University
Indiana University at Bloomington
Kansas State Teachers College
Keene State College
Kellogg Community College
Kent State University
Knox College
Lamar University
Longwood College
Lorain County Community College
Luther College
Lynchburg College
Madison College
Mankato State College
Mary Washington College
McPherson College
Mesa Community College
Michigan State University
Millersville State College
Mills College
Mississippi State College for Women
Morgan State College
Mount San Antonio College
Mount Union College
Nasson College
North Dakota State University
Newcomb College
Northeastern Illinois State
 University
Northeastern Junior College

Northeastern University
Northern Illinois University
Northern State College (S.D.)
Northwest Missouri State College
Oakland College
Occidental College
Ocean County College
Old Dominion University
Ohio University
Oklahoma State University
Oregon College of Education
Oregon State University
Pacific Lutheran University
Palm Beach Junior College
Pennsylvania State University
Phoenix College
PMC Colleges
Pomona College
Portland State University
Princeton University
Purdue University
Queens College
Randolph-Macon Women's College
Rangely Junior College
Rhode Island College
Ricks College
Sacramento State College
Salisbury State College
San Diego State College
San Fernando Valley State College
South Dakota State University
Skidmore College
Southern Connecticut State College
Southern Illinois University
 (Carbondale)
Springfield College
St. Andrews Presbyterian College
State College at Salem
Stephen F. Austin State College

Stratford College

State University of New York College at Buffalo

State University of New York College at Cortland

State University of New York at Albany

State University of New York at Buffalo

Southwest Missouri State College

Sweet Briar College

Syracuse University

Texas Christian University

Temple University

Towson State College

Trenton State College

Trinity College

University of Arizona

University of Chicago

University of Dayton

University of Denver

University of Florida

University of Georgia

University of Idaho

University of Illinois at Urbana-Champaign

University of Iowa

University of Maine at Farmington

University of Maine at Machias

University of Maine at Orono

University of Maine at Portland-Gorham

University of Maryland

University of Minnesota

University of Nebraska at Omaha

University of Nebraska (Lincoln)

University of Nevada at Reno

University of Northern Colorado

University of Northern Iowa

University of Oregon

University of Santa Clara

University of Washington

University of North Carolina at Greensboro

University of San Diego

Utah State University

University of Virginia

University of Wisconsin at Lacrosse

University of Wisconsin (Madison)

Valparaiso University

Virginia Polytechnic Institute and State University

Washburn University

Wayne State University

Washington State University

Western Carolina University

West Georgia College

Western Illinois University

Western Michigan University

Western Washington State College

Westfield State College

Whittier College

Wichita State University

Wilson College

Winthrop College

Worcester State College

University of Wyoming

York College

APPENDIX C

•

DRAFT REGULATIONS FOR INTERSCHOLASTIC AND INTERCOLLEGIATE ATHLETICS (1974)

Published May 18 1974, *Federal Register*, 39, no. 120 (June 20, 1974): 22236.

(a) General. No person shall, on the basis of sex, be excluded from participation in, be denied the benefits of being treated differently from another person or otherwise be discriminated against in any physical education or athletic program operated by a recipient, and no recipient shall provide any physical education or athletic program separately on such basis; provided, however, that a recipient may operate or sponsor separate teams for members of each sex where selection for such teams is based upon competitive skill.

(b) Determination of student interest. A recipient which operates or sponsors athletics shall determine at least annually, using a method to be selected by the recipient which is acceptable to the director, in what sports members of each sex would desire to compete.

(c) Affirmative efforts. A recipient which operates or sponsors athletic activities shall, with regard to members of a sex for which athletic opportunities previously have been limited, make affirmative efforts to:

(1) inform members of such sex of the availability for them of athletic opportunities equal to those available for members of the other sex and of the nature of those opportunities, and

(2) provide support and training activities for members of such sex designed to improve and expand their capabilities and interests to participate in such opportunities.

(d) Equal opportunity. A recipient which operates or sponsors athletics shall make affirmative efforts to provide athletic opportunities in such sports and through such teams as will most effectively equalize such opportunities for members of both sexes, taking into consideration the determination made pursuant to paragraph (b).

(e) Separate teams. A recipient which operates or sponsors separate teams for members of each sex shall not discriminate on the basis of sex therein in the provision of necessary equipment or supplies for each team, or in any other manner.

Expenditures. Nothing in this section shall be interpreted to require equal aggregate expenditures for athletics for members of each sex.

APPENDIX D

•

FINAL REGULATIONS CONCERNING TITLE IX AND SCHOLASTIC-COLLEGIATE SPORTS (1975)

Title 34, Code of Federal Regulations, Part 106: Nondiscrimination on the Basis of Sex in Education Programs or Activities Receiving Federal Financial Assistance

106.41 Athletics.

(a) General. No person shall, on the basis of sex, be excluded from participation in, be denied the benefits of, be treated differently from another person or otherwise be discriminated against in any interscholastic, intercollegiate, club or intramural athletics offered by a recipient, and no recipient shall provide any such athletics separately on such basis.

(b) Separate teams. Notwithstanding the requirements of paragraph (a) of this section, a recipient may operate or sponsor separate teams for members of each sex where selection for such teams is based upon competitive skill or the activity involved is a contact sport. However, where a recipient operates or sponsors a team in a particular sport for members of one sex but operates or sponsors no such team for members of the other sex, and athletic opportunities for members of that sex have previously been limited, members of the excluded sex must be allowed to try-out for the team offered unless the sport involved is a contact sport. For the purposes of this part, contact sports include boxing, wrestling, rugby, ice hockey, football, basketball and other sports the purpose or major activity of which involves bodily contact.

(c) Equal opportunity. A recipient which operates or sponsors interscholastic, intercollegiate, club or intramural athletics shall provide equal athletic opportunity for members of both sexes. In determining whether equal opportunities are available the Director will consider, among other factors:

(1) Whether the selection of sports and levels of competition effectively accommodate the interests and abilities of members of both sexes;

(2) The provision of equipment and supplies;

(3) Scheduling of games and practice time;

(4) Travel and per diem allowance;

(5) Opportunity to receive coaching and academic tutoring;

(6) Assignment and compensation of coaches and tutors;

(7) Provision of locker rooms, practice and competitive facilities;

(8) Provision of medical and training facilities and services;

(9) Provision of housing and dining facilities and services;

(10) Publicity.

Unequal aggregate expenditures for members of each sex or unequal expenditures for male and female teams if a recipient operates or sponsors separate teams will not constitute noncompliance with this section, but the Assistant Secretary may consider the failure to provide necessary funds for teams for one sex in assessing equality of opportunity for members of each sex.

(d) Adjustment period. A recipient which operates or sponsors interscholastic, intercollegiate, club or intramural athletics at the elementary school level shall comply fully with this section as expeditiously as possible but in no event later than one year from the effective date of this regulation. A recipient which operates or sponsors interscholastic, intercollegiate, club or intramural athletics at the secondary or post-secondary school level shall comply fully with this section as expeditiously as possible but in no event later than three years from the effective date of this regulation.

APPENDIX E

•

PROPOSED POLICY INTERPRETATION (1978)

The Federal Register 58070. 43 no. 238 (December 11, 1978):

Agency: Office for Civil Rights, Office of the Secretary, HEW.

Action: Proposed Policy Interpretation.

Summary: The following proposed Policy Interpretation applies the provisions of Title IX of the Education Amendments of 1972 and its implementing regulation to intercollegiate athletics. It is being published in proposed form for public comment.

In developing this policy interpretation, a broad range of alternatives and views were considered. For example, some urged adoption of policies requiring immediate equality of expenditures on men's and women's sports based on enrollment. Others urged that receipts generated by revenue-producing sports be exempt from Title IX.

The proposed Policy Interpretation attempts to accommodate many of the concerns expressed, consistent with the Department's obligations under the law passed by the Congress. The policy bases compliance on participation rates, not enrollment, but requires that procedures be established to increase opportunities for women to participate in competitive athletics. The policy also bases compliance on a calculation that includes all revenue, regardless of source, but recognizes that certain sports that produce revenue, such as football and basketball, may require greater expenditures without having a discriminatory effect. The Policy Interpretation recognizes the higher costs of sports involving large teams, large coaching staffs, expensive equipment and facilities, and additional costs of travel, recruiting, publicity and the like, associated with national competition.

Date: etc.

Supplementary Information: The Department is seeking public comment on this approach as well as on all other aspects of the proposed Preamble and Policy Interpretation. In particular:

1. Is the description of the current status and development of intercollegiate athletics for men and women accurate? What other factors should be considered?

2. Is the proposed two stage approach to compliance practical? Should it be modified? Are there other approaches that should be considered?

3. Is the equal average per capita standard based on participation rates practical? Are there alternatives or modifications that should be considered?

4. Is there a basis for treating part of the expense of a particular revenue-producing sport differently because the sport produces income used by the university for non-athletic operating expenses on a non-discriminatory basis? If so, how should such funds be identified and treated?

5. Is the grouping of financially measurable benefits into three categories practical? Are there alternatives that should be considered? Specifically, should recruiting expenses be considered together with all other financially measurable benefits?

6. Are the factors used to justify differences in equal average per capita expenditures for financially measurable benefits and opportunities fair? Are there other factors that should be considered?

7. Is the comparability standard for benefits and opportunities that are not financially measurable fair and realistic? Should other factors controlling comparability be included? Should the comparability standard be revised? Is there a different standard that should be considered?

8. Is the proposal for increasing the opportunity for women to participate in competitive athletics appropriate and effective? Are there other procedures that should be considered? Is there a more effective way to ensure that the interests and abilities of both men and women are equally accommodated?

This policy interpretation establishes a two-stage approach to compliance and enforcement:

Part I is designed to eliminate discrimination against men or women currently participating in intercollegiate programs. It requires the immediate elimination of discrepancies in average per capita expenditures for financially measurable benefits and opportunities unless the institution can demonstrate that the discrepancies are based on differences in the costs of particular sports (e.g., equipment), their scope of competition (e.g., national, regional, or local), or other nondiscriminatory factors. Part I also requires comparability with respect to those benefits and services that are not readily financially measurable.

Part II is designed to eliminate, over a reasonable period of time, the discriminatory effects of the historic emphasis on men's intercollegiate sports, and to facilitate the continued growth of women's athletics. It requires adoption of procedures for the expansion of women's athletic programs to provide the number of participation opportunities needed to accommodate the interests and abilities of women.

Together, Parts I and II are designed to ensure that intercollegiate athletic programs at colleges and universities provide equal opportunities for both sexes. They are designed to ensure that women's intercollegiate athletic programs receive the resources and commitments to which they are entitled. This will not necessarily result in identical men's and women's intercollegiate athletic programs. Finally, Parts I and II take account of the size and cost of football by measuring present compliance in terms of actual, rather than potential participation rates, by recognizing the fact that the costs of some sports are greater than others, and where appropriate, by taking account of the scope of competition.

. . . A college or university intercollegiate athletic program will be in compliance with Title IX if:

I. It has eliminated discrimination in financial support and other benefits and opportunities in its existing athletic program; and

II. It follows an institutional policy that includes procedures and standards for developing an athletic program that provides equal opportunities for men and women to accommodate their interests and abilities.

I. Eliminating Discrimination in Existing Programs

To determine whether a college or university has eliminated discrimination on the basis of sex in its existing athletic program, benefits and opportunities that are readily financially measurable and those that are not will be examined separately. An institution provides equal athletic opportunities in its existing programs if:

A. Substantially equal average per capita funds are allocated to participating male and female athletes for:

1. Financial assistance awarded on the basis of athletic ability;

2. Recruitment; and

3. All other readily financially measurable benefits and opportunities;

Provided, however, that differences in average per-capita expenditures for such financially measurable benefits and opportunities will be considered consistent with Title IX if the institution can demonstrate that the differences result from non-discriminatory factors such as the nature or level of competition of a particular sport.

B. Comparable benefits and opportunities which are not readily financially measurable, are provided for participating male and female athletes.

A. Financially Measurable Benefits and Opportunities

Equality of benefits and opportunities for men and women in many aspects of a recipient's intercollegiate athletic program can best be measured in financial terms. Financially measurable benefits and opportunities covered by the Title IX regulation [45 C.F. 86:41(c)] include but are not limited to:

1. Financial assistance awarded on the basis of athletic ability;
2. Recruitment of athletes;
3. Provision and maintenance of equipment and supplies;
4. Living and travel expenses related to competitive events; and
5. Publicity.

In assessing whether an institution's present intercollegiate athletic program complies with Title IX, the Department will initially determine whether the institution's average per capita expenditures for male and female athletes on financially measurable benefits and opportunities are substantially equal. Average per capita expenditures will be calculated by dividing total expenditures on financially measurable benefits for each sex by the total number of participating athletes of each sex.

All funds spent on benefits or opportunities for athletes of each sex, regardless of source (gate receipts, student fees, earmarked donations, booster-club funds, etc.) will be considered in computing the total expenditures for athletes of that sex. Funds that are generated by athletic events but allocated to non-athletic activities (e.g., general institutional operating expenses, libraries) will not be included.

An institution may measure the number of participants in intercollegiate athletics by any non-discriminatory method. For example, institutions can use certified eligibility lists developed in accordance with NCAA or AIAW standards that are non-discriminatory.

In evaluating per capita expenditures for financially measurable benefits and opportunities, the Department will examine expenditures for athletic financial assistance and recruitment individually and will examine all other financially measurable items—equipment and supplies, travel and per diem, publicity, etc.—as a group. If the average per capita expenditures for participating males and females are substantially equal for the group of all other financially measurable items, the institution will be presumed to be in compliance as to each of the separate items that constitute the group.

If average per capita expenditures are not substantially equal, the Department will examine the reasons advanced by the institution as justification for the differences. Variations in average per capita expenditures may be caused by differences in costs, levels of competition, and other nondiscriminatory factors. Some of the reasons that the Department may accept for variations from the equal average per capita standard are set out below.

1. Financial assistance. Greater per capita expenditures for athletic financial assistance in either men's or women's programs will be consistent with Title IX if they result from nondiscriminatory circumstances or decisions. For example, an athletic director may decide not to award the usual number of scholarships in a particular year because he/she believes some support should be deferred until a later year for purposes of program development. This is a programmatic decision concerning the building of a team or total program which may result in different expenditures that do not violate Title IX. Also, the necessary extra cost of tuition for some out-of-state athletes of either sex may cause greater average per capita expenditures that are not discriminatory.

2. Recruiting. Similarly, greater per capita expenditures for recruiting in either men's or women's programs will be consistent with Title IX if they result from non-discriminatory programmatic decisions. For example, where the current area of intercollegiate competition is regional rather than national, less expensive regional recruitment may currently be appropriate. Likewise, greater competition for a particular athlete may make it necessary for an institution to approach that athlete more often, thereby increasing the cost of recruitment for athletes of that sex. Although identical recruitment methods or techniques are not required, the level of effort and methods used to recruit must be based on non-discriminatory criteria.

3. Other financially measurable benefits and opportunities. In the case of other readily financially measurable benefits and opportunities, per capita expenditures for men and women may differ simply because of intrinsic sex-neutral differences in the particular men's and women's sports sponsored by the recipient. Variations in average per capita expenditures are non-discriminatory if they result from:

a. Differences controlled by the nature of the sport, such as variations in the cost of equipment and supplies; and/or

b. Differences resulting from the scope of competition (i.e. local, regional, or national) such as cost of travel to distant locations for competition, living expenses while in those locations, more extensive publicity, or the cost of other activities that may vary in accordance with the requirements of local, regional, or national competition.

Differences in per capita expenditures that result in discrimination cannot be excused by different rules of men's and women's athletic associations. The Title IX regulation specifically states:

The obligation to comply is not obviated or alleviated by any rule or regulation of any . . . athletic or other league, or association . . . (45 CFR 86.6(c))

B. Benefits That Are Not Financially Measurable

Equality of opportunity in aspects of an intercollegiate athletic program that cannot readily be measured in financial terms will be determined by assessing whether the program offers comparable benefits and opportunities for men and women. Such non-financially measurable benefits and opportunities covered by the Title IX regulation [45 CFR 86.4(c)] include, but are not limited to:

1. Opportunity to compete and practice;
2. Opportunity to receive coaching and academic tutoring;
3. Provision of locker rooms, practice and competitive facilities;
4. Provision of medical and training services and facilities; and
5. Provision of housing and dining services and facilities.

1. Opportunity to compete and practice. Comparability of opportunity to compete and practice will be determined by examining the institution's scheduling of games and practice times. Opportunities will be comparable if:

a. Decisions regarding scheduling are based on non-discriminatory criteria;

b. Facilities provided for games and practice are made available at times that are convenient for participants of each sex; and

c. Game schedules are arranged so that each sex has the opportunity to compete before an audience.

2. Opportunity to receive coaching and academic tutoring. The Department will presume that comparable opportunity to receive coaching exists where the ratio of full-time coaches (or their equivalent) to participating athletes is substantially equal for males and females. Discrepancies in the ratio will be accepted if they are the result of non-discriminatory factors required by the nature of a particular sport. Title IX does not

require that particular men's and women's teams have an equal number of coaches. If tutoring services are provided, tutors must be made available to student athletes on the basis of non-discriminatory criteria.

3. Facilities. The elements to be considered in determining comparability of facilities include:

a. Access to those facilities by student athletes; and

b. Suitability to the sports to be played (e.g., size, safety, maintenance, spectator and media capacity).

Comparable facilities can be offered by providing separate, comparable facilities or sharing the game facilities. For example, if an institution has spacious, well-equipped facilities for men but not for women, it has one of two choices. It may expand the women's facilities to a comparable standard, or it may meet its obligation to provide comparable facilities by making the same facilities available to men and women at different times on an equitable basis. The latter could be accomplished either by rotating the use of the entire facility or by alternating use of the previously separate men's and women's facilities. The regulation does not require identical facilities.

4. Provision of medical and training services and facilities. If an institution supplies doctors, trainers, physical therapists, or other health and training personnel and facilities to athletes, they must be made available on a nondiscriminatory basis. For example, the pattern of injuries and thus the cost of insurance may vary from sport to sport. An institution may offer different athletic insurance policies tailored to injuries occurring in a particular sport. But the policies must provide similar benefits for similar injuries.

5. Provision of housing and dining services and facilities. Housing and dining services and facilities provided to athletes need not be identical, but they must be comparable. An institution may provide a separate dormitory for male athletes but not for female athletes so long as there are no additional services or benefits that accrue to residents of the separate dormitory. However, differences in housing, dining, and related services and facilities will be accepted if they are made on a non-discriminatory basis.

II. Equally Accommodating the Interests and Abilities of Women

The Title IX regulation does not require an equal number of men and women participants or an equal number of men's and women's sports. Rather, it requires that the interests and abilities of men and women be equally accommodated. In recent years, there has been a significant growth in the athletic interests and abilities of women.

An institution that satisfied Part I of this Policy Interpretation will be considered in compliance with Title IX if in addition it follows an institutional policy that insures that the interests and abilities of women are effectively accommodated in its intercollegiate program. Specifically, such a policy must include procedures and standards:

A. To encourage an increase in the number of women participants at the club, intramural, and intercollegiate level;

B. To increase the number of women's sports at the club, intramural, and intercollegiate level;

C. To publicize on campus and feeder schools athletic opportunities for women at the institution; and

D. To elevate the scope of women's intercollegiate competition (e.g., from local to State, State to regional, and from regional to national).

An institution that does not choose to have the above procedures may, nevertheless, be satisfying the athletic interests and abilities of its female students. Such an institution should be able to demonstrate that it is doing so, for example,

A. By showing that the club, intramural, and intercollegiate sports currently offered accommodate the interests and abilities of women by providing opportunities comparable to those of men at all levels (i.e., intramural, club, and intercollegiate);

B. By showing that there is at the institution a pattern of increased participation by women in athletic activities at all levels; or

C. By showing that the institution's overall athletic program at all levels reflects the growth in the athletic interests and abilities of women evidenced in regional or area interscholastic program.

APPENDIX F

•

POLICY INTERPRETATION: TITLE IX AND INTERCOLLEGIATE ATHLETICS (1979)

Federal Register 44, no. 239 (Tuesday, December 11, 1979);
www.ed.gov/about/offices/list/ocr/docs/t9interp.html.

This Policy Interpretation clarifies the obligations which recipients of Federal aid have under Title IX to provide equal opportunities in athletic programs. In particular, this Policy Interpretation provides a means to assess an institution's compliance with the equal opportunity requirements of the regulation which are set forth at 45 CFR 88.37(c) and 88.4a(c).

A. Athletic Financial Assistance (Scholarships)

1. The Regulation-Section 86.37(c) of the regulation provides:

[Institutions] must provide reasonable opportunities for such award (of financial assistance) for member of each sex in proportion to the number of students of each sex participating in inter-collegiate athletics.

2. The Policy—The Department will examine compliance with this provision of the regulation primarily by means of a financial comparison to determine whether proportionately equal amounts of financial assistance (scholarship aid) are available to men's and women's athletic programs. The Department will measure compliance with this standard by dividing the amounts of aid available for the members of each sex by the numbers of male or female participants in the athletic program and comparing the results. Institutions may be found in compliance if this comparison results in substantially equal amounts or if a resulting disparity can be explained by adjustments to take into account legitimate, nondiscriminatory factors. Two such factors are:

a. At public institutions, the higher costs of tuition for students from out-of-state may in some years be unevenly distributed between men's and women's programs. These differences will be considered non-discriminatory if they are not the result of policies or practices which disproportionately limit the availability of out-of-state scholarships to either men or women.

b. An institution may make reasonable professional decisions concerning the awards most appropriate for program development. For example, team development initially may require spreading scholarships over as much as a full generation (four years) of student athletes. This may result in the award of fewer scholarships in the first few years than would be necessary to create proportionality between male and female athletes.

3. Application of the Policy—a. This section does not require a proportionate number of scholarships for men and women or individual scholarships of equal dollar value. It does mean that the total amount of scholarship aid made available to men and women must be substantially proportionate to their participation rates.

b. When financial assistance is provided in forms other than grants, the distribution of non-grant assistance will also be compared to determine whether equivalent benefits are proportionately available to male and female athletes. A disproportionate amount of work-related aid or loans in the assistance made available to the members of one sex, for example, could constitute a violation of Title IX.

4. Definition—For purposes of examining compliance with this Section, the participants will be defined as those athletes:

a. Who are receiving the institutionally-sponsored support normally provided to athletes competing at the institution involved, e.g., coaching, equipment, medical and training room services, on a regular basis during a sport's season; and

b. Who are participating in organized practice sessions and other team meetings and activities on a regular basis during a sport's season; and

c. Who are listed on the eligibility or squad lists maintained for each sport, or

d. Who, because of injury, cannot meet a, b, or c above but continue to receive financial aid on the basis of athletic ability.

B. Equivalence in Other Athletic Benefits and Opportunities

1. The Regulation. The Regulation requires that recipients that operate or sponsor interscholastic, intercollegiate, club or intramural athletics "provide equal athletic opportunities for members of both sexes." In determining whether an institution is providing equal opportunity in intercollegiate athletics the regulation requires the Department to consider, among others, the following factors:

(1) [Accommodation of student interests and abilities];
(2) Provision and maintenance of equipment and supplies;
(3) Scheduling of games and practice times;
(4) Travel and per diem expenses;

(5) Opportunity to receive coaching and academic tutoring;

(6) Assignment and compensation of coaches and tutors;

(7) Provision of locker rooms, practice and competitive facilities;

(8) Provision of medical and training services and facilities;

(9) Provision of housing and dining services and facilities; and

(10) Publicity.

Section 86.41(c) also permits the Director of the Office for Civil Rights to consider other factors in the determination of equal opportunity. Accordingly, this Section also addresses recruitment of student athletes and provision of support services.

This list is not exhaustive. Under the regulation, it may be expanded as necessary at the discretion of the Director of the Office for Civil Rights.

2. The Policy—The Department will assess compliance with both the recruitment and the general athletic program requirements of the regulation by comparing the availability, quality and kinds of benefits, opportunities, and treatment afforded members of both sexes. Institutions will be in compliance if the compared program components are equivalent, that is, equal or equal in effect. Under this standard, identical benefits, opportunities, or treatment are not required, provided the overall effects of any differences is [sic] negligible.

If comparisons of program components reveal that treatment, benefits, or opportunities are not equivalent in kind, quality or availability, a finding of compliance may still be justified if the differences are the result of nondiscriminatory factors. Some of the factors that may justify these differences are as follows:

a. Some aspects of athletic programs may not be equivalent for men and women because of unique aspects of particular sports or athletic activities. This type of distinction was called for by the "Javits' Amendment" to Title IX which instructed HEW to make "reasonable [regulatory] provisions considering the nature of particular sports" in intercollegiate athletics.

Generally, these differences will be the result of factors that are inherent to the basic operation of specific sports. Such factors may include rules of play, nature/replacement of equipment, rates of injury resulting from participation, nature of facilities required for competition, and the maintenance/upkeep requirements of those facilities. For the most part, differences involving such factors will occur in programs offering football, and consequently these differences will favor men. If sport-specific needs are met equivalently in both men's and women's programs, however, differences in particular program components will be found to be justifiable.

b. Some aspects of athletic programs may not be equivalent for men and women because of legitimately sex-neutral factors related to special circumstances of a temporary nature. For example, large disparities in recruitment activity for any particular year may be the result of annual fluctuations in team needs for first-year athletes. Such differences are justifiable to the extent that they do not reduce overall equality of opportunity.

c. The activities directly associated with the operation of a competitive event in a single-sex sport may, under some circumstances, create unique demands or imbalances in particular program components. Provided any special demands associated with the activities of sports involving participants of the other sex are met to an equivalent degree, the resulting differences may be found nondiscriminatory. At many schools, for example, certain sports—notably football and men's basketball—traditionally draw large crowds. Since the costs of managing an athletic event increase with crowd size, the overall support made available for event management to men's and women's programs may differ in degree and kind. These differences would not violate Title IX if the recipient does not limit the potential for women's athletic events to rise in spectator appeal and if the levels of event management support available to both programs are based on sex-neutral criteria (e.g. facilities used, projected attendance, and staffing needs).

d. Some aspects of athletic programs may not be equivalent for men and women because institutions are undertaking voluntary affirmative actions to overcome effects of historical conditions that have limited participation in athletics by the members of one sex. This is authorized at 86.3(b) of the regulation.

3. Application of the Policy—General Athletic Program Components

a. Equipment and Supplies (§86.41(c)(2)). Equipment and supplies include but are not limited to uniforms, other apparel, sport-specific equipment and supplies, general equipment and supplies, instructional devices, and conditioning and weight training equipment.

Compliance will be assessed by examining, among other factors, the equivalence for men and women of:

(1) The quality of equipment and supplies;

(2) The amount of equipment and supplies;

(3) The suitability of equipment and supplies;

(4) The maintenance and replacement of the equipment and supplies; and

(5) The availability of equipment and supplies.

b. Scheduling of Games and Practice Times (§86.41(c)(3)). Compliance will be assessed by examining, among other factors, the equivalence for men and women of:

(1) The number of competitive events per sport;

(2) The number and length of practice opportunities;

(3) The time of day competitive events are scheduled;

(4) The time of day practice opportunities are scheduled; and

(5) The opportunities to engage in available pre-season and post-season competition.

c. Travel and Per Diem Allowances (§ 86.41(c)(4)). Compliance will be assessed by examining, among other factors, the equivalence for men and women of:

(1) Modes of transportation;

(2) Housing furnished during travel:

(3) Length of stay before and after competitive events:

(4) Per diem allowances: and

(5) Dining arrangements.

d. Opportunity to Receive Coaching and Academic Tutoring (86.41 (c)(5)).

(1) Coaching—Compliance will be assessed by examining, among other factors:

(a) Relative availability of full-time coaches:

(b) Relative availability of part-time and assistant coaches; and

(c) Relative availability of graduate assistants.

(2) Academic tutoring—Compliance will be assessed by examining, among other factors, the equivalence for men and women of:

(a) The availability of tutoring; and

(b) Procedures and criteria for obtaining tutorial assistance.

e. Assignment and Compensation of Coaches and Tutors (§86.41(c)(6)). In general, a violation of Section 86.41(c)(6) will be found only where compensation or assignment policies or practices deny male and female athletes coaching of equivalent quality, nature, or availability.

Nondiscriminatory factors can affect the compensation of coaches. In determining whether differences are caused by permissible factors, the range and nature of duties, the experience of individual coaches, the number of participants for particular sports, the number of assistant coaches supervised, and the level of competition will be considered.

Where these or similar factors represent valid differences in skill, effort, responsibility or working conditions they may, in specific circumstances, justify differences in compensation. Similarly, there may be unique situations in which a particular person may possess such an outstanding record of achievement as to justify an abnormally high salary.

(1) Assignment of Coaches—Compliance will be assessed by examining, among other factors, the equivalence for men's and women's coaches of:
(a) Training, experience, and other professional qualifications;
(b) Professional standing.
(2) Assignment of Tutors—Compliance will be assessed by examining, among other factors, the equivalence for men's and women's tutors of:
(a) Tutor qualifications;
(b) Training, experience, and other qualifications.
(3) Compensation of Coaches—Compliance will be assessed by examining, among other factors, the equivalence for men's and women's coaches of:
(a) Rate of compensation (per sport, per season);
(b) Duration of contracts;
(c) Conditions relating to contract renewal;
(d) Experience;
(e) Nature of coaching duties performed;
(f) Working conditions; and
(g) Other terms and conditions of employment.
(4) Compensation of Tutors—Compliance will be assessed by examining, among other factors, the equivalence for men's and women's tutors of:
(a) Hourly rate of payment by nature subjects tutored;
(b) Pupil loads per tutoring season;
(c) Tutor qualifications;
(d) Experience;
(e) Other terms and conditions of employment.
f. Provision of Locker Rooms, Practice and Competitive Facilities (86.41(c)(7)). Compliance will be assessed by examining, among other factors, the equivalence for men and women of:
(1) Quality and availability of the facilities provided for practice and competitive events;
(2) Exclusivity of use of facilities provided for practice and competitive events;
(3) Availability of locker rooms;
(4) Quality of locker rooms;
(5) Maintenance of practice and competitive facilities; and
(6) Preparation of facilities for practice and competitive events.
g. Provision of Medical and Training Facilities and Services (86.41(c)(8)). Compliance will be assessed by examining, among other factors, the equivalence for men and women of:
(1) Availability of medical personnel and assistance;
(2) Health, accident and injury insurance coverage;
(3) Availability and quality of weight and training facilities;

(4) Availability and quality of conditioning facilities; and

(5) Availability and qualifications of athletic trainers.

h. Provision of Housing and Dining Facilities and Services (§86.41(c)(9). Compliance will be assessed by examining, among other factors, the equivalence for men and women of:

(1) Housing provided;

(2) Special services as part of housing arrangements (e.g., laundry facilities, parking space, maid service).

i. Publicity (86.41(c)(10)). Compliance will be assessed by examining, among other factors, the equivalence for men and women of:

(1) Availability and quality of sports information personnel;

(2) Access to other publicity resources for men's and women's programs; and

(3) Quantity and quality of publications and other promotional devices featuring men's and women's program.

4. Application of the Policy—Other Factors (86.41(c)). a. Recruitment of Student Athletes. The athletic recruitment practices of institutions often affect the overall provision of opportunity to male and female athletes. Accordingly, where equal athletic opportunities are not present for male and female students, compliance will be assessed by examining the recruitment practices of the athletic programs for both sexes to determine whether the provision of equal opportunity will require modification of those practices.

Such examinations will review the following factors:

(1) Whether coaches or other professional athletic personnel in the programs serving male and female athletes are provided with substantially equal opportunities to recruit;

(2) Whether the financial and other resources made available for recruitment in male and female athletic programs are equivalently adequate to meet the needs of each program; and

(3) Whether the differences in benefits, opportunities, and treatment afforded prospective student athletes of each sex have a disproportionately limiting effect upon the recruitment of students of either sex.

b. Provision of Support Services. The administrative and clerical support provided to an athletic program can affect the overall provision of opportunity to male and female athletes, particularly to the extent that the provided services enable coaches to perform better their coaching functions.

In the provision of support services, compliance will be assessed by examining, among other factors, the equivalence of:

(1) The amount of administrative assistance provided to men's and women's programs;

(2) The amount of secretarial and clerical assistance provided to men's and women's programs

5. Overall Determination of Compliance. The Department will base its compliance determination under § 86.41(c) of the regulation upon an examination of the following:

a. Whether the policies of an institution are discriminatory in language or effect; or

b. Whether disparities of a substantial and unjustified nature exist in the benefits, treatment, services, or opportunities afforded male and female athletes in the institution's program as a whole; or

c. Whether disparities in benefits, treatment, services, or opportunities in individual segments of the program are substantial enough in and of themselves to deny equality of athletic opportunity.

C. Effective Accommodation of Student Interests and Abilities.

1. The Regulation. The regulation requires institutions to accommodate effectively the interests and abilities of students to the extent necessary to provide equal opportunity in the selection of sports and levels of competition available to members of both sexes.

Specifically, the regulation, at 86.41(c)(1), requires the Director to consider, when determining whether equal opportunities are available—

Whether the selection of sports and levels of competition effectively accommodate the interests and abilities of members of both sexes.

Section 86.41(c) also permits the Director of the Office for Civil Rights to consider other factors in the determination of equal opportunity. Accordingly, this section also addresses competitive opportunities in terms of the competitive team schedules available to athletes of both sexes.

2. The Policy. The Department will assess compliance with the interests and abilities section of the regulation by examining the following factors:

a. The determination of athletic interests and abilities of students;

b. The selection of sports offered; and

c. The levels of competition available including the opportunity for team competition.

3. Application of the Policy—Determination of Athletic Interests and Abilities.

Institutions may determine the athletic interests and abilities of students by nondiscriminatory methods of their choosing provided:

a. The processes take into account the nationally increasing levels of women's interests and abilities;

b. The methods of determining interest and ability do not disadvantage the members of an underrepresented sex;

227
•

c. The methods of determining ability take into account team performance records; and

d. The methods are responsive to the expressed interests of students capable of intercollegiate competition who are members of an underrepresented sex.

4. Application of the Policy—Selection of Sports.

In the selection of sports, the regulation does not require institutions to integrate their teams nor to provide exactly the same choice of sports to men and women. However, where an institution sponsors a team in a particular sport for members of one sex, it may be required either to permit the excluded sex to try out for the team or to sponsor a separate team for the previously excluded sex.

a. Contact Sports—Effective accommodation means that if an institution sponsors a team for members of one sex in a contact sport, it must do so for members of the other sex under the following circumstances:

(1) The opportunities for members of the excluded sex have historically been limited; and

(2) There is sufficient interest and ability among the members of the excluded sex to sustain a viable team and a reasonable expectation of intercollegiate competition for that team.

b. Non-Contact Sports—Effective accommodation means that if an institution sponsors a team for members of one sex in a non-contact sport, it must do so for members of the other sex under the following circumstances:

(1) The opportunities for members of the excluded sex have historically been limited;

(2) There is sufficient interest and ability among the members of the excluded sex to sustain a viable team and a reasonable expectation of intercollegiate competition for that team; and

(3) Members of the excluded sex do not possess sufficient skill to be selected for a single integrated team, or to compete actively on such a team if selected.

5. Application of the Policy—Levels of Competition.

In effectively accommodating the interests and abilities of male and female athletes, institutions must provide both the opportunity for individuals of each sex to participate in intercollegiate competition, and for athletes of each sex to have competitive team schedules which equally reflect their abilities.

a. Compliance will be assessed in any one of the following ways:

(1) Whether intercollegiate level participation opportunities for male and female students are provided in numbers substantially proportionate to their respective enrollments; or

(2) Where the members of one sex have been and are underrepresented among intercollegiate athletes, whether the institution can show a history and continuing practice of program expansion which is demonstrably responsive to the developing interest and abilities of the members of that sex; or

(3) Where the members of one sex are underrepresented among intercollegiate athletes, and the institution cannot show a continuing practice of program expansion such as that cited above, whether it can be demonstrated that the interests and abilities of the members of that sex have been fully and effectively accommodated by the present program.

b. Compliance with this provision of the regulation will also be assessed by examining the following:

(1) Whether the competitive schedules for men's and women's teams, on a program-wide basis, afford proportionally similar numbers of male and female athletes equivalently advanced competitive opportunities; or

(2) Whether the institution can demonstrate a history and continuing practice of upgrading the competitive opportunities available to the historically disadvantaged sex as warranted by developing abilities among the athletes of that sex.

c. Institutions are not required to upgrade teams to intercollegiate status or otherwise develop intercollegiate sports absent a reasonable expectation that intercollegiate competition in that sport will be available within the institution's normal competitive regions. Institutions may be required by the Title IX regulation to actively encourage the development of such competition, however, when overall athletic opportunities within that region have been historically limited for the members of one sex.

6. Overall Determination of Compliance.

The Department will base its compliance determination under §86.41(c) of the regulation upon a determination of the following:

a. Whether the policies of an institution are discriminatory in language or effect; or

b. Whether disparities of a substantial and unjustified nature in the benefits, treatment, services, or opportunities afforded male and female athletes exist in the institution's program as a whole; or

c. Whether disparities in individual segments of the program with respect to benefits, treatment, services, or opportunities are substantial enough in and of themselves to deny equality of athletic opportunity.

•

THE CIVIL RIGHTS RESTORATION ACT OF 1987

Congressional Record, January 26, 1988, vol. 134, pt. 2: 96.

Interpretation of "Program or Activity"

Sec. 908. For the purposes of this title, the term "program or activity" and "program" mean all of the operations of—

(1)(A) a department, agency, special purpose district, or other instrumentality of a State or of a local government; or

(B) the entity of such State or local government that distributes such assistance and each such department or agency (and each other State or local government entity) to which the assistance is extended, in the case of assistance to a State or local government;

(2)(A) a college, university, or other postsecondary institution, or a public system of higher education; or

(B) a local educational agency (as defined in section 198(a)(10) of the Elementary and Secondary Education Act of 1965), system of vocational education, or other school system;

(3)(A) an entire corporation, partnership, or other private organization, or an entire sole proprietorship—

(i) if assistance is extended to such corporation, partnership, private organization, or sole proprietorship as a whole; or

(ii) which is principally engaged in the business of providing education, health care, housing, social services, or parks and recreation; or

(B) the entire plant or other comparable, geographically separate facility to which Federal financial assistance is extended, in the case of any other corporation, partnership, private organization, or sole proprietorship; or

(4) any other entity which is established by two or more of the entities described in paragraph (1), (2), or (3); any part of which is extended

Federal financial assistance, except that such term does not include any operation of an entity which is controlled by a religious organization if the application of section 901 to such operation would not be consistent with the religious tenets of such organization.

APPENDIX H

•

CLARIFICATION OF INTERCOLLEGIATE ATHLETIC POLICY GUIDANCE: THE THREE-PART TEST (1996)

Selections from the policy guidance issued January 16, 1996, by the Office for Civil Rights, U.S. Department of Education

Part One: Are Participation Opportunities Substantially Proportionate to Enrollment?

Under part one of the three-part test (part one), where an institution provides intercollegiate level athletic participation opportunities for male and female students in numbers substantially proportionate to their respective full-time undergraduate enrollments, OCR will find that the institution is providing nondiscriminatory participation opportunities for individuals of both sexes.

. . . The Policy Interpretation defines participants as those athletes:

Who are receiving the institutionally-sponsored support normally provided to athletes competing at the institution involved, e.g., coaching, equipment, medical and training room services, on a regular basis during a sport's season; and

Who are participating in organized practice sessions and other team meetings and activities on a regular basis during a sport's season; and

Who are listed on the eligibility or squad lists maintained for each sport, or

Who, because of injury, cannot meet a, b, or c above but continue to receive financial aid on the basis of athletic ability.

. . . OCR's analysis next determines whether athletic opportunities are substantially proportionate. . . . the Policy Interpretation examines whether participation opportunities are "substantially" proportionate to enrollment rates. Because this determination depends on the institution's specific circumstances and the size of its athletic program, OCR makes this determination on a case-by-case basis, rather than through use of a statistical test. [That is to say, there is no fixed percentage for colleges to use as a guide. However,]

. . . If an institution's enrollment is 52 percent male and 48 percent female and 52 percent of the participants in the athletic program are male and 48 percent female, then the institution would clearly satisfy part one. However, OCR recognizes that natural fluctuations in an institution's enrollment and/or participation rates may affect the percentages in a subsequent year. For instance, if the institution's admissions the following year resulted in an enrollment rate of 51 percent males and 49 percent females, while the participation rates of males and females in the athletic program remained constant, the institution would continue to satisfy part one because it would be unreasonable to expect the institution to fine tune its program in response to this change in enrollment. . . .

Part Two: Is There a History and Continuing Practice of Program Expansion for the Underrepresented Sex?

Under part two of the three-part test (part two), an institution can show that it has a history and continuing practice of program expansion which is demonstrably responsive to the developing interests and abilities of the underrepresented sex.

. . . OCR will review the entire history of the athletic program, focusing on the participation opportunities provided for the underrepresented sex. First, OCR will assess whether past actions of the institution have expanded participation opportunities for the underrepresented sex in a manner that was demonstrably responsive to their developing interests and abilities. . . . There are no fixed intervals of time within which an institution must have added participation opportunities. Neither is a particular number of sports dispositive. Rather, the focus is on whether the program expansion was responsive to developing interests and abilities of the underrepresented sex. In addition, the institution must demonstrate a continuing (i.e., present) practice of program expansion as warranted by developing interests and abilities.

OCR will consider the following factors, among others, as evidence that may indicate a history of program expansion that is demonstrably responsive to the developing interests and abilities of the underrepresented sex:

- an institution's record of adding intercollegiate teams, or upgrading teams to intercollegiate status, for the underrepresented sex;

233
•

- an institution's record of increasing the numbers of participants in intercollegiate athletics who are members of the underrepresented sex; and
- an institution's affirmative responses to requests by students or others for addition or elevation of sports.

... In the event that an institution eliminated any team for the underrepresented sex, OCR would evaluate the circumstances surrounding this action in assessing whether the institution could satisfy part two of the test. However, OCR will not find a history and continuing practice of program expansion where an institution increases the proportional participation opportunities for the underrepresented sex by reducing opportunities for the overrepresented sex alone or by reducing participation opportunities for the overrepresented sex to a proportionately greater degree than for the underrepresented sex.

... In addition, OCR will not find that an institution satisfies part two where it established teams for the underrepresented sex only at the initiation of its program for the underrepresented sex or where it merely promises to expand its program for the underrepresented sex at some time in the future. ...

Part Three: Is the Institution Fully and Effectively Accommodating the Interests and Abilities of the Underrepresented Sex?

Under part three of the three-part test (part three) OCR determines whether an institution is fully and effectively accommodating the interests and abilities of its students who are members of the underrepresented sex—including students who are admitted to the institution though not yet enrolled. Title IX provides that a recipient must provide equal athletic opportunity to its students. Accordingly, the Policy Interpretation does not require an institution to accommodate the interests and abilities of potential students.

While disproportionately high athletic participation rates by an institution's students of the overrepresented sex (as compared to their enrollment rates) may indicate that an institution is not providing equal athletic opportunities to its students of the underrepresented sex, an institution can satisfy part three where there is evidence that the imbalance does not reflect discrimination, i.e., where it can be demonstrated that, notwithstanding disproportionately low participation rates by the institution's students of the underrepresented sex, the interests and abilities of these students are, in fact, being fully and effectively accommodated.

In making this determination, OCR will consider whether there is (a) unmet interest in a particular sport; (b) sufficient ability to sustain a team in the sport; and (c) a reasonable expectation of competition for the team. If all three conditions are present OCR will find that an institution has not fully and effectively accommodated the interests and abilities of the underrepresented sex.

If an institution has recently eliminated a viable team from the intercollegiate program, OCR will find that there is sufficient interest, ability, and available competition to sustain an intercollegiate team in that sport unless an institution can provide strong evidence that interest, ability, or available competition no longer exists.

. . . In addition, OCR will look at participation rates in sports in high schools, amateur athletic associations, and community sports leagues that operate in areas from which the institution draws its students in order to ascertain likely interest and ability of its students and admitted students in particular sport(s). For example, where OCR's investigation finds that a substantial number of high schools from the relevant region offer a particular sport which the institution does not offer for the underrepresented sex, OCR will ask the institution to provide a basis for any assertion that its students and admitted students are not interested in playing that sport. OCR may also interview students, admitted students, coaches, and others regarding interest in that sport. . . .

FURTHER CLARIFICATION OF INTERCOLLEGIATE ATHLETICS POLICY GUIDANCE REGARDING TITLE IX COMPLIANCE (2003)

July 11, 2003

Dear Colleague:

It is my pleasure to provide you with this Further Clarification of Intercollegiate Athletics Policy Guidance Regarding Title IX Compliance.

Since its enactment in 1972, Title IX has produced significant advancement in athletic opportunities for women and girls across the nation. Recognizing that more remains to be done, the Bush Administration is firmly committed to building on this legacy and continuing the progress that Title IX has brought toward true equality of opportunity for male and female student-athletes in America.

In response to numerous requests for additional guidance on the Department of Education's (Department) enforcement standards since its last written guidance on Title IX in 1996, the Department's Office for Civil Rights (OCR) began looking into whether additional guidance on Title IX requirements regarding intercollegiate athletics was needed. On June 27, 2002, Secretary of Education Rod Paige created the Secretary's Commission on Opportunities in Athletics to investigate this matter further, and to report back with recommendations on how to improve the application of the current standards for measuring equal opportunity to participate in athletics under Title IX. On February 26, 2003, the Commission presented Secretary Paige with its final report, "Open to All: Title IX at Thirty," and in addition, individual members expressed their views.

After eight months of discussion and an extensive and inclusive fact-finding process, the Commission found very broad support throughout the country for the goals and spirit of Title IX. With that in mind, OCR today issues this Further Clarification in order to strengthen Title IX's promise of non-discrimination in the athletic programs of our nation's schools.

Title IX establishes that: "No person in the United States shall, on the basis of sex, be excluded from participation in, be denied the benefits of, or be subjected to discrimination under any education program or activity receiving Federal financial assistance."

In its 1979 Policy Interpretation, the Department established a three-prong test for compliance with Title IX, which it later amplified and clarified in its 1996 Clarification. The test provides that an institution is in compliance if 1) the intercollegiate-level participation opportunities for male and female students at the institution are "substantially proportionate" to their respective full-time undergraduate enrollments, 2) the institution has a "history and continuing practice of program expansion" for the underrepresented sex, or 3) the institution is "fully and effectively" accommodating the interests and abilities of the underrepresented sex.

First, with respect to the three-prong test, which has worked well, OCR encourages schools to take advantage of its flexibility, and to consider which of the three prongs best suits their individual situations. All three prongs have been used successfully by schools to comply with Title IX, and the test offers three separate ways of assessing whether schools are providing equal opportunities to their male and female students to participate in athletics. If a school does not satisfy the "substantial proportionality" prong, it would still satisfy the three-prong test if it maintains a history and continuing practice of program expansion for the underrepresented sex, or if "the interests and abilities of the members of [the underrepresented] sex have been fully and effectively accommodated by the present program." Each of the three prongs is thus a valid, alternative way for schools to comply with Title IX.

The transmittal letter accompanying the 1996 Clarification issued by the Department described only one of these three separate prongs—substantial proportionality—as a "safe harbor" for Title IX compliance. This led many schools to believe, erroneously, that they must take measures to ensure strict proportionality between the sexes. In fact, each of the three prongs of the test is an equally sufficient means of complying with Title IX, and no one prong is favored. The Department will continue to make clear, as it did in its 1996 Clarification, that "[i]nstitutions have flexibility in providing nondiscriminatory participation opportunities to their students, and OCR does not require quotas."

In order to ensure that schools have a clear understanding of their options for compliance with Title IX, OCR will undertake an education campaign to help educational institutions appreciate the flexibility of the law, to explain that each prong of the test is a viable and separate means of compliance, to give practical examples of the ways in which schools can comply, and to provide schools with technical assistance as they try to comply with Title IX.

In the 1996 Clarification, the Department provided schools with a broad range of specific factors, as well as illustrative examples, to help schools understand the flexibility of the three-prong test. OCR reincorporates those factors, as well as those illustrative examples, into this Further Clarification, and OCR will continue to assist schools on a case-by-case basis and address any questions they have about Title IX compliance. Indeed, OCR encourages schools to request individualized assistance from OCR as they consider ways to meet the requirements of Title IX. As OCR works with schools on Title IX compliance, OCR will share information on successful approaches with the broader scholastic community.

Second, OCR hereby clarifies that nothing in Title IX requires the cutting or reduction of teams in order to demonstrate compliance with Title IX, and that the elimination of teams is a disfavored practice. Because the elimination of teams diminishes opportunities for students who are interested in participating in athletics instead of enhancing opportunities for students who have suffered from discrimination, it is contrary to the spirit of Title IX for the government to require or encourage an institution to eliminate athletic teams.

Therefore, in negotiating compliance agreements, OCR's policy will be to seek remedies that do not involve the elimination of teams.

Third, OCR hereby advises schools that it will aggressively enforce Title IX standards, including implementing sanctions for institutions that do not comply. At the same time, OCR will also work with schools to assist them in avoiding such sanctions by achieving Title IX compliance.

Fourth, private sponsorship of athletic teams will continue to be allowed. Of course, private sponsorship does not in any way change or diminish a school's obligations under Title IX.

Finally, OCR recognizes that schools will benefit from clear and consistent implementation of Title IX. Accordingly, OCR will ensure that its enforcement practices do not vary from region to region.

OCR recognizes that the question of how to comply with Title IX and to provide equal athletic opportunities for all students is a challenge for many academic institutions. But OCR believes that the three-prong test has provided, and will continue to provide, schools with the flexibility to provide greater athletic opportunities for students of both sexes.

OCR is strongly reaffirming today its commitment to equal opportunity for girls and boys, women and men. To that end, OCR is committed to continuing to work in partnership with educational institutions to ensure that the promise of Title IX becomes a reality for all students.

Thank you for your continuing interest in this subject.

Sincerely,

Gerald Reynolds

Assistant Secretary for Civil Rights

NOTES

•

Introduction

1. Data provided by the National Center for Education Statistics, U.S. Department of Education.

2. National Federation of State High School Associations, participation survey, 2002–3, http://www.nfhs.org/scriptcontent/VA_Custom/SurveyResources/2002_03_Participation.pdf, 4, accessed July 9, 2004.

3. Title IX of the Education Amendments of 1972, vol. 20, U.S.C. sec. 1681.

4. Office for Civil Rights, U.S. Department of Health, Education, and Welfare, policy interpretation of Title IX of the Education Amendments of 1972, *Federal Register* 44, no. 239 (December 11, 1979): 71415–17.

5. Mabel Lee, "Sports and Games—an Educational Dynamic Force," delivered at meeting of the Women's Division of the National Amateur Athletic Federation, New York City, January 3–5, 1929, http://www.barnard.columbia.edu/amstud/resources/women/lee.htm, accessed July 9, 2004.

Chapter 1

1. Clifford Putney, *Muscular Christianity: Manhood and Sports in Protestant America, 1880–1920* (Cambridge: Harvard University Press, 2001), 20.

2. Putney, *Muscular Christianity*, 22.

3. Putney, *Muscular Christianity*, 26.

4. Putney, *Muscular Christianity*, 29.

5. Dudley Allen Sargent, *An Autobiography*, ed. Ledyard W. Sargent (Philadelphia: Lea and Fobinger, 1927), 141.

6. Sargent, *An Autobiography*, 136–37.

7. Mark F. Bernstein, *Football: The Ivy League Origins of an American Obsession* (Philadelphia: University of Pennsylvania Press, 2001), 37.

8. Edmund Morris, *The Rise of Theodore Roosevelt* (New York: Coward, McCann, and Geoghegan, 1979), 90–91.

9. This history adapted from John R. Thelin, *Games Colleges Play: Scandal and Reform in Intercollegiate Athletics* (Baltimore: Johns Hopkins University Press, 1993); and Allen L. Sack and Ellen J. Staurowsky, *College Athletes for Hire: The Evolution and Legacy of the NCAA's Amateur Myth* (Westport, Conn.: Praeger, 1998).

10. *Princeton Alumni Weekly*, December 15, 1909, 6, cited in Bernstein, *Football*, 9.

11. Bernstein, *Football*, 14.

12. Monroe H. Little, "The Extra-curricular Activities of Black College Students, 1868–1940," *Journal of Negro History* 65, no. 2 (1980): 143.

13. Donald J. Mrozek, *Sport and American Mentality, 1880–1910* (Knoxville: University of Tennessee Press, 1983), 69.

14. Mrozek, *Sport and American Mentality*, 81.

15. Ellen W. Gerber, et al., *The American Woman in Sport* (Reading, Mass.: Addison-Wesley, 1974), 51.

16. Mrozek, *Sport and American Mentality*, 141–42.

17. Roberta J. Park and Joan S. Hult, "Women as Leaders in Physical Education and School-Based Sports, 1865 to the 1930s," *Journal of Physical Education, Recreation and Dance* 64 (1993): 36.

18. Reet Howell, ed., *Her Story in Sport: A Historical Anthology of Women in Sport* (West Point, N.Y.: Leisure Press, 1982).

19. Joan Paul, "Heroines Paving the Way," in *Women in Sport: Issues and Controversies*, ed. Greta L. Cohen (Newbury Park, Calif.: Sage, 1993), 28.

20. Lynne Emery, "The First Intercollegiate Contest for Women: Basketball, April 4, 1896," in Howell, *Her Story in Sport*.

21. Susan K. Cahn, *Coming on Strong: Gender and Sexuality in Twentieth Century Women's Sport* (New York: Free Press, 1994), 25.

22. *The Silhouette*, Agnes Scott College yearbook, 1909, Agnes Scott College library, 94.

23. Attributed to Ethel Perrin, National Amateur Athletic Federation, 1928, http://library.usask.ca/herstory/hockey.html.

24. Karen Kenney, "The Realm of Sports and the Athletic Women, 1850–1900," in Howell, *Her Story in Sport*.

25. Attributed to Mabel Lee, director of physical education for women at the University of Nebraska at Lincoln, 1930, in article titled "Sport and Games—an Educational Dynamic Force," in *Her Story: An Exhibition*, http://library.usask.ca/herstory/hockey.html, accessed July 9, 2004.

26. Gerber, *American Woman in Sport*, 37–38.

27. Discussed in David E. Diles, "A Historical Overview of Title IX," written while he was an assistant athletics director at Auburn University (photocopy).

28. Gerber, *American Woman in Sport*, 70–71.

29. Charlotte West, speech to the Snell Symposium at Ursinus College, 1999; notes taken by the author.

30. Gerber, *American Woman in Sport*, 64.

31. John Sayle Watterson, *College Football: History, Spectacle, Controversy* (Baltimore: Johns Hopkins University Press, 2000), 69.

32. Watterson, *College Football*, 74–79.

33. W. H. Cowley, "Athletics in American Colleges," *Journal of Higher Education* 1, no. 1 (1930): 29–30. This was a summary of the Carnegie Commission's report published, in the author's words, to "make for a more-widespread knowledge of the report's findings."

34. Cowley, "Athletics in American Colleges," 31.

35. Cowley, "Athletics in American Colleges," 32.

36. Cowley, "Athletics in American Colleges," 34–35.

37. Cited in Little, "Extra-curricular Activities," 140.

38. Cited in Murray A. Sperber, "*Onward to Victory: The Crises That Shaped College Sports*" (New York: Henry Holt, 1998), 181.

39. Sperber, *Onward to Victory*, 171.

40. Adapted from interviews for Welch Suggs, "Anti-gambling Seminar at U. of Kentucky Stars Athlete Charged in Betting Scandal," *Chronicle of Higher Education*, March 12, 1999, A43.

41. Jack Falla, *NCAA: The Voice of College Sports: A Diamond Anniversary History, 1906–1981* (Overland Park, Kans.: NCAA, 1981), 145.

Chapter 2

1. David B. Filvaroff and Raymond E. Wolfinger, "The Origin and Enactment of the Civil Rights Act of 1964," in *Legacies of the 1964 Civil Rights Act*, ed. Bernard Grofman (Charlottesville: University of Virginia Press, 2000), 12–13.

2. Charles V. Hamilton, *Adam Clayton Powell Jr.: The Political Biography of an American Dilemma* (New York: Macmillan, 1991), 227.

3. Cited at http://usinfo.state.gov/usa/infousa/facts/democrac/39.htm, accessed July 9, 2004.

4. See Grofman, *Legacies*; Robert D. Loevy, *To End All Segregation: The Politics of the Passage of the Civil Rights Act of 1964* (Lanham, Md.: University Press, 1990); Charles Whalen and Barbara Whalen, *The Longest Debate: A Legislative History of the 1964 Civil Rights Act* (Washington, D.C.: Seven Locks Press, 1985).

5. U.S.C., vol. 42, sec. 2000d.

6. U.S.C., vol. 42, sec. 2000e-2.

7. Filvaroff, and Wolfinger, "Origin and Enactment," 22.

8. Mary Frances Berry, *Why ERA Failed* (Bloomington: Indiana University Press, 1988), 61.

9. U.S.C., vol. 42, sec. 2000e-2(j).

10. Code of Federal Regulations, Title 41, chap. 60, pt. 2, subpart A.

11. Hugh Davis Graham, *The Civil Rights Era: Origins and Development of National Policy, 1960–72* (New York: Oxford University Press, 1990), 291.

12. Graham, *The Civil Rights Era*, 295.

13. Graham, *The Civil Rights Era*, 321.

14. Graham, *The Civil Rights Era*, 325.

15. Graham, *The Civil Rights Era*, 327.

16. Prepared testimony of Hugh Davis Graham before the House Committee on the Judiciary Subcommittee on the Constitution, Federal News Service, April 3, 1995.

17. Graham, prepared testimony.

18. Jeffrey H. Orleans, interview by the author.

19. Jeffrey H. Orleans, "An End to the Odyssey: Equal Athletic Opportunities for Women," *Duke Journal of Gender Law and Policy* 3 (1996): 137.

20. Discussion of Sandler's actions is taken from the account on her personal website, www.bernicesandler.com, and a 2003 interview. Other higher-education sources vouch for the general accuracy of her story.

21. *Congressional Record*, August 6, 1971, vol. 117, pt. 23: 30407.

22. Testimony before the U.S. Secretary's Commission on Opportunity in Athletics, August 27, 2002, http://www.ed.gov/about/bdscomm/list/athletics/transcript-082702.pdf.

23. Senate Conference Report 92-798, contained in 12971-3, *Senate Miscellaneous Reports on Public Bills* III, 148–50.

Chapter 3

1. All quotations from Hatchell, Rose, Summitt, and Lopiano in this chapter are drawn from interviews conducted in 2003 and 2004.

2. Patricia Ann Rosenbrock, "Persistence and Accommodation in a Decade of Struggle and Change: The Case of Women Administrators in Division I-A Intercollegiate Athletics Programs," Ph.D. diss., University of Iowa, 1987, 44–45.

3. Falla, *NCAA*, 33 and 164.

4. Affidavit of Donna A. Lopiano, president of the AIAW, in *Association for Intercollegiate Athletics for Women v. National Collegiate Athletic Association*, 588 F. Supp. 487 (D. D.C., 1983), affirmed, 735 F. 2d 577 (D.C. Cir. 1984).

5. AAHPER news release, December 7, 1967.

6. AAHPER news release.

7. AIAW Policy Statement, adopted May 1974, AIAW records archives, University of Maryland.

8. Christine H. B. Grant, "The Gender Gap in Sport: From Olympic to Intercollegiate Level," *Arena Review*, July 1984, 43.

9. Margaret J. Dunkle, "What Constitutes Equality for Women in Sport? Federal Law Puts Women in the Running," report for Project on the Status and Education of Women, April 1974, 10.

10. *Athletic Director*, 1. February 1974.

11. Dorothy McKnight and Joan Hult, untitled and undated memorandum, AIAW records archives, College Park, Md.

12. *AIAW newsletter* 2, no. 1, p. 3.

13. Lopiano affidavit, 35–36.

14. Lopiano affidavit, 36.

15. Falla, *NCAA*, 161–62.

16. Lopiano affidavit, 39.

17. Lopiano affidavit, 42–43.

18. Lopiano affidavit, 43.

19. Lopiano affidavit, 49.

20. Charles S. Neinas, interview by the author, 2003.

21. Lopiano affidavit, 45.

22. Walter F. Byers with Charles Hammer, *Unsportsmanlike Conduct: Exploiting College Athletes* (Ann Arbor: University of Michigan Press, 1993), 242.

23. Minutes of AIAW Delegates Assembly, January 5–8, 1975, AIAW records archives.

24. Minutes of AIAW Delegates Assembly, January 5–8, 1975, AIAW records archives.

25. Quoted in Rosenbrock, "Persistence and Accommodation," 51–52.

26. NCAA, *1982–00 Participation Statistics Report* (Indianapolis: NCAA, 2001). Available online at http://www.ncaa.org/library/research/participation_rates/1982-2000/153-164.pdf, accessed July 14, 2004.

27. Quoted in Rosenbrock, "Persistence and Accommodation," 53.

28. Addendum to AIAW executive board minutes for meeting June 1–4, 1972, AIAW records archives.

29. DGWS statement of philosophy, April 1, 1973, AIAW records archives.

30. Quoted in Rosenbrock, "Persistence and Accommodation," 53.

31. Thelin, *Games Colleges Play*, 395.

32. Thelin, *Games Colleges Play*, 396.

33. Falla, *NCAA*, 164.

34. Falla, *NCAA*, 164–65.

35. Byers, *Unsportsmanlike Conduct*, 244.

36. Falla, *NCAA*, 168–74.

37. Byers, *Unsportsmanlike Conduct*, 244.

Chapter 4

1. Cheryl Fields, "Woman Gets Spot on Varsity Basketball Team," *Chronicle of Higher Education*, November 4, 1974, 2, and Fields, "Big Gains for Women's Sports," *Chronicle of Higher Education*, December 9, 1974, 4.

2. *Congressional Record 1974*, May 20, 1974, vol. 120, pt. 15: 322.

3. *Congressional Record 1974*, May 20, 1974, vol. 120, pt. 15: 322.

4. Senate Conference Report No. 1026, 93rd, Congress, 2d sess., 1974, 139.

5. Lopiano affidavit, 100.

6. Caspar W. Weinberger, letter to Gerald R. Ford, reprinted in *Chronicle of Higher Education*, April 7, 1975, 11.

7. The regulation never uses the words *men* or *women*, but instead refers to the sex for which "opportunities have previously been limited." Women are the sex for which opportunities have been and continue to be limited, so I refer to them in the interest of simplicity.

8. Peter E. Holmes, "Elimination of Sex Discrimination in Athletic Programs," letter to Chief State School Officers, Superintendents of Local Educational Agencies, and University Presidents, September 1975, http://www.ed.gov./about/offices/list/ocr/docs/holmes/html.

9. Testimony before the House Committee on Education and Labor, June 17, 1975.

10. Falla, *NCAA*, 211.

11. Darrell Royal, testimony before the House Committee on Education and Labor, 94th Cong., 1st sess., June 17, 1975.

12. Motti's response to Royal, House Committee on Education and Labor, June 17, 1975.

13. Marcia D. Greenberger, interview by the author, 2003.

14. Dallin H. Oaks, "Title IX: Administrative, Legal, and Constitutional Aspects, the Future of Independent Higher Education," speech delivered to the Western College Association, San Francisco, March 10, 1977, *Vital Speeches of the Day*, March 1, 1978.

15. *National Collegiate Athletic Association v. Califano*, 444 F. Supp. 425 (D. Kans., 1978), affirmed, 622 F. 2d 1382 (10th Cir. 1980).

16. *Federal Register* 43, no. 238 (December 11, 1978): 58070.

17. *Federal Register* 44, no. 239 (December 11, 1979): 71420.

18. *Federal Register* 44, no. 239 (December 11, 1979): 71420.

19. *Federal Register* 44, no. 239 (December 11, 1979): 71413.

Chapter 5

1. U.S. Commission on Civil Rights, *More Hurdles to Clear: Women and Girls in Competitive Athletics*, Clearinghouse Publication no. 63 (July 1980), 2 and 11.

2. U.S. Department of Health, Education, and Welfare, Office for Civil Rights, *Title IX Intercollegiate Athletics Investigator's Manual (Interim)* (1980), 7.

3. U.S. Commission on Civil Rights, *The Federal Civil Rights Enforcement Effort to Ensure Equal Educational Opportunity* (1975), 41.

4. "About US: Now Legal Defense and Education Fund's History," http://www.nowldef.org/html/about/history.shtml, accessed July 9, 2004.

5. U.S. Commission on Civil Rights, *More Hurdles to Clear*, 33.

6. Lamar Daniel, interview by the author, 2003.

7. *Cannon v. U. of Chicago, et al.*, 406 F. Supp. 1257 (N.D. Ill. 1976), affirmed, 559 F. 2d [*1105] 1063 (7th Cir. 1976), reversed, 441 U.S. 677 (1979).

8. Holmes, "Elimination of Sex Discrimination."

9. Noted in U.S. Commission on Civil Rights, *More Hurdles to Clear*, 34; *Pavey v. University of Alaska*, 490 F. Supp. 1011 (D. Ark. 1980).

10. *U. of Richmond v. Bell*, 543 F. Supp. 321 (E.D. Va. 1982).

11. *U. of Richmond v. Bell*, 321.

12. *Haffer et al. v. Temple U. of the Commonwealth System of Higher Education et al.*, 524 F. Supp. 531 (E.D. Pa. 1981), affirmed, 688 F. 2d 14 (3d Cir. 1982).

13. *Grove City College v. Bell*, 687 F. 2d 691 (3d Cir. 1982), affirmed, 465 U.S. 555 (1984).

14. Julia Leighton, "Where Is Title IX?" Off Our Backs, May 31, 1982, 34.

15. Terrel H. Bell, *The Thirteenth Man: A Reagan Cabinet Memoir* (New York: Free Press, 1988), 2.

16. Bell, *The Thirteenth Man*, 104.

17. Bell, *The Thirteenth Man*, 107.

18. Charles R. Babcock, "University of Richmond Cleared; U.S. Won't Press Sex-Bias Case," *Washington Post*, September 9, 1982, A23.

19. "U.S. Won't Appeal Bias Case," *New York Times*, September 9, 1982, A20.

20. Byron Rosen, "Fan Fare," *Washington Post*, April 21, 1981, D5.

21. Christine Terp, "Title IX: More Races to Run," *Christian Science Monitor*, May 20, 1981, 12.

22. Bart Barnes, "Lack of Money Halts Boom in Women's Sports," *Washington Post*, July 5, 1981, D4.

23. Robert Pear, "Justice Department Open to New Rights Bill," *New York Times*, March 3, 1984, sec. 1, p. 11.

24. *Federal Register* 47 (January 13, 1982): 1662.

25. Bell, *The Thirteenth Man*, 112.

26. *Grove City College v. Bell*.

27. "Bell Assails Role of U.S. on Colleges," Associated Press, December 22, 1982.

28. Bell, *The Thirteenth Man*, 112.

29. *Grove City College v. Bell*.

30. Ruth Marcus, "Grove City Decision Has Stifled Hundred of Bias Complaints," *Washington Post*, March 7, 1988, A8.

31. Cited in HR 5430, Civil Rights Act of 1984, *Congressional Record*, June 26, 1984, vol. 130, pt. 13: 18835.

32. *Haffer*.

33. Martin Tolchin, "Baker Tries to Mediate Dispute on Scope of Civil Rights Bill," *New York Times*, September 21, 1984, B13.

34. Numbers taken from analysis of the NCAA's annual participation study, using reports covering academic years 1981–82 through 1989–90.

35. Robert Pear, "Justice Dept. Open to New Rights Bill," *New York Times*, March 3, 1984, sec. 1, p. 11.

36. Robert Pear, "Bill to Expand Rights Coverage Sets Off Dispute," *New York Times*, March 3, 1984, sec. 1, p. 1.

37. *Congressional Record*, June 25, 1984, vol. 130, p. 13: 18524.

38. Helen Dewar, "Rights Bill Is Shelved in Senate; Path Is Cleared for Enactment of Spending Measure," *Washington Post*, October 3, 1984, A1.

39. *Congressional Record*, January 26, 1988, vol. 134, pt. 2: S76.

40. Senate Bill 557, *Congressional Record*, January 26, 1988, vol. 134, pt. 2: S40.

41. *Congressional Record*, March 2, 1988, vol. 134, pt. 23: H565.

42. Veto Message on Senate Bill 557, Civil Rights Restoration Act, *Congressional Record*, March 17, 1988, vol. 134, pt. 33: S2489.

43. Veto Message, S2489.

44. Julie Johnson, "Foes of Civil Rights Bill Mount Eleventh-Hour Drive," *New York Times*, March 22, 1988, A22.

45. Helen Dewar, "Congress Overrides Civil Rights Law Veto; Antibias Legislation Is Voted into Effect," *Washington Post*, March 23, 1988, A1.

46. Motion for Reconsideration, *Haffer*, 678 F. Supp. 541.

47. "Temple Settlement," *New York Times*, June 14, 1988, B14.

48. Welch Suggs, "Players Off the Field," *Chronicle of Higher Education*, November 24, 2000, A59.

49. Mark Asher, "NCAA Convention to Begin; USOC, Women's Sports Foundation Wary of Certain Proposals," *Washington Post*, June 29, 1987, C2.

50. Erik Brady, "Title IX Gains a Measure of Success," *USA Today*, June 18, 1990, C1.

51. Jon Roe, "Gender Equity Key Issue; Schultz to Form Task Force on Hiring Women in Top Jobs," *Minneapolis Star-Tribune*, April 3, 1992, D1.

52. Douglas Lederman, "NCAA Releases Report on Sex Equity," *Chronicle of Higher Education*, March 18, 1992, online ed.

53. Douglas Lederman, "NCAA Panel Addresses Sex Equity in Sports," *Chronicle of Higher Education*, May 26, 1993, online ed.

54. NCAA, *Gender Equity Task Force Report* (Overland Park, Kans.: NCAA, July 26, 1993), 3.

55 Bill Sullivan, "Gender Equity Troubles CFA," *Houston Chronicle*, June 5, 1993, Sports, 8.

56. NCAA, *Achieving Gender Equity* (Overland Park, Kans.: NCAA, 1997), sec. 1, 1.

57. NCAA, *Gender Equity Task Force Report*, 6.

58. Numbers taken from analysis of NCAA's annual participation study, using reports covering academic years 1981–82 through 1989–90. Some of the increase in both men's and women's teams is due to the growth of the NCAA's membership as a whole, but that growth was very small in the 1980s compared to both prior and later decades.

Chapter 6

1. www.coachsummitt.com.

2. Travis Haney, "Lady Vols Fans an Older Crowd," *Chattanooga Times Free Press*, February 28, 2002, D4.

3. This section adapted from Welch Suggs, "U. of Tennessee's Lady Vols Find Success—and Profit—on the Court," *Chronicle of Higher Education*, December 17, 1999, A54.

4. All statistics from the NCAA's website, http://www.ncaa.org/stats.

5. Anson Dorrance, telephone interview by the author, December 2003. Unless otherwise noted, quotations from Dorrance are from this interview.

6. Anson Dorrance and Gloria Averbuch, *The Vision of a Champion* (Chelsea, Mich.: Sleeping Bear Press, 2002), 43.

7. Dorrance and Averbuch, *Vision of a Champion*, 44.

8. R. Vivian Acosta and Linda Jean Carpenter, "Women in Intercollegiate Sport: A Longitudinal Study—Twenty-seven Year Update, 1977–2004," http://webpages.charter.net/womeninsport/, 2004, 13, accessed July 14, 2004.

9. Acosta and Carpenter, "Women in Intercollegiate Sport," 12.

10. Acosta and Carpenter, "Women in Intercollegiate Sport," 2.

Chapter 7

1. *Franklin v. Gwinnett County Public Schools*, 911 F. 2d 617 (11th Cir. 1990), reversed, 503 U.S. 60 (1992).

2. Franklin.

3. *Favia et al. v. Indiana University of Pennsylvania et al.*, 812 F. Supp. 578 (W.D. Pa. 1992).

4. Favia.

5. *Roberts v. Colorado State Univ.*, 814 F. Supp. 1507 (D. Colo. 1993), affirmed, 998 F. 2d 824 (10th Cir. 1993), cert. denied.

6. Associated Press, no byline, no headline, May 9, 1991, Lexis-Nexis.

7. "Brown Abolishes Four Varsity Teams," *New York Times*, April 30, 1991, B10.

8. William G. Bowen and James L. Shulman, *The Game of Life: College Sports and Educational Values* (Princeton: Princeton University Press, 2001), 33. Figures apply only to Columbia, Princeton, Penn, and Yale, but are undoubtedly comparable in the other four Ivy League institutions.

9. Paula D. Welch, *Silver Era, Golden Moments: A Celebration of Ivy League Women's Athletics* (Lanham, Md.: Madison, 1999), 12.

10. Welch, *Silver Era, Golden Moments*, 25.

11. "Yale Women Strip to Protest a Lack of Crew's Showers," *New York Times*, March 3, 1976, reprinted in Welch, *Silver Era, Golden Moments*, 22. This episode is chronicled in the documentary *A Hero for Daisy*, prod. and dir. Mary Mazzio, 50 Eggs Productions, 2001.

12. Welch, *Silver Era, Golden Moments*, 25.

13. Trial Lawyers for Public Justice, press release, April 9, 1992.

14. *Cohen et al. v. Brown University et al.*, 809 F. Supp. 978 (D. R.I. 1992).

15. Cohen, 809 F. Supp.

16. Brown University, press release, April 9, 1992.

17. Debra E. Blum, "Suit Accuses Brown U. of Discriminating against Its Female Athletes," *Chronicle of Higher Education*, April 15, 1992, A44.

18. "Brown Sex Discrimination Suit Underway," Associated Press, October 27, 1992, Lexis-Nexis.

19. "Judge Said He Hopes to Decide Brown Discrimination Suit," Associated Press, November 17, 1992, Lexis-Nexis.

20. *Cohen*, 809 F. Supp.

21. *Federal Register*, 44, no. 239 (December 11, 1979): 71415.

22. *Cohen*, 809 F. Supp. Pettine used some creative accounting to come up with numbers for varsity athletes. He resolved to count only funded, varsity athletes, thus excluding male and female fencers (whose team was an unfunded club that competed against varsity athletes from other colleges), yet he counted a freshman football team as a varsity squad, even though freshman teams are usually considered junior varsity. He assigned it an arbitrary roster count of fifty athletes. Both decisions increased the number of male athletes relative to female, adding weight to the plaintiffs' claims of discrimination.

23. Brown University, press release, December 21, 1992.

24. Jessica Gavora, *Tilting the Playing Field: School Sports, Sex, and Title IX* (San Francisco: Encounter, 2002), chap. 6.

25. *Cohen et al. v. Brown University et al.*, 809 F. Supp. 978 (D. R.I. 1992), affirmed, 991 F. 2d 888 (1st Cir. 1993).

26. *Cohen et al. v. Brown University et al.*, 879 F. Supp. 185 (D. R.I. 1995), affirmed, 101 F. 3d 155 (1st Cir. 1996), cert. denied.

27. Ibid.

28. Trial Lawyers for Public Justice, press release, April 16, 1993.

29. "Brown Responds to Court Ruling," Associated Press, June 13, 1993, Lexis-Nexis.

30. Brown University, press release, September 23, 1994.

31. Respondents' brief, *Cohen*, 809 F. Supp. 978.

32. Douglas Lederman, "A Key Sports Equity Case," *Chronicle of Higher Education*, October 5, 1994, A51.

33. Trial Lawyers for Public Justice, press release, March 29, 1995.

34. Mary Swerczek, "Before Ruling, Women Athletes Saw Upgrades," *Brown Daily Herald*, April 4, 1995, online ed.

35. Brown University, press release, December 5, 1994.

36. Figures from surveys by the National Federation of State High School Associations, the U. S. Department of Education's National Center for Education Statistics, and the College board quotes are found in Brown University, press release, December 5, 1994.

37. *Cohen*, 809 F. Supp. 978.

38. Brown University, press release, March 29, 1995.

39. Trial Lawyers for Public Justice, press release, March 29, 1995.

40. Pettine actually stayed his ordered pending appeal, then reversed himself to resolve the order before the appeal took place. In August 1995 he ruled that the plan submitted by Brown was inadequate, allowing the appeals court to hear the case in December. Cited in *Cohen*, 879 F. Supp. 185 (D. R.I. 1995), affirmed, 101 F. 3d 155 (1st Cir. 1996), cert. denied.

41. Ibid.

42. Ibid.

43. *Cohen*. Also note that the options in the three-part tests are often referred to as "prongs" by Title IX insiders.

44. Adapted from *Cohen*, brief of appellants to U.S. Court of Appeals for the First Circuit, filed June 26, 1995, 1.

45. *Cohen*, 3.

46. *Cohen*, 879 F. Supp. 185 (D. R.I., 1995), affirmed, 101 F.3d 155 (1ˢᵗ Cir. 1996), cert. denied.

47. Ibid.

48. Ibid.

49. *Brown University, et al. v. Amy Cohen et al.*, Supreme Court 96-1321, appellants' brief, February 20, 1997.

50. All of these briefs, including Brown's and Cohen's, can be found on the *Chronicle of Higher Education*'s website at http://chronicle.com/indepth/titleix/documents.htm.

51. Jim Naughton, "Judge Approves Settlement of Brown U.'s Title IX Case," *Chronicle of Higher Education*, July 3, 1998, online ed.

52. Testimony of Beverly E. Ledbetter, Brown University general counsel, before the Secretary [of Education]'s Commission on Opportunity in Athletics, August 2002, Atlanta, http://www.ed.gov/about/bdscomm/list/athletics/transcript-082702.pdf.

Chapter 8

1. Jeremy Gerard, "In $1 Billion Deal, CBS Locks Up N.C.A.A. Basketball Tournament," *New York Times*, November 22, 1989, A1.

2. Welch Suggs, "Players Off the Field," *Chronicle of Higher Education*, November 24, 2000, A59.

3. Welch Suggs, "More Women Participate in Intercollegiate Athletics," *Chronicle of Higher Education*, May 21, 1999, A44.

4. *Kelley v. Board of Trustees of the University of Illinois*, 832 F. Supp. 237 (C.D. Ill. 1993), affirmed, 35 F. 3d 265 (7th Cir. 1994), cert. denied.

5. Kimberly Schuld, "Dangerous Waters in the (Title IX) Safe Harbor," *Federalist Society Civil Rights Practice Group Newsletter*, summer 1999, online ed.

6. "Gender Equity in Intercollegiate Athletics: The Inadequacy of Title IX Enforcement by the U.S. Office for Civil Rights," project directed by Kenneth W. Tolo, Working Paper No. 69, Lyndon B. Johnson School of Public Affairs, University of Texas at Austin, July 1993, 5.

7. "Gender Equity," 1–2.

8. "Gender Equity," 19.

9. "Gender Equity," 22–23.

10. General Accounting Office, "Intercollegiate Athletics: Status of Efforts to Promote Gender Equity," HEHS-97-10, October 25, 1996.

11. General Accounting Office, "Gender Equity: Men's and Women's Participation in Higher Education," December 15, 2000.

12. Harry Blauvelt, "Title IX Enforcement Hit Hard at Hearing," *USA Today*, May 10, 1995, C3.

13. Blauvelt, "Title IX Enforcement," C3.

14. Letter from Rep. J. Dennis Hastert to Norma V. Cantù, October 30, 1995, photocopy.

15. Letter from Greg Waggoner to Norma V. Cantù, October 20, 1995, photocopy.

16. Letter from Phil Webster, Peoria Manual High School, to Norma V. Cantù, October 17, 1995, photocopy.

17. Letter from Margaret J. Bradley-Doppes to Norma V. Cantù, October 10, 1995, photocopy.

18. Office for Civil Rights, U.S. Department of Education, "Clarification of Intercollegiate Athletic Policy Guidance: The Three-Part Test," issued January 16, 1996.

19. Norma V. Cantù, "Dear Colleague" letter accompanying the January 19, 1996 policy clarification, http://www.ed.gov/about/offices/list/ocr/title9guidance-Final.html.

20. *Cohen*, 879 F. Supp. 185 (D. R.I. 1995), affirmed, 101 F. 3d 155 (1st Cir. 1996), cert. Denied.

21. Jim Naughton, "Advocacy Group Charges Twenty-five Colleges with Violating Title IX," *Chronicle of Higher Education*, June 13, 1997, online ed.

22. Norma V. Cantù, letter to Nancy S. Footer, general counsel, Bowling Green State University, July 24, 1998.

23. Welch Suggs, "Sports Administrators Remain Disturbed as U.S. Acts on Gender-Equity Complaints," *Chronicle of Higher Education*, January 8, 1999, A57.

24. Suggs, "Sports Administrators," A57.

25. Welch Suggs, "Education Dept. Resolves Last of Twenty-five Bias Complaints Filed by Women's Group," *Chronicle of Higher Education*, January 11, 2000, A49.

26. EEOC Notice 915.002, "Enforcement Guidance on Sex Discrimination in the Compensation of Sports Coaches in Educational Institutions," November 3, 1997, http://www.eeoc.gov/policy/does/coaches.html.

27. EEOC, "Enforcement Guidance."

28. General Accounting Office, "Gender Equity: Men's and Women's Participation in Higher Education," December 15, 2000, 38.

29. *Kelley v. Board of Trustees of the U. of Illinois*.

30. Welch Suggs, "Miami U. Drops Three Men's Sports," *Chronicle of Higher Education*, April 30, 1999, A44.

31. Welch Suggs, "Colleges Consider Fairness of Cutting Men's Teams to Comply with Title IX," *Chronicle of Higher Education*, February 19, 1999, A53.

32. Denise K. Magner, "Judge Blocks Cal State–Bakersfield's Plan to Cap Size of Wrestling Team," *Chronicle of Higher Education*, March 12, 1999, A44.

33. *Neal et al. v. California State Board of Trustees et al.*, 198 F. 3d 763 (9th Cir. 1999), cert. denied.

34. Welch Suggs, "Two Appeals Courts Uphold Right of Universities to Reduce Number of Male Athletes," *Chronicle of Higher Education*, January 7, 2000, A64.

35. *Pederson et al. v. Louisiana State University et al.*, 912 F. Supp. 892 (M.D. La. 1996), affirmed, 213 F. 3d 858 (5th Cir. 2000).

36. Ibid.

37. Welch Suggs, "Judge Rules against Duke U. in Female Football Player's Lawsuit," *Chronicle of Higher Education*, March 15, 2001, online ed.

38. Welch Suggs, "Foes of Title IX Try to Make Equity in College Sports a Campaign Issue," *Chronicle of Higher Education*, February 4, 2000, A55.

39. General Accounting Office, "Gender Equity."

40. Lori Nickel, "Arm-Twisting: Alumni Save MU wrestling program," *Milwaukee Journal-Sentinel*, October 20, 1998, Sports, 7.

41. Welch Suggs, "Poll Finds Strong Public Backing for Gender Equity in College Athletics," *Chronicle of Higher Education*, July 7, 2000, A40.

Chapter 9

1. National Federation of State High School Associations, press release, September 3, 2003.

2. National Federation of State High School Associations, participation survey, 2000–2001, reprinted by NCAA, http://www.ncaa.org/library/research/participation_rates/1982-2001/175-192.pdf, accessed July 10, 2004.

3. Gavora, *Tilting the Playing Field*.

4. *Mercer v. Duke University and Fred Goldsmith*, 32 F. Supp. 2d 836 (M.D. N.C. 1998), reversed, 190 F. 3d 643 (4th Cir. 1999).

5. Ibid.

6. Peter Monaghan, "Supreme Court Favors NCAA in Title IX Ruling, but Sends Two Questions to Lower Court," *Chronicle of Higher Education*, February 28, 1999, online ed.

7. Horner et al. v. *Kentucky High School Athletic Association* et al., 43 F. 3d 265 (6th Cir. 1994).

8. Ibid, emphasis added.

9. Ibid.

10. *Landow v. School Board of Brevard County*, 132 F. Supp. 2d 958 (M.D. Fla. 2000).

11. "Ruling Ends Unequal girls' Softball Fields," *Florida Times-Union*, December 18, 2000, B2.

12. National Federation of State High School Associations, 2001–2 participation report, http://www.nfhs.org/scriptcontent/Va_custom/va_cm/contentpagedisplay.cfm?content_ID-215.

13. Mike Fish and David A. Milliron, "The Gender Gap: Georgia Treats Girl Athletes Second-Class," *Atlanta Journal-Constitution*, December 12, 1999, 1A.

14. Fish and Milliron, "The Gender Gap," 1A.

15. Kevin Walls, "Gender Numbers Game Requires Balancing Act," *Tampa Tribune*, June 29, 1999, Sports, 1.

16. Mike Fish and David A. Milliron, "The Gender Gap: Equity Backers Stirring," *Atlanta Journal-Constitution*, December 19, 1999, 1E.

17. National Federation of State High School Associations, 2001–2 participation report.

18. Herb Dempsey, email to the author.

19. *Communities for Equity et al. v. Michigan High School Athletic Association*, 80 F. Supp. 2d 729 (M.D. Mich. 2000).

20. Tim Martin, "Federal Appeals Court Says Michigan Prep Schedule Unfair to Girls, Associated Press, state and regional wites, July 28, 2004.

21. *Communtics for Equity.*

22. Ibid.

23. Larry Colson, *Counting Coup: A True Story of Basketball and Honor on the Little Big Horn* (New York: Warner, 2001), 106.

24. Mike Fish and David A. Milliron, "Private Schools: Private Practice Close to Parity," *Atlanta Journal-Constitution*, December 16, 1999, G7.

25. Analysis of data on Georgia High School Association and Florida High School Athletic Association websites, http://ghsa.net and http://www.fhsaa.org, accessed July 10, 2004.

26. Fish and Milliron, "Private Schools," G7.

Chapter 10

1. Welch Suggs, "Foes of Title IX Try to Make Equity in College Sports a Campaign Issue," *Chronicle of Higher Education*, February 25, 2000, A55.

2. Suggs, "Foes of Title IX," A55.

3. "Q&A: The Candidates on College Issues," *Chronicle of Higher Education*, February 25, 2000, A32.

4. Jeffrey Selingo, "Republicans Seek a New Tone on Many Education Issues," *Chronicle of Higher Education*, August 11, 2000, A28.

5. Stephen Burd, "Bush Nominates Houston Official to Be Secretary of Education," *Chronicle of Higher Education*, January 12, 2001, A21.

6. Ben Gose, "Civil-Rights Nominee Faces Tough Grilling in Senate Confirmation Hearing," *Chronicle of Higher Education*, March 8, 2002, A41.

7. Gose, "Civil-Rights Nominee," A41.

8. Welch Suggs, "Defying Rumors, Bush Administration Defends Status Quo on Title IX," *Chronicle of Higher Education*, June 7, 2002, A41.

9. Suggs, "Defying Rumors," A41.

10. Welch Suggs, "Can a Commission Change Title IX?" *Chronicle of Higher Education*, July 12, 2002, A38.

11. U.S. Department of Education, "Members—Secretary's Commission on Opportunity in Athletics," http://www.ed.gov/about/bdscomm/list/athletics/members.html, accessed July 10, 2004.

12. Suggs, "Can a Commission Change," A38.

13. U.S. Department of Education, "Charter—Secretary's Commission on Opportunity in Athletics," http://www.ed.gov/about/bdscomm/list/athletics/charter.html, accessed July 10, 2004.

14. These critiques are the author's, but a similar question-by-question analysis was written by Valerie Bonnette of Good Sports Inc. and submitted to the commissioners and others.

15. Suggs, "Can a Commission Change," A38.

16. Welch Suggs, "Federal Commission Considers Reinterpreting Title IX," *Chronicle of Higher Education*, September 6, 2002, online ed.

17. Suggs, "Commission Considers Reinterpreting."

18. Welch Suggs, "A Federal Commission Wrestles with Gender Equity in Sports," *Chronicle of Higher Education*, January 3, 2003, A41.

19. Suggs, "Federal Commission Wrestles," A41.

20. Dick Aronson, e-mail to author, December 17, 2003.

21. Suggs, "Federal Commission Wrestles," A41.

22. "Federal Panelists' Ideas for Changing Title IX," *Chronicle of Higher Education*, January 3, 2003, A43.

23. Welch Suggs, "Advocates for Men's and Women's Sports Trade Charges as Title IX Panel Gets Ready to Vote," *Chronicle of Higher Education*, January 29, 2003, online ed.

24. Suggs, "Advocates."

25. Welch Suggs, "Skirmishes Begin over Commission's Report on Title IX," *Chronicle of Higher Education*, January 30, 2003, online ed.

26. Welch Suggs, "Smoke Obscures Fire in Title IX Debate as Federal Panel Adjourns," *Chronicle of Higher Education*, February 7, 2003, A31.

27. "Open to All: Title IX at Thirty," The Secretary of Education's Commission on Opportunity in Athletics, U.S. Department of Education, February 2003, 5.

28. Suggs, "Smoke Obscures Fire," A31.

29. Suggs, "Smoke Obscures Fire," A31.

30. Welch Suggs, "Getting Ready for the Next Round: Proposals on Title IX Intensify the Debate over Gender Equity," *Chronicle of Higher Education*, February 14, 2003, A39.

31. Suggs, "Getting Ready."

32. Welch Suggs, "U.S. Commission on Title IX Calls for Protecting Men's Teams," *Chronicle of Higher Education*, February 28, 2003, online ed.

33. Secretary's Commission on Title IX in Athletics, "Open to All: Title IX at 30," U.S. Department of Education, February 2003, http://www.ed.gov/about/bdscomm/list/athletics/report.html.

34. Secretary's Commission, "Open to All," 28.

35. Welch Suggs, "Cheers and Condemnation Greet Report Card on Gender Equity," *Chronicle of Higher Education*, March 7, 2003, A40.

36. Donna de Varona and Julie Foudy, "Minority Views on the Report of the Commission on Opportunity in Athletics," February 26, 2003, 1; distributed at press conference.

37. Suggs, "Cheers and Condemnation," A40.

38. Suggs, "Cheers and Condemnation," A40.

39. Suggs, "Cheers and Condemnation," A40.

40. Suggs, "Cheers and Condemnation," A40.

41. Welch Suggs, "A Quiet Convention," *Chronicle of Higher Education*, January 24, 2003, A35.

42. Welch Suggs, "NCAA Leader Defends Title IX," *Chronicle of Higher Education*, March 14, 2003, A38.

43. Welch Suggs, "Wrestling Complaints Denied in Title IX Ruling," *Chronicle of Higher Education*, June 20, 2003, A34.

44. *National Wrestling Coaches Association et al. v. U.S. Department of Education*, 263 F. Supp. 2d 82 (D. D.C. 2003).

45. Gerald Reynolds, "Further Clarification of Intercollegiate Athletics Policy Guidance Regarding Title IX Compliance," July 11, 2003, http://www.ed.gov/about/offices/list/ocr/title9guidanceFinal.html.

46. Welch Suggs, "Education Department Stands Pat on Title IX," *Chronicle of Higher Education*, July 25, 2003, A33.

Chapter 11

1. Bob Sterken, e-mail to the author, November 18, 2003.

2. Welch Suggs, "The Big-Time Cost of Small-Time Sports," *Chronicle of Higher Education*, September 19, 2003, A35.

3. McKinsey and Co., "Intercollegiate Athletics at Rice University," private report to Rice University's Board of Trustees, April 2004, 32 and 39.

4. Welch Suggs, "Left Behind," *Chronicle of Higher Education*, November 30, 2001, A35.

5. Jennifer Jacobson, "Why Do So Many Female Athletes Enter ACL Hell?" *Chronicle of Higher Education*, March 9, 2001, A45.

6. Peter Cary, "Fixing Kids' Sports," *U.S. News & World Report*, June 7, 2004, 48. Data cited from American Sports Data Inc. and the Sporting Goods Manufacturers Association.

7. Brenda J. Buote, "Schools Shirking Workouts," *Boston Globe*, June 24, 2004, 1.

8. *Tampa Tribune*, "The Upshot on Physical Education: Waistlines Up, Classes Down," February 24, 2004, 12.

Chapter 12

1. Data obtained from the U.S. Department of Education's Office for Post-secondary Education and analyzed by staff of the *Chronicle of Higher Education*.

2. National Federation of State High School Associations, "Survey Resources: Participation Sets Record for Fifth Straight Year," press release, September 2, 2003.

3. Welch Suggs, "Non-bowl Athletes Lose Male Athletes," *Chronicle of Higher Education*, June 18, 2004, A33.

4. *National Wrestling Coaches Association et al. v. U.S. Department of Education*, 263 F. Supp. 2d 82 (D. D.C. 2003) affirmed, 366 F. 3d 930 (D.C. Cir. 2004).

5. Bob Clark, "Locker Room Pairs Luxury, Technology," *Register-Guard* (Eugene, Ore.), August 24, 2003, http://www.registerguard.com/news/2003/08/24/d1.sp.lockers.0824.html, accessed July 10, 2004.

6. Data obtained from the U.S. Department of Education's Office for Postsecondary Education and analyzed by staff of the *Chronicle of Higher Education*.

7. Welch Suggs, "Colleges Make Slight Progress toward Gender Equity in Sports," *Chronicle of Higher Education*, July 25, 2003, A30.

8. Suggs, "Colleges Make Slight Progress," A30.

9. Suggs, "Colleges Make Slight Progress," A30.

10. Emily Badger, "U-M Makes Cheerleading a Sport," *Washington Post*, September 27, 2003, D1.

BIBLIOGRAPHY

•

Acosta, R. Vivian, and Linda Jean Carpenter. "Women in Intercollegiate Sport: A Longitudinal Study—Twenty-seven Year Update, 1977–2004." Typescript.

AIAW Newsletter 2, no. 1, undated.

Athletic Director, February 1974.

Asher, Mark. "NCAA Convention to Begin; USOC, Women's Sports Foundation Wary of Certain Proposals." *Washington Post*, June 29, 1987, C2.

Babcock, Charles R. "University of Richmond Cleared; U.S. Won't Press Sex-Bias Case." *Washington Post*, September 9, 1982, A23.

Badger, Emily. "U-M Makes Cheerleading a Sport." *Washington Post*, September 27, 2003, D1.

Barnes, Bart. "Lack of Money Halts Boom in Women's Sports." *Washington Post*, July 5, 1981, D4.

Becker, Susan D. *The Origins of the Equal Rights Movement*. Westport, Conn.: Greenwood Press, 1981.

Bell, Terrel H. *The Thirteenth Man: A Reagan Cabinet Memoir*. New York: Free Press, 1988.

"Bell Assails Role of U.S. on Campus." Associated Press, December 22, 1982, Lexis-Nexis.

Bernstein, Mark F. *Football: The Ivy League Origins of an American Obsession*. Philadelphia: University of Pennsylvania Press, 2001.

Berry, Mary Frances. *Why ERA Failed*. Bloomington: Indiana University Press, 1988.

Blauvelt, Harry. "Title IX Enforcement Hit Hard at Hearing." *USA Today*, May 10, 1995, 3C.

Blum, Debra E. "Suit Accuses Brown U. of Discriminating against Its Female Athletes." *Chronicle of Higher Education*, April 15, 1992, A44.

Bowen, William G., and James L. Shulman. *The Game of Life: College Sports and Educational Values*. Princeton: Princeton University Press, 2001.

Bradley-Doppes, Margaret J. Letter to Norma V. Cantù, October 10, 1995. Photocopy in author's possession.

Brady, Erik. "Title IX Gains a Measure of Success." *USA Today*, June 18, 1990, C1.

"Brown Abolishes Four Varsity Teams." *New York Times*, April 30, 1991, B10.

"Brown Responds to Court Ruling." *New York Times*, June 13, 1993.

"Brown Sex Discrimination Suit Underway." Associated Press, October 27, 1992, Lexis-Nexis.

Burd, Stephen. "Bush Nominates Houston Official to Be Secretary of Education." *Chronicle of Higher Education*, January 12, 2001, A21.

Byers, Walter F. *Unsportsmanlike Conduct: Exploiting College Athletes*. Ann Arbor: University of Michigan Press, 1993.

Cahn, Susan K. *Coming on Strong: Gender and Sexuality in Twentieth Century Women's Sport*. New York: Free Press, 1994.

Cantù, Norma V. "Dear Colleague" letter accompanying U.S. Department of Education's "Clarification of Intercollegiate Athletic Policy Guidance: The Three-Part Test." January 16, 1996. http://www.ed.gov/about/offices/list/ocr/docs/clarific.html#one.

Cantù, Norma V. Letter to Nancy S. Footer, June 24, 1998. Photocopy in author's possession.

Carpenter, Linda Jean, and R. Vivan Acosta. *Title IX*. Champaign, Ill.: Human Kinetics, 2004.

Clark, Bob. "Locker Room Pairs Luxury, Technology." *Register-Guard* (Eugene, Ore.), August 24, 2003, online ed.

Cohen, Greta L. *Women in Sport: Issues and Controversies*. Newbury Park, Calif.: Sage, 1993.

Colson, Larry. *Counting Coup: A True Story of Basketball and Honor on the Little Big Horn*. New York: Warner Books, 2001.

Cowley, W. H. "Athletics in American Colleges." *Journal of Higher Education* 1 no. 1 (1930), reprinted 70, no. 5 (1999): 494–503.

de Varona, Donna, and Julie Foudy. "Minority Views on the Report of the Commission on Opportunity in Athletics." February 26, 2003. Photocopy.

Dewar, Helen. "Congress Overrides Civil Rights Law Veto; Antibias Legislation Is Voted into Effect." *Washington Post*, March 23, 1988, A1.

———. "Rights Bill Is Shelved in Senate; Path Is Cleared for Enactment of Spending Measure." *Washington Post*, October 3, 1984, A1.

Diles, David E. "A Historical Overview of Title IX." Photocopy.

Dorrance, Anson, and Gloria Averbuch. *The Vision of a Champion*. Chelsea, Mich.: Sleeping Bear Press, 2002.

Dunkle, Margaret J. "What Constitutes Equality for Women in Sport? Federal Law Puts Women in the Running." Report for Project on the Status and Education of Women. Washington, D.C.: April 1974.

Equal Employment Opportunity Commission. "Enforcement Guidance on Sex Discrimination in the Compensation of Sports Coaches in Educational Institutions." EEOC Notice No. 915.002, November 3, 1997.

Falla, Jack. *NCAA: The Voice of College Sports: A Diamond Anniversary History, 1906–1981*. Overland Park, Kans.: NCAA, 1981.

"Federal Panelists' Ideas for Changing Title IX." *Chronicle of Higher Education*, January 3, 2003, A43.

Fields, Cheryl. "Big Gains for Women's Sports." *Chronicle of Higher Education*, December 9, 1974, 4.

———. "Woman Gets Spot on Varsity Basketball Team." *Chronicle of Higher Education*, November 4, 1974, 2.

——. "The Gender Gap: George Treats Girl Athletes Second-Class." *Atlanta Journal-Constitution*, December 12, 1999, 1A.

Fish, Mike, and David A. Milliron. "The Gender Gap: Equity Backers Stirring." *Atlanta Journal-Constitution*, December 19, 1999, 1E.

——. "Private Practice: Private Schools Close to Parity." *Atlanta Journal-Constitution*, December 16, 1999, G7.

Gavora, Jessica. *Tilting the Playing Field: School, Sports, Sex, and Title IX*. San Francisco: Encounter Books, 2002.

"Gender Equity in Intercollegiate Athletics: The Inadequacy of Title IX Enforcement by the U.S. Office for Civil Rights," project directed by Kenneth W. Tolo, Working Paper No. 69, Lyndon B. Johnson School of Public Affairs, University of Texas at Austin, July 1993.

General Accounting Office. "Gender Equity: Men's and Women's Participation in Higher Education." December 15, 2000.

——. "Intercollegiate Athletics: Status of Efforts to Promote Gender Equity." HEHS-97-10, October 26, 1996.

Gerard, Jeremy. "In $1 Billion Deal, CBS Locks Up N.C.A.A. Basketball Tournament." *New York Times*, November 22, 1989, A1.

Gerber, Ellen W., ed. *The American Woman in Sport*. Boston: Addison-Wesley, 1974.

Gose, Ben. "Civil-Rights Nominee Faces Tough Grilling in Senate Confirmation Hearing." *Chronicle of Higher Education*, March 8, 2002, A41.

Graham, Hugh Davis. *The Civil Rights Era: Origins and Development of National Policy, 1960–72*. New York: Oxford University Press, 1990.

——. Prepared testimony before the House Committee on the Judiciary Subcommittee on the Constitution, Federal News Service, April 3, 1995.

Grofman, Bernard, ed. *Legacies of the 1964 Civil Rights Act*. Charlottesville: University of Virginia Press, 2000.

Hamilton, Charles V. *Adam Clayton Powell, Jr.: The Political Biography of an American Dilemma*. New York: Macmillan, 1991.

Haney, Travis. "Lady Vols Fans an Older Crowd." *Chattanooga Times Free Press*, February 28, 2002, D4.

Hastert, J. Dennis. Letter to Norma V. Cantù, October 30, 1995. Photocopy in author's possession.

Holmes, Peter E. "Elimination of Sex Discrimination in Athletic Programs." Letter to Chief State School Officers, Superintendents of Local Educational Agencies, and College and University Presidents, September 1975.

Howell, Reet, ed. *Her Story in Sport: A Historical Anthology of Women in Sport*. West Point, N.Y.: Leisure Press, 1982.

Jacobson, Jennifer. "Why Do So Many Female Athletes Enter ACL Hell?" *Chronicle of Higher Education*, March 9, 2001, A45.

Johnson, Julie. "Foes of Civil Rights Bill Mount Eleventh-Hour Drive." *New York Times*, March 22, 1988, A22.

"Judge Said He Hopes to Decide Brown Discrimination Suit." Associated Press, November 17, 1992, Lexis-Nexis.

Lederman, Douglas. "A Key Sports Equity Case." *Chronicle of Higher Education*, October 5, 1994, A5.

———. "NCAA Panel Addresses Sex Equity in Sports." *Chronicle of Higher Education*, May 26, 1993, A3.

———. "NCAA Releases Report on Sex Equity." *Chronicle of Higher Education*, March 18, 1992, A1.

Leighton, Julia. "Where Is Title IX?" Off Our Backs, May 31, 1982, 34.

Little, Monroe H. "The Extra-curricular Activities of Black College Students, 1868–1940." *Journal of Negro History*, 65 no. 2 (1980): 135–48.

Loevy, Robert D. *To End All Segregation: The Politics of the Passage of the Civil Rights Act of 1964*. Lanham, Md.: University Press, 1990.

Magner, Denise K. "Judge Blocks Cal State–Bakersfield's Plan to Cap Size of Wrestling Team." *Chronicle of Higher Education*, March 12, 1999, A44.

Marcus, Ruth. "Grove City Decision Has Stifled Hundreds of Bias Complaints." *Washington Post*, March 7, 1988, A8.

Mazzio, Mary, dir. and pro. *A Hero for Daisy*, 50 Eggs Productions, 2001.

McKinsey and Co. "Intercollegiate Athletics at Rice University." Report to Rice University Board of Trustees, April 2004.

Monaghan, Peter. "Supreme Court Favors NCAA in Title IX Ruling, but Sends Two Questions to Lower Court." *Chronicle of Higher Education*, February 28, 1999, online ed.

Morris, Edmund. *The Rise of Theodore Roosevelt*. New York: Coward, McCann, and Geoghegan, 1979.

Mrozek, Donald J. *Sport and American Mentality, 1880–1910*. Knoxville: University of Tennessee Press, 1983.

National Collegiate Athletic Association. *Achieving Gender Equity*. Overland Park, Kans.: NCAA, 1997.

———. *Gender Equity Task Force Report*. Overland Park, Kans.: NCAA, July 26, 1993.

———. *1982–00 Participation Statistics Report*. Indianapolis: NCAA, 2001.

National Federation of State High School Associations, "Participation Survey, 2000–1." Reprinted by NCAA in *"Participation Rates in College Sports 1982–2001."* (Indianapolis: NCAA, 2001).

———. Participation Report, 2002–3. http://www.nfhs.org/scriptcontent/Va_custom/va_cm/contentpagedisplay.cfm?content_ID=215.

Naughton, Jim. "Advocacy Group Charges 25 Colleges with Violating Title IX." *Chronicle of Higher Education*, June 13, 1997. Online ed.

———. "Judge Approves Settlement of Brown U.'s Title IX Case." *Chronicle of Higher Education*, July 3, 1998. Online ed.

Nickel, Lori. "Arm-Twisting: Alumni Save MU Wrestling Program." *Milwaukee Journal-Sentinel*, October 20, 1998, Sports, 7.

Oaks, Dallin H. "Title IX: Administrative, Legal, and Constitutional Aspects: The Future of Independent Higher Education." Speech delivered to the Western College Association, San Francisco, March 10, 1977. *Vital Speeches of the Day*, March 1, 1978.

Office for Civil Rights, U.S. Department of Health, Education and Welfare. "Title IX of the Education Amendments of 1972; A Policy Interpretation: Title IX and Intercollegiate Athletics." *Federal Register*, vol. 44, no. 239 (December 11, 1979). Online ed.

Office for Civil Rights, U.S. Department of Education. "Clarification of Intercollegiate Athletic Policy Guidance: The Three-Part Test." January 16, 1996.

Orleans, Jeffrey H. "An End to the Odyssey: Equal Athletic Opportunities for Women." *Duke Journal of Gender Law and Policy* 3 (1996): 131–61.

Park, Roberta J., and Joan S. Hult. "Women as Leaders in Physical Education and School-based Sports, 1865 to the 1930s." *Journal of Physical Education, Recreation, and Dance* 64 (1993): 36.

Pear, Robert. "Bill to Expand Rights Coverage Sets Off Dispute." *New York Times*, March 3, 1984, A1.

———. "Justice Department Open to New Rights Bill." *New York Times*, March 3, 1984, A11.

Putney, Clifford. *Muscular Christianity: Manhood and Sports in Protestant America 1880–1920*. Cambridge: Harvard University Press, 2001.

"Q&A: The Candidates on Campaign Issues." *Chronicle of Higher Education*, February 25, 2000, A32.

Reagan, Ronald W. Veto Message on S. 557, The Civil Rights Restoration Act. *Congressional Record*, March 17, 1988, vol. 134, pt. 33: S2489.

Reynolds, Gerald. "Further Clarification of Intercollegiate Athletics Policy Guidance Regarding Title IX Compliance." July 11, 2003. http://www.ed.gov./about/offices/list/ocr/title9guidanceFinal.html.

Roe, Jon. "Gender Equity Key Issue; Shultz to Form Task Force on Hiring Women in Top Jobs." *Minneapolis Star Tribune*, April 3, 1992, D1.

Rosen, Byron. "Fan Fare." *Washington Post*, April 21, 1981, D5.

Rosenbrock, Patricia Ann. "Persistence and Accommodation in a Decade of Struggle and Change: The Case of Women Administrators in Division I-A Intercollegiate Athletics Programs." Ph.D. diss., University of Iowa, 1987.

"Ruling Ends Unequal Girls Softball Fields." *Florida Times-Union*, December 18, 2000, B2.

Sack, Allen L., and Ellen J. Staurowsky. *College Athletes for Hire: The Evolution and Legacy of the NCAA's Amateur Myth*. Westport, Conn.: Praeger, 1998.

Sargent, Dudley Allen. *An Autobiography*. Ed. Ledyard W. Sargent. Philadelphia: Lea and Fobinger, 1927.

Schuld, Kimberly. "Dangerous Waters in the (Title IX) Safe Harbor." *Civil Rights Practice Group Newsletters* 3, no. 2 (1999).

Secretary's Commission on Opportunity in Athletics. Hearing transcripts, 2002–3. Available at http://www.ed.gov/about/bdscomm/list/athletics/transcripts.html, accessed July 14, 2004.

Secretary's Commission on Title IX in Athletics, "Open to All: Title IX at 30." U.S. Department of Education. http://www.ed.gov/about/bdscomm/list/athletics/report.html. February 2003.

Selingo, Jeffrey. "Republicans Seek a New Tone on Many Education Issues." *Chronicle of Higher Education*, August 11, 2000, A28.

Sperber, Murray A. *Onward to Victory: The Crises That Shapes College Sports.* New York: Henry Holt, 1998.

Suggs, Welch. "Advocates for Men's and Women's Sports Trade Charges as Title IX Panel Gets Ready to Vote." *Chronicle of Higher Education*, January 29, 2003, online ed.

———. "Big-Time Cost of Small-Time Sports." *Chronicle of Higher Education*, September 19, 2003.

———. "Can a Commission Change Title IX?" *Chronicle of Higher Education*, July 12, 2002, A38.

———. "Cheers and Condemnation Greet Report Card on Gender Equity." *Chronicle of Higher Education*, March 7, 2003, A40.

———. "Colleges Consider Fairness of Cutting Men's Teams to Comply with Title IX." *Chronicle of Higher Education*, February 19, 1999, A53.

———. "Colleges Make Slight Progress toward Gender Equity in Sports." *Chronicle of Higher Education*, July 25, 2003, A30.

———. "Defying Rumors, Bush Administration Defends Status Quo on Title IX." *Chronicle of Higher Education*, June 7, 2002, A41.

———. "Education Department Stands Pat on Title IX." July 25, 2003, A33.

———. "Education Dept. Resolves Last of Twenty-Five Bias Complaints Filed by Women's Group." *Chronicle of Higher Education*, January 11, 2000, A49.

———. "Federal Commission Considers Reinterpreting Title IX." *Chronicle of Higher Education*, September 6, 2002, online ed.

———. "A Federal Commission Wrestles with Gender Equity in Sports." *Chronicle of Higher Education*, January 3, 2003, A41.

———. "Foes of Title IX Try to Make Equity in College Sports a Campaign Issue." *Chronicle of Higher Education*, February 4, 2000, A55.

———. "Getting Ready for the Next Round: Proposals on Title IX Intensify the Debate over Gender Equity." *Chronicle of Higher Education*, February 7, 2003, A31.

———. "Getting Ready for the Next Round: Proposals on Title IX Intensify the Debate over Gender Equity." *Chronicle of Higher Education*, February 14, 2003, A39.

———. "Left Behind." *Chronicle of Higher Education*, November 30, 2001, A35.

———. "Miami U. Drops Three Men's Sports." *Chronicle of Higher Education*, April 30, 1999, A44.

———. "More Women Participate in Intercollegiate Athletics." *Chronicle of Higher Education*, May 21, 1999, A44.

———. "NCAA Leader Defends Title IX." *Chronicle of Higher Education*, March 14, 2003, A38.

———. "Non-bowl Colleges Lose Male Athletes." *Chronicle of Higher Education*, June 18, 2004, A33.

————. "Players Off the Field." *Chronicle of Higher Education*, November 24, 2000, A59.

————. "Poll Finds Strong Public Backing for Gender Equity in College Athletics." *Chronicle of Higher Education*, July 7, 2000, online ed.

————. "A Quiet Convention." *Chronicle of Higher Education*, January 24, 2003, A35.

————. "Skirmishes Begin over Commission's Report on Title IX." *Chronicle of Higher Education*, January 30, 2003, online ed.

————. "Sports Administrators Remain Disturbed as U.S. Acts on Gender-Equity Complaints." *Chronicle of Higher Education*, January 8, 1999, A57.

————. "Two Appeals Courts Uphold Right of Universities to Reduce Number of Male Athletes." *Chronicle of Higher Education*, January 7, 2000, A64.

————. "U. of Tennessee's Lady Vols Find Success—and Profit—On the Court." *Chronicle of Higher Education*, December 17, 1999, A54.

————. "U.S. Commission on Title IX Calls for Protecting Men's Teams." *Chronicle of Higher Education*, February 28, 2003, online ed.

————. "Wrestling Complaints Denied in Title IX Ruling." *Chronicle of Higher Education*, June 20, 2003, A34.

Sullivan, Bill. "Gender Equity Troubles CFA." *Houston Chronicle*, June 5, 1993, Sports, 8.

Swerczek, Mary. "Before Ruling, Women Athletes Saw Upgrades." *Brown Daily Herald*, April 4, 1995, online ed.

"Temple Settlement." *New York Times*, June 14, 1988, B14.

Terp, Christine. "Title IX: More Races to Run." *Christian Science Monitor*, May 20, 1981, 12.

Thelin, John R. *Games Colleges Play: Scandal and Reform in Intercollegiate Athletics*. Baltimore: Johns Hopkins University Press, 1993.

Tolchin, Martin. "Baker Tries to Mediate Dispute on Scope of Civil Rights Bill." *New York Times*, September 21, 1984, B13.

U.S. Commission on Civil Rights. *More Hurdles to Clear: Woman and Girls in Competitive Athletics*. Clearinghouse Publication no. 63, July 1980.

"U.S. Won't Appeal Bias Case." *New York Times*, September 9, 1982, A20.

Waggoner, Greg. Letter to Norma V. Cantù, October 20, 1995. Photocopy in author's possession.

Walls, Kevin. "Gender Numbers Game Requires Balancing Act." *Tampa Tribune*, June 29, 1999, Sports, 1.

Watterson, John Sayle. *College Football: History, Spectacle, Controversy*. Baltimore: Johns Hopkins University Press, 2000.

Webster, Phil. Letter to Norma V. Cantù, October 17, 1995. Photocopy in author's possession.

Weinberger, Casper W. Letter to Gerald R. Ford. Reprinted in *Chronicle of Higher Education*, April 7, 1975, 11.

Welch, Paula D. *Silver Era, Golden Moments: A Celebration of Ivy League Women's Athletics*. Lanham, Md.: Madison Books, 1999.

Whalen, Charles, and Barbara Whalen. *The longest Debate: A Legislative History of the 1964 Civil Rights Act.* Washington, D.C.: Seven Locks Press, 1985.

Wushanley, Ying. *Playing Nice and Losing: The Struggle for Control of Women's Intercollegiate Athletics, 1960–2000.* Syracuse, N.Y.: Syracuse University Press, 2004.

LANDMARK TITLE IX LAWSUITS

•

Association for Intercollegiate Athletics for Women v. National Collegiate Athletic Association, 588 F. Supp. 487 (D. D.C. 1983), affirmed, 735 F. 2d 577 (D.C. Cir. 1984).

Cannon v. U. of Chicago, et al., 406 F. Supp. 1257 (N.D. Ill. 1976), affirmed, 559 F. 2d [*1105] 1063 (7th Cir. 1976), reversed, 441 U.S. 677 (1979).

Cohen et al. v. Brown University et al., 809 F. Supp. 978 (D. R.I., 1992), affirmed, 991 F. 2d 888 (1st Cir. 1993).

Cohen et al. v. Brown University et al., 879 F. Supp. 185 (D. R.I. 1995), affirmed, 101 F. 3d 155 (1st Cir. 1996), cert. denied.

Communities for Equity et al. v. Michigan High School Athletic Association, 80 F. Supp. 2d 729 (M.D. Mich. 2000).

Favia et al. v. Indiana University of Pennsylvania et al., 812 F. Supp. 578 (W.D. Pa. 1992), affirmed, 7 F. 3d 332 (3d Cir. 1993).

Franklin v. Gwinnett County Public Schools, 911 F. 2d 617 (11th Cir. 1990), reversed, 503 U.S. 60 (1992).

Grove City College v. Bell, 687 F. 2d 691 (3d Cir. 1982), affirmed 465 U.S. 555 (1984).

Haffer et al. v. Temple U. of the Commonwealth System of Higher Education et al., 524 F. Supp. 531 (E.D. Pa. 1981), affirmed, 688 F. 2d 14 (3d Cir. 1982).

Haffer et al. v. Temple University of Commonwealth System of Higher Education et al., 115 F.R.D. 506 (E.D. Pa. 1987).

Horner et al. v. Kentucky State High School Athletic Association et al., 43 F. 3d 265 (6th Cir. 1994).

Kelley v. Board of Trustees of the University of Illinois, 832 F. Supp. 237 (C.D. Ill. 1993), affirmed, 35 F. 3d 265 (7th Cir. 1994), cert. denied.

Landow v. School Board of Brevard County, 132 F. Supp. 2d 958 (M.D. Fla. 2000).

Mercer v. Duke University and Fred Goldsmith, 32 F. Supp. 2d 836 (M.D. N.C. 1998), reversed, 190 F. 3d 643 (4th Cir. 1999).

National Collegiate Athletic Association v. Califano, 444 F. Supp. 425 (D. Kan. 1978), affirmed, 622 F. 2d 1382 (10th Cir. 1980).

National Wrestling Coaches Association et al. v. U.S. Department of Education, 263 F. Supp. 2d 82 (D. D.C. 2003) affirmed, 366 F. 3d 930 (D.C. Cir. 2004).

Neal et al. v. California State Board of Trustees et al., 198 F. 3d 763 (9th Cir. 1999), cert. denied.

Pavey v. University of Alaska, 490 F. Supp. 1011 (D. Ak. 1980).

Pederson et al. v. Louisiana State University et al., 912 F. Supp. 892 (M.D. La. 1996), affirmed, 213 F. 3d 858 (5th Cir. 2000).

Roberts v. Colorado State Univ., 814 F. Supp. 1507 (D. Colo. 1993), affirmed, 998 F. 2d 824 (10th Cir. 1993), cert. denied.

U. of Richmond v. Bell, 543 F. Supp. 321 (E. D. Va. 1982).

INDEX

•